Chocolate and Sangria

A STORY ABOUT
LOVING NEIGHBOURS

ANNELIESE SAWATZKY

◆ FriesenPress

One Printers Way
Altona, MB R0G 0B0
Canada

www.friesenpress.com

www.anneliesesawatzky.ca

ISBN
978-1-03-832071-1 (Hardcover)
978-1-03-832070-4 (Paperback)
978-1-03-832072-8 (eBook)

1. BIOGRAPHY & AUTOBIOGRAPHY, WOMEN

Distributed to the trade by The Ingram Book Company

Sharing our stories brings us closer, no matter who we are or where we come from.

Harold,

Enjoy!

Anneliese Sawatzky

To my beloved children and grandchildren.
My love for each of you is a timeless bond,
deeper than words will ever capture.

Chapter One

"Mothers of little boys work from son up to son down." The framed quote—a gift from my sister—sat beside a pot of African violets on my kitchen windowsill, a daily reminder of my reality. With four boys born in just six years, my life was a blur of nonstop activity, and the truth of those words only deepened over time.

As I rinsed a large mixing bowl, I glanced out the window at my sons playing in the backyard. David and Mark were on the swing set, their little legs pumping with determination, each trying to outdo the other as they reached for the sky. Nearby, Tim was perfecting his front flip on the trampoline. On the far side of the yard, my oldest, George Matthew, playfully wrestled with Bruno, the puppy we had gotten for free a year ago.

Mark flew off the swing, tumbled across the grass, and rolled to a stop. I froze, waiting to see if my youngest was hurt. But he sprang to his feet, wiped his hands on his pants, and climbed right back on. I felt a tinge of pride over not being needed every minute of the day anymore. And now that Mark was five, the boys' frequent squabbles were beginning to be tempered by a growing bond, giving me some moments—though still rare—to catch my breath.

A sudden barrage of loud knocks shattered the stillness of the house, echoing like a thunderclap. I grabbed the dish towel, wondering who it could be, and quickly dried my hands as I made my way to the front door. When I swung the door open, I was confronted by an elderly man, stern and red-faced, furiously shaking his cane in the air.

In a booming, thick British accent, he shouted, "It's bedlam at this house! I can't stand it anymore!"

I stepped back instinctively, but he had already turned and marched down the driveway, his cane thudding against the pavement like an extension of his fury. I stared in disbelief as he made his way toward the house next door.

Tears filled my eyes as I closed the door. I blinked them away, grateful the boys hadn't witnessed his outburst. In my thirty-seven years of life, I had never been yelled at like that before. I walked back into the kitchen to finish the dishes, my heart pounding anew every time I imagined the man's angry face.

The incident was completely contrary to my previous experiences of our neighbourhood. My husband George and I moved to Fort Langley in 1990, drawn to the charm of the historic town nestled in the Fraser Valley. With its tree-lined streets, spacious backyards, and a vibrant community of young families, it was the perfect place to raise our children. Or so I'd thought.

George arrived home just after the boys had settled for the night.

As I descended the stairs, I heard the door to the garage close. "Anne?" he called out in his familiar way, his voice mingling with the soft thud of his shoes and the rustle of his jacket being hung in the mudroom closet.

I met him in the hallway and wrapped my arms around him. "Are you hungry?"

"No, I already ate," he replied. "It's been a long day."

He traded his dress pants, shirt, and tie for lightweight track pants and a T-shirt before getting comfortable on the couch in the family room. When I walked in carrying two glasses of water, he was already fiddling with the TV remote.

I set the glasses down on the coffee table and knelt beside him on the couch. He shifted slightly, already anticipating the neck and shoulder massage I was about to give him. Leaning in, I pressed my thumb and fingers into the tense muscles, finding the knots and easing them with just enough pressure.

"That feels so good. Ohhh, right there."

His left shoulder was even more tense than usual, so I kept kneading while he talked about his day.

"... and on one of our major projects, the building permit was delayed because of staff shortages at the Vancouver planning department. It's dragging everything out, so it will be hard to make our deadline."

Eventually, we both sank back into the couch facing the TV. Then I told George about how the neighbour had shown up in a fit of rage.

"Stan? Next door?" George gave me a concerned look. "He had no right to yell at you."

"Is that his name? Stan?" I pictured the scene again in my mind. "That's the first time I ever met him... and it's not like the boys were being super loud this afternoon."

"I've talked to him a few times over the fence. He's not very friendly." George turned his attention back to the TV.

"I've been trying to figure out what triggered his anger. I think his frustration must have accumulated over the years. Maybe when we demolished the old house and spent a year building?"

George flicked on the nightly news. "That was four years ago," he scoffed. "That's no reason to come over now."

George was right, but I still found myself trying to see things through Stan's eyes.

"Bruno's barking can be annoying." We'd tried obedience training, but the mixed-breed dog was still showing signs of aggression. I made a mental note to ensure the dog had water in his bowl overnight. "Stan probably misses the peace and quiet he had when that old Austrian couple lived here."

George glanced at me, then back at the TV. "What does he expect? We have young kids who enjoy playing in the yard. That's normal. We have nothing to apologize for."

"Still..." I murmured, fully aware that George's attention had shifted to the hockey scores, and he was no longer listening to my words, "I don't like the idea of our neighbours hating us."

The next morning, I pulled out my binder of handwritten recipes and paged through the cookie section, although I was pretty sure I had this one memorized. Years of refinement had perfected these chocolate chip cookies, striking the ideal balance of crunch and softness.

I whipped up a triple batch, ensuring there would be enough for school lunches and extra for the freezer. While the cookies were still warm, I stacked some decoratively on a paper plate and headed next door.

Stan's house, a small, modest, blueish-grey rancher, was nestled in the centre of an overgrown lawn. I trod carefully up the cracked pathway to the front door. Up close, I saw that the sun had started to peel the faded paint from the wood siding.

I exhaled softly and rang the doorbell, shifting the plate of cookies to my other hand. As I waited, I wondered if I should have knocked instead. Just then, the lock clicked, and the door swung open. Stan stood in the doorway, staring at me with a blank expression.

I held out the plate, a peace offering between neighbours, and smiled. "I baked cookies and thought you might like some."

Stan cautiously took a guarded half-step toward me, his face paler and more wrinkled than I remembered from the previous day. He inspected the plate, then with a faint nod, took it and shut the door. I heard the lock click back into place before I headed home.

I felt a curious combination of bemusement and determination, knowing that it would take time and patience to forge any kind of friendship with this man.

Chapter Two

Chopped onions and minced garlic tumbled into the shimmering olive oil, sizzling on contact and filling the kitchen with their savoury aroma. As they softened, I added lean ground beef, breaking it apart with my wooden spoon and watching as it browned to a deep, rich colour. A dash of salt and pepper followed, then crushed tomatoes and a dollop of tomato paste. I stirred until the sauce thickened to the perfect consistency, ready for a slow simmer.

The boys were kicking a soccer ball in the backyard, shrieking with laughter as they chased it across the grass. I stepped out the back door to snip fresh parsley and oregano from my herb pots, the extent of my garden in this season of my life. I'd had the privilege of growing up on a farm surrounded by cattle, acres of raspberries, fruit trees, and a vegetable garden ten times the size of our current property. Every fall we gathered the abundant harvest, then enjoyed it fresh, canned, or frozen throughout the year. These days, though, tending to a few herb pots was all I had time for.

Stepping back into the kitchen, my mind was already racing ahead to the next day. David had violin lessons at four o'clock, followed by George Matthew's baseball practice at six thirty. I planned to make enough spaghetti to have leftovers tomorrow, but the day after would be just as hectic. I'd promised to help with Hot Lunch Day at school, and then look after Mark's friend Thomas until six. I'd have to whip up a meal before Tim's soccer practice at seven. I sighed, reminding myself to call a dishwasher repairman. The machine had been acting up for days, and washing dishes by hand was eating into precious time.

Suddenly, a sharp cry pierced the air, and I rushed outside. Mark was sitting on the grass, clutching his leg with tears streaming down his face. I knelt and wrapped my arms around him.

Tim stood a few feet away, shifting uncomfortably, "I didn't mean to hit him, I was just kicking the ball."

"I know," I said softly, glancing at Tim with a reassuring smile. "It was an accident." I pulled Mark close. His sobs quieted as I held him, gently rocking back and forth. "You'll be okay," I whispered, wiping tears from his cheeks. Within a few minutes, he was running around again.

George arrived home surprisingly early. His eyes were brighter and more alive than usual as he came into the kitchen and gave me a hug.

"I finally got that raise," he announced.

"Great! So that's why you're in such a good mood." I gave him a long congratulatory kiss, wondering if the extra income would be enough to ease the stress of counting every penny during grocery shopping.

George went upstairs to change and returned in his favourite Nike T-shirt, the iconic swoosh sweeping across his chest. He sat at the kitchen table, quickly absorbed in the daily newspaper. I chopped the fresh herbs I'd gathered earlier, then stirred them into the simmering sauce, deepening the vibrant aromas that filled the kitchen.

"Have you seen Stan since you brought him the cookies?" he asked, turning the page.

"No, I haven't."

"Probably best to just leave him alone. Remember what the old Austrian lady told us?"

"Yeah." I remembered it clearly. When we moved in seven years ago, the European widow who sold us the property had warned us about Stan and his wife. "Don't bother getting to know those neighbours," she'd hissed. "They're reclusive, and the curtains are always closed." Her words stuck with me, especially the way she'd concluded: "The woman's an alcoholic. Plus, they're British." She'd spat out the last part as if that explained everything.

"But you do have a way with people," George added.

A warm smile spread across my face as I dropped the pasta into the boiling water. George was never the romantic type, but I'd come to recognize his roundabout compliments as expressions of love. I let the moment linger.

The next day, when Mark and I got home from walking the older boys to school, he busied himself with a pile of building blocks. Seeing him happily engaged, I seized the moment to dial my best friend, Liz. I knew her phone number by heart.

We chatted about what we'd be bringing to the church potluck on Sunday, and I told her about Stan. I easily multi-tasked, folding laundry as I watched Mark build a huge tower, all the while cradling the landline phone in the crook of my neck.

"You brought him cookies?" The phone made crackling noises— not a great connection. "That's very neighbourly of you."

Her gentle voice carried the warmth of a smile, and I knew she would have done the same. Even during her battle with breast cancer, her kindness and selflessness never wavered. Thankfully, she was now in remission.

"Hey, I gotta go," she said. "Let's get together Friday afternoon. How about we meet at the park so you can bring Mark along?"

"Sounds good, see you then," I replied, grabbing a pen to write it down. My calendar always stayed beside the phone so I could keep track of our entire family's ever-changing schedule.

As I hung up the phone, the tower of blocks toppled into Mark's lap. His eyes sparkled, and his laughter was so infectious that I couldn't help but smile along with him.

Mark and I leisurely walked to the park at the end of our street that Friday, reaching it just as Liz's car pulled into the parking lot. I noticed Liz discretely wiping her eyes and tucking a tissue into her pocket as she walked toward us. As she got closer, I saw the redness around her eyes and asked, "What's wrong?"

She waited until Mark was climbing up the slide to reply. "I had a doctor's appointment yesterday." She took a deep breath before she continued. "The cancer is back. It's spread into my lymph nodes and spine."

I couldn't hold back tears as I imagined the pain she was about to face and the impact it would have on her family. We wrapped each other in a comforting hug. When we slowly pulled apart, it took a moment before I managed to say, "I'll do whatever I can to help you get through this."

She pulled her sweater tighter across her body as if bracing herself against the chill of dread that lay ahead. "One day at a time," she said with sincerity. "I'm so grateful that I'm surrounded by so much love."

Her quiet strength steadied my own emotions. Liz's husband provided unwavering support, and her sons, siblings, and the entire church community surrounded her with a strong network of encouragement and love. I thought about how she'd always been there for me, like the time I was dealing with four sick children and she'd brought me treats from a bakery—a luxury I never allowed myself. I vowed to be there for her as well.

I was still blinking away tears as Mark and I left to pick up the other boys from school. I had to shift my focus, walking home, as they shared with me about their days. David said his friend lost a tooth on the monkey bars during recess. Tim proudly announced that his teacher had commented on his good work in math.

I glanced at Stan's place when it came into view. Sure enough, the curtains were drawn, making the place look abandoned. From the road, there was a stark difference between our two homes. Stan's rundown bungalow looked small and outdated next to our three-story Craftsman-style house that George had designed.

The boys ran ahead just as Stan was coming out of his front door with a bag of trash. I slowed my step and waited beside his garbage bin.

"Hi, Stan. I'm Anne, by the way."

He stared at me blankly without responding.

I pushed on. "So, how long have you lived in this house?"

His eyebrows went up as if he was stunned that I'd had the audacity to ask such a personal question. After a moment, he replied in his clipped style, "Twelve years. Now you know all our secrets."

He dropped his trash in the can, slammed down the lid, and walked away with a determined stride, each step punctuating the message that he was very much done talking.

The boys were finally out of school for the summer. They raced barefoot through the grass in the backyard, embracing the freedom of long, unstructured days. I hadn't made much of an effort to speak to Stan since our awkward exchange, but every now and then, I brought over some fresh baking.

Arriving home after dropping off an apple strudel, I felt I had finally made some progress. The moment the fresh smell of warm apples and cinnamon had wafted in Stan's direction, his face had softened, and a rare smile had broken through his usual reserve.

I joined the boys in the backyard, uncoiled the garden hose, and set up the sprinkler so they could cool off in the sweltering heat. They sprinted through the refreshing spray, their laughter echoing above the steady hiss of the water. I stepped back into the house to get some towels when the doorbell rang. To my surprise, it was Stan.

"Are the boys too loud? I could—"

"Honeysuckle," he blurted out as he thrust a mason jar full of delicate pink flowers toward me. "It's from my garden."

He watched me inhale the rich floral scent. It was unlike anything I had ever smelled before.

"Thank you," I smiled, bringing the bouquet to my nose once more. Stan gave me a sheepish grin before turning to go.

Chapter Three

With October came shorter days, accompanied by a thick, lingering fog that shrouded the landscape in a ghostly veil until midday.

Soup weather.

Waiting at Stan's doorstep with a jar of homemade chicken noodle soup and a bag of freshly baked buns, I listened for his approaching footsteps. The door opened, and as usual, Stan took the food from my hands. But this time, instead of shutting the door, he paused.

Tentatively, as if he was unsure of the idea himself, he asked, "Would you like to meet my wife, Vera?"

I couldn't help but feel honoured by the offer. "Yes, I'd love to."

He stepped back and gestured into the dimly lit home. The first thing that struck me as I entered was the smell. A musty odour, like mothballs mixed with stale cigarette smoke, hovered in the stagnant air. It was as if they hadn't opened a window in years. I tried not to show my displeasure. As I followed Stan, my eyes caught sight of an old piano resting against the wall in their den.

Vera was sitting at the dining room table, hunched to one side in her wheelchair. She held a smouldering cigarette between two fingers, absently tapping ash into an overflowing tray. She looked me up and down from her perch in the corner of the room.

"Hello," she managed, her voice raspy from years of smoke and age. Taking a final puff, she flicked the butt onto the growing pile, a wisp of smoke curling around her greying hair, where traces of red dye still clung to the ends.

I stifled a cough. "Hello. It's nice to finally meet you, Vera."

She nodded. Stan nodded. And with that, I was guided back to the front door.

"Thanks for the soup," Stan said. He shut the door behind me before I could reply.

Once back inside my own home, I could hear the boys already waiting for me in the kitchen.

"Can I have a bun with jam?" David asked.

"Me too," Mark grinned.

"Okay, but just one each. We'll save the rest for dinner."

Tim showed me some cool karate moves that made me laugh. "Mom, can I sign up for karate? Some of my friends are doing it, and they said it's really fun."

"Maybe," I said. "I'll have to find out when the classes are and see if we can fit it in."

I spread butter and homemade strawberry jam onto four buns as the boys crowded around the counter. I noticed that George Matthew's pants were too short, his legs having grown during the summer. I made a mental note to add pants to my shopping list.

David pulled a crumpled paper from his backpack. "My friend James is having a birthday party, and I need to get him a present," he said, showing me the invitation.

"We can pick something out for James when we go shopping next week," I replied, pouring four glasses of milk and setting them on the kitchen table. Then I grabbed my shopping list and added "pants and birthday present" to the bottom.

13

"Can we go to the *liberry*?" Mark asked between gulps. "I wanna get some more books."

Mark was in kindergarten now and was already starting to learn how to read. I was glad he was excited about books.

"Let's stop at the library before we pick up the guys from school tomorrow," I told him.

The phone rang. It was the music leader from church, giving me the list of songs I would be playing on the piano for congregational singing that Sunday. While I jotted down the list of hymns, Tim accidentally knocked over his glass of milk while practising his karate moves. I motioned for him to grab some paper towels and clean it up. After I hung up the phone, I got a rag from the laundry room, wet it, and got down on my hands and knees to properly wipe the area.

"I'm still hungry," David said. "Can I have another bun?"

"Me too," Mark echoed.

"How about some apple slices while you start on your homework?"

"I don't have any homework today, so can I watch TV?" Tim asked.

"No fair," David frowned.

"You can all sit at the table for twenty minutes and work on something, even if it's just colouring a picture."

I reached for my calendar and shopping list once more, remembering that I also needed to plan Thanksgiving dinner for George's side of the family. This year, it was my turn to host and make the turkey.

As the boys took their seats, I looked up from my planning and found myself assessing the lengths of their hair. I had given them all back-to-school haircuts at the end of summer, but they were already starting to look a bit shaggy. I reviewed my daily planner and saw that I could squeeze in four haircuts on Wednesday evening. George requested a trim every three weeks as well, which made it feel like I was always sweeping hair from my laundry room floor.

After dinner, with the leftovers stored and the dishes put away, I tossed in a load of laundry before getting the boys ready for bed. No matter what happened during the day or how exhausted I felt, bedtime was my favourite time with my sons. I dedicated at least ten minutes to each child individually every night. I cherished these moments, enjoying the opportunity to hear their thoughts and delve into the intricacies of their worlds.

Most of the boys had already fallen asleep by the time I came downstairs. When George got home, he headed straight for the couch while I put the laundry in the dryer.

"Have you had anything to eat?" I said as I passed through the family room on my way to the kitchen.

"I had a big lunch with clients today, but I could still eat something."

I heated a bowl of soup in the microwave and carried it in on a tray along with a fresh bun, generously buttered, knowing he enjoyed dipping it into the soup. Between mouthfuls, he described his day, and I listened patiently until he asked, "How was your day?"

"I was invited in to meet Vera today."

He had the TV remote in his hand, already scrolling through the channels. "Who?"

"I met Vera, Stan's wife."

George tried to keep his expression neutral, but I saw something in his eyes. He sighed as he said, "Don't get too involved. You're already so busy with the boys, church, and Liz."

I was part of a small support group of women from church who were helping to transport Liz to her appointments and deliver meals to her family. George's concern was valid in that there were only so many hours in every day, but I was taught that genuine happiness came from serving others, an unwavering truth intricately woven into the fabric of my life.

"I know I'm busy. But I'm just trying to be a good neighbour."

Chapter Four

The phone startled me out of a deep sleep around five-thirty in the morning. George, already up and getting ready for work, answered it. He turned toward me, holding out the receiver, whispering, "It's Stan."

"Stan?" I sat up, sliding my legs over the side of the bed. "Hello?"

The voice on the other end was quiet, distant. "Could you pick me up from Langley Memorial Hospital?" A brief pause. "Vera died."

After I hung up, I shared the news with George.

"I don't have any meetings this morning, so I'll stay with the boys until you're back," he said as I threw on some jeans and a shirt. I thanked him, grabbed my jacket, and rushed to the hospital, not knowing what to expect.

Stan was easily recognizable waiting at the entrance. He looked small and fragile, as if one good gust of the cold October air could shatter him and carry the pieces away. His head was bowed.

As he opened the door and slipped into the car, an apology came out in a nervous rush. "I'm sorry. I found your name in the phone book. I didn't know who to call."

"Please, don't be sorry." I reached over and helped him with the seatbelt. "I'm glad you called."

I pulled out onto the road and noticed Stan staring down at the plastic bag in his lap.

"These are Vera's things," he said slowly. I heard him sniffle as we turned left to begin the fifteen-minute drive back to Fort Langley.

I tried to gather my thoughts in the darkness, but before I could speak, Stan broke the silence again, "I fought in the Second World War."

I let the silence reply. The streetlights cast a soft glow on the wet pavement, their reflections shimmering in the drizzle.

He continued. "Most of my friends didn't make it. Some came back wounded, others in coffins, but very few of us came home." He sniffled again, pulling a handkerchief out of his pocket. "I watched my best friend get blown apart. To this day, I don't know how I made it out alive."

"That must have been terrible!" I realized he was grappling with years of trauma and grief.

He sighed and the windshield wiper held time until he spoke again. "I've been looking after Vera for the past fifteen years. It hasn't been easy."

I nodded. My throat felt dry as I swallowed.

"And then our son, our only son, died four years ago. Vera really went downhill after that." His voice was quivering as he turned away to the window. "So did I, maybe, but I had to be strong for her." He pressed the handkerchief to his nose.

After a brief silence, I softly said, "You've really been through a lot!"

I calculated the timing in my head, and it hit me. While Stan and his wife were mourning the loss of their only son, we had been busy building our house, completely oblivious to the difficulties our neighbours were facing.

We pulled into Stan's driveway. I turned off the engine and sat quietly, not sure what he needed right then. That was the most I'd ever heard him say, so I thought he might want to continue talking about his life.

"Would you like some company?"

"No, thank you." Stan opened the door. "I would rather be alone at the moment."

I gave him an encouraging smile, hoping he could sense that he wasn't alone. "How about if I come by early next week? I could help you tidy up a bit?"

He nodded. "That would be nice."

Stan closed the door behind him and slowly walked away. His shoulders were slumped forward, burdened not only by the weight of grief but also by the uncertainty of facing his home without his wife. I watched as he paused at the door, fumbling with his keys, and only pulled out of his driveway once the light came on and he was safely inside.

The following week, after dropping Mark off at kindergarten, I knocked on Stan's door, waiting patiently until I heard the slow shuffle of his feet coming closer. The door cracked open slightly, revealing the sunken shell of a man—frail and weighed down.

"Hi, Stan." A profound sadness lingered in the contours of his expression. My voice softened with genuine concern. "What can I do to help?"

He didn't reply, just opened the door and walked back the way he came. I slipped in and looked around. The house seemed cold and empty, as if the home itself was lost without Vera. I ducked under a long cobweb and followed him into the dining room.

"I have absolutely no idea where to start," Stan said as he sank into a chair that still faced the spot where Vera had been the last time I visited.

With my mind in cleaning mode, I looked around to assess the situation.

"How about we start with some light and fresh air?" I suggested, moving around him to pull the soiled curtains wide and crack open the window. A rush of fresh air spilled into the room.

He didn't look up. "Do whatever you like."

With the light streaming in, the house was even grimier than it had appeared at first glance. Years of smoking had stained the walls and left a film on the windows. Dirt had gathered around light switches and door handles. I stepped into the kitchen. The laminate floor tiles were lifted in several places and probably hadn't had a good scrub in a long time.

"Did you install this floor yourself?"

Stan got up and stepped into the doorway of the small galley kitchen. "Laid each and every one of them myself. Peel 'n stick. Fantastic things," he bragged, pressing down a lifting tile with his slippered toe. "It was quite a job getting them all lined up straight."

He paused, then headed toward the living room. I watched him slowly lower himself into an old leather reclining chair, then turned my attention back to the kitchen sink, where a towering stack of dishes precariously extended onto the counter.

I did a rough count and figured the bottom ones had been there for weeks. On the opposite counter, a layer of dust had settled between piles of bills and a stack of empty cans and more dishes. When I opened the refrigerator, the smell of rotten vegetables took my breath away, and I quickly closed it. I formulated a plan of action in my mind. Unfortunately, the slimy vegetables were at the top of the list.

"Stan, do you mind if I use your phone?"

"No, go ahead."

I called my oldest sister, Elsie, who lived just across the street from the boys' elementary school. She said they could come to her place after school and stay until I picked them up later. I really appreciated how often she was willing to help me out.

It took hours to make noticeable progress in the kitchen, and Stan didn't come in once. I wondered if he was okay and took a quick peek into the living room. He had fallen asleep in the recliner, his slippers piled onto the avocado-coloured shag carpet.

Eventually, he shuffled into the kitchen, and instead of commenting on the clean sink and counters, he asked, "Why are you digging through the cupboards?"

I pulled out a box of rock-hard bouillon cubes. "Did you know these expired twelve years ago?" I gave the box a shake to emphasize my point.

"Goodness me." With a subtle blush colouring his cheeks, he said, "I still make soup out of those. Carry on."

He left the room again, but this time, instead of the low groan of the recliner, I heard the soft creak of the piano lid being lifted. The moment he began to play, I was surprised at how graceful and confident his fingers sounded on the keys. I recognized that he was playing "As Time Goes By," and I quietly hummed along as I continued checking dates and throwing out absurdly expired items.

He ended the song with a flourish and called out, "That was from the movie *Casablanca*."

I yelled back, "Keep playing! I love it," as I wiped out yet another cupboard before giving each can and box a designated spot on its shelf.

Although Stan wasn't in the kitchen cleaning, it felt like he was doing what he could, and the house detected its first sign of hope.

Once I'd started the project, my motivation only grew. During my next cleaning visit, I finished organizing the entire kitchen and then moved on to the dining room. The more effort I put in, the more the house seemed to come alive. The walls changed colour when I wiped the soot from them, and the curtains, which I took home to wash, got rehung, looking renewed in their original cream colour instead of the previous dingy grey.

Stan's old vacuum barely lifted the first layer of dust from his shag carpet, so I hauled over my heavy-duty Miracle Mate and finished the job. That afternoon, Stan asked me to make him a cup of tea.

I reached for the white porcelain teapot, then hesitated—it was stained, inside and out. I flicked on the electric kettle and located the baking soda to tackle the teapot while I waited for the water to boil. The stains, however, clung stubbornly after years of buildup, and by the time the kettle clicked off, there wasn't much improvement. Still, I kept scrubbing, refusing to give up.

I heard Stan huff audibly from the living room before asking, "Everything okay in there?"

Disregarding his impatience, I said, "Yup," while rinsing the teapot. I frowned at the stains and abandoned the scrubbing. Instead, I grabbed a cup from the newly organized shelf and poured in the water. I rarely drank tea myself, so I hastily dipped a tea bag up and down a few times. He had mentioned he took milk and sugar, so I added some before handing him the cup.

He lifted it to his lips, took a sip, and immediately spat it back into the cup. "You call this tea?" he exclaimed, glaring at the offending brew. "This is not a proper cup of tea. It needs to be hot and strong and sweet and milky."

His previous fatigue had seemingly evaporated at this catastrophe. He jumped to his feet and insisted I join him in the kitchen. "I'll show you how to make a proper cup of tea."

Stan looked at the teapot I had attempted to scrub and scoffed, shaking his head as he pointed to the stains. "You don't need to clean the teapot, it enhances the flavour!"

I chuckled at his dramatic tone and noticed the twinkle in his eye.

"First, the water has to be boiling hot." He put the kettle on again and started pulling tea bags out of the box. "Two for a full pot, and let it steep for at least five minutes to make it strong enough." He took out another cup and said, "I'll make one for you as well."

Curious, I watched as he poured a generous amount of milk into two cups and added a heaping spoonful of sugar. Then he pulled a plate and a package of cookies from the cupboard, saying, "And biscuits must always accompany the tea."

We sat at the dining room table, now clean and neatly arranged, sipping tea. It was a new experience for me—something I hadn't grown up with—but I appreciated how it offered a much-needed pause in the day. It felt like an invitation to slow down.

From that moment on, I never got it wrong again. I always made the tea hot and strong and sweet and milky.

Mark's half-day kindergarten schedule had been a welcome change this fall, offering me a few uninterrupted hours each day for the first time in eleven years. It didn't mean I suddenly had more free time, but it provided an opportunity to accomplish a few things without distractions.

I went to Stan's house a couple of times a week, steadily making progress. During breaks from cleaning, we would sip tea and chat casually. As we spent more time together, Stan began to relax, and I slowly started asking more personal questions.

"How did you and Vera meet?" I ventured one day, studying Stan's features to make sure I wasn't crossing a line. He held my gaze for a while before speaking.

"I was in the army at the time. We met through a mutual friend." He closed his eyes for a moment, and his expression softened as he told the story. "I was immediately drawn to her flaming red hair. And that personality!" Stan laughed. "Her nickname was Bubbles."

For a moment, Stan looked almost youthful, a glimpse of his younger self shining through. "We'd really only known each other a few weeks when we got married, but everyone was getting married quickly in those days. You see, us men needed a reason to fight, and someone to come back home to."

I listened with rapt attention.

"Our marriage was no bed of roses, mind you. We didn't even celebrate our anniversary these last few years, you know, with Vera in and out of the hospital so much. She always enjoyed her drink, but it got much worse when our son Stanley died."

At this, Stan stopped, finished his tea, and stared silently into his empty cup. Uncertain of the right words, I chose to sit quietly. Eventually, he looked up at me again.

"I've never told anyone this next part, not even Vera."

He took a long breath, his eyes became glossy, and he cleared his throat. "Stanley used to come over every Sunday for dinner. He'd gone through a nasty divorce. His wife took custody of their three kids and their house, leaving him to live alone in an apartment about half an hour's drive from here. One Sunday, he didn't show up. I called and called, but no answer. Three days later, I drove over to check on him."

Stan swallowed hard, his voice barely audible. "Before I even unlocked the door, I knew... I could... I knew the smell of death."

Tears spilled over the old man's cheeks, and I didn't even try to hold back my own. I could feel the full weight of this event, being voiced out loud, landing heavily in the space between us.

"It was dreadful—his motionless body on the bed. There were pills and pill bottles scattered around him." Stan took out his pocket handkerchief and blew his nose. "I threw everything into the bin in the alley before I called the police. I couldn't tell Vera it was a suicide, so I told her it must have been a heart attack. There was no autopsy done."

For a few minutes, we wept silently—he, a grieving husband and father, finally unburdening a secret about his son that he had carried for far too long, and I, a mother of young sons, recognizing life's capacity for unexpected twists that can change the course of one's life in an instant.

Chapter Five

Stan and I discovered we had something in common. We both played piano by ear, and neither of us read music very well. Stan's talent had developed in London at the age of seven. According to my parents, at four years old, I would rush to the piano after church and plunk out the tunes I had just heard.

I brewed a pot of tea and brought it into the living room, letting it steep while Stan continued talking about his piano playing. Then he asked, "Do you play any other instruments?"

"Yes. When I was nineteen, a family at our church had a Paraguayan harp that no one was using, so I borrowed it and taught myself how to play. Eventually, I was asked to play at weddings and funerals. Years later, when someone donated a harp to the hospital, my pastor, knowing I loved to play, arranged to have me volunteer in the waiting room where they wheeled patients down to listen."

I poured Stan's tea just how he liked it—with milk and sugar— then poured my own and left it black. "I asked the hospital receptionist if she knew who had donated that beautiful folk harp. It turned out to be a retired man named Emil Geering, who lived nearby in South Langley. I visited his workshop and saw that he didn't just make folk harps—he also crafted these unique cross-strung harps, where the strings crisscrossed like the black and white keys of a piano, meeting at an angle through the middle. I could only play in the key of C on my harp, so I thought it would be fun to have sharps and flats."

I noticed that Stan had perked up a bit at the word "piano." I paused to test the temperature of my tea and took a sip. "I was about three months pregnant when I asked Emil if he would consider building me a cross-strung harp. He not only agreed but gave me such a good deal. Even then, I knew we couldn't afford it, but my sister Mary agreed to lend me the money."

Stan looked out the window, possibly bored, so I summarized the rest of the story. "Six months later, Mr. Geering let me know the harp was ready. Even though I started having contractions that morning, I was so eager to see the harp that I convinced George to drive me over to pick it up right away. I played it all afternoon, through the waves of labour pains, and later that evening, Mark was born."

I took another sip of my tea. "After a few weeks I went back to thank Mr. Geering. I introduced him to Mark and told him that the day I picked up the harp, my baby boy was born. With soft eyes, he said, 'My wife passed away that very same night.' And then he said something I'll never forget: 'Well isn't that the way life should be? The old ones move on, and the young ones are born.'"

I stopped talking and finished my tea. Stan nodded slowly, seeming tired. After washing the mugs, I slipped on my shoes and jacket by the door. "See you tomorrow."

Stan looked up, his voice sincere, "Thank you for telling me that story. I think that man, Emil, has a remarkable attitude."

"I think so too," I replied as I closed his door.

My days settled into a routine of dropping the kids off at school and either running errands or spending time at Stan's before picking up Mark from kindergarten. After-school and evenings were reserved for the boys and for cooking, cleaning, and catching up on paperwork at home.

One night, as I sat at the kitchen table going over our weekly budget, the phone rang. Liz's voice sounded weak on the other end, clearly affected by the toll of her chemotherapy treatments. The cancer was aggressive, so the treatments needed to be as well.

After the usual updates about our families, she told me that she'd signed up for a relaxation therapy class and was wondering if I would join her. I agreed immediately—not only would I do anything for her, but I also figured I could use a little relaxation myself.

During our first session, we reclined on mats, cocooned ourselves in blankets, and luxuriated in the soothing comfort of eye pillows. All the while, the soft voice of the instructor guided us through various breathing techniques.

My mind was scattered at first, leaping from one task to another—the kids' schedules and the endless errands piling up. But as the minutes passed and my body slowly began to unwind, I felt the shift. The tightness started to release, like a weight off my shoulders. With each deep breath, the tension ebbed away, leaving me lighter, calmer, and far more at ease than I had been in a while.

The way the instructor ended the session was magical. She gently strummed a guitar as she hummed a beautiful, soothing melody that seemed to settle over us like a warm embrace.

As we walked to the van after the class, Liz asked, "So, what did you think?"

"I loved it! I didn't even realize how much stress I was carrying until about halfway through, when I felt it begin to release."

"Me too." She rested her head back against the seat as we started the drive home. "I wasn't expecting to feel such a difference. It was nice, even just for an hour, to be transported to a different world—just being in the moment."

"I agree. Thanks for inviting me."

"Thanks for coming," she replied.

I glanced at Liz and noticed the contented glow on her face.

In a November downpour, rain slashing sideways, I ran over to Stan's house, unsuccessfully using my jacket held above my head like an umbrella. Once safely inside, I carefully hung up the dripping jacket and sat on the edge of his floral couch, facing him. He sank back in his leather recliner and sighed, gazing out the window at the steady rain. The droplets trickled down the glass in gentle streams, turning the world outside into a hazy blur.

"Did I tell you the funeral home dropped off Vera's ashes the other day?"

A drip of water trailed down my forehead, and I wiped it with the back of my hand. "No, you didn't."

"It was strange. The doorbell rang. A man handed me a heavy paper bag and left without a word. Honestly, I was a bit taken aback." He shifted in his chair. "The thought of it, you know? This used to be my wife."

I was accustomed to ornate caskets being lowered into freshly dug graves in the stillness of traditional cemeteries. Funerals in my world were elaborate events with hundreds of loved ones, followed by food and sharing memories of the deceased. I tried to imagine a whole person—a breathing, thinking, feeling, human being—reduced to a mere pile of ashes.

"I buried her in the backyard under the tree. We planted that tree beside the patio when Stanley died. His ashes are there as well." Before I could say anything in response, Stan segued into his next request. "I think I'm ready to go through Vera's things. Would you be able to help me with that?"

True to my nature as an organizer, I replied, "Of course. We can start right now."

Some of Vera's dresses looked like they hadn't been worn in over thirty years, judging both by their style and the layer of dust that had gathered on their shoulders. I folded them neatly and stacked them into the boxes Stan had set aside for me, wondering who would buy them—or would they become Halloween costumes?

Soon enough, three boxes of clothing were ready to be taken to the "Sally Ann," as Stan referred to it affectionately. The Salvation Army had helped the troops during the war back in the day, and he insisted that everything be donated there.

After loading the donation boxes into my van, I turned my attention to the bathroom drawers. This job was easy. All the crumpled tubes of hand cream and outdated medications went straight into a garbage bag. I came across quite a few pairs of tweezers and set them aside. I found another half dozen in the drawer of Vera's bedside table just as Stan walked by.

"Ah yes," he smiled as he looked at the pile of tweezers. "My wife had quite a tweezer fetish. She would spend hours in front of a magnifying mirror pulling stray hairs from her face... Bless her heart."

He said this last part with such affection that I silently decided to adopt the expression myself when referring to people's endearing quirks. After all, why judge someone when it's far more enjoyable to see their eccentricities as the traits that make them truly unique?

Once Stan's house was in order, he began coming to our place in the afternoons, especially when I was too busy to visit him. He'd show up in his checked cotton shirt and his favourite well-worn brown cardigan, with a handkerchief neatly tucked into the front pocket. The grease stains on his beige pants made me wonder how frequently he did his laundry.

Perched on a stool at the kitchen counter, Stan called out the crossword clues while I cooked or baked or signed field trip forms, and we'd endeavour to finish the puzzles together. With great precision, he penned the letters into the squares, methodically moving from one clue to the next, his glasses resting low on his nose.

"What's a five-letter word for overreact?" he read aloud.

From the next room, a high-pitched scream rang out, and the rapid thump of small feet approached.

"Mooooommmmmmmmm," David wailed upon entering the kitchen, "Tim is bugging me." Tears revealed the depth of his feelings.

"That's it!" Stan exclaimed, taking in the situation. "What perfect timing!" He chuckled as he filled in the letters.

I gave David a reassuring hug, and he glanced at Stan in confusion before running into the other room as if nothing had happened. I leaned over Stan's shoulder and saw E-M-O-T-E proudly penned into the crossword puzzle.

"Are you staying for dinner tonight?" He was staying more and more often, and the family was getting used to having him around.

Stan nodded enthusiastically and said, "Yes, please," before returning his attention to the next clue. I peeled an extra potato.

Once the meal was finished, Stan would always slip on his shoes, give us one last glance, and exit with the same sheepish grin and signature line, "Same time tomorrow?"

Christmas filled the air as the town of Fort Langley hung its decor. The historic Community Hall looked especially festive, adorned with lights and garlands. At the centre of the front lawn stood a magnificent Christmas tree, decorated with oversized round ornaments.

Liz and I visited a nearby garden shop where we each picked out a pot of white poinsettias. The outing visibly brightened Liz's spirits. She said the delicate white flowers always brought her a sense of hope and peace during the holiday rush.

Later, on my way home, I made a stop at the post office. A poster on the bulletin board caught my eye. A Christmas harp concert was coming to Fort Langley. I had never actually seen a professional harpist play in person. On a whim, I bought three tickets.

The night of the concert, Stan, George, and I arrived early to get good seats. The stage of the Community Hall was beautifully decorated with candles, baskets of holly, and draping cedar boughs wrapped with twinkling lights. I watched with rapt attention as the harpist allowed her fingers to trail expertly over the strings.

Observing the positioning of her hands and the way she plucked the strings, I realized that my self-taught technique was totally wrong. Nevertheless, the familiar, soothing sound resonated with how my heart felt when I played.

Just before the intermission, the harpist addressed the crowd.

"And now I'd like to pay tribute to a man named Emil Geering." She extended her right arm to the back of the room where an elderly man rose from his seat, and people started clapping. "Emil resurrected the cross-strung harp," she shared enthusiastically with the assembled guests, "which hadn't been built since the seventeenth century. There are only about a dozen of his special, handcrafted cross-strung harps in the world."

As she started listing the countries where these harps were located, a shiver crept up my spine.

Stan leaned in, gently resting his hand on my arm and whispered, "Is that the man who built your harp?"

"Yes!" We gave each other an excited grin, my eyes wide with surprise as I realized that my harp, the harp that shared a birthday with my youngest, was one of those rare instruments.

I looked over at George, noticing his raised eyebrows, a clear sign of his own astonishment at the news. The room erupted with applause over Mr. Geering's lifetime accomplishments, and we joined in the standing ovation. I didn't get a chance to speak with him, as he left shortly after.

A few weeks later, I invited Stan to our church's Christmas Eve service. By eight o'clock, the service was over, and the boys couldn't wait to get home to open their gifts. As we drove, Stan commented, "I enjoyed all the music immensely, especially the singing."

I nodded, "Mennonites are well-known for their four-part harmony."

"It was wonderful. Absolutely wonderful," he said.

"The kid's choir did a good job too." I turned my attention to the boys. "What song did you like the best?"

"Away in a Manger," Mark answered.

"Jingle Bells," David joked as the other boys snickered.

"What's your favourite?" Tim asked me.

"Silent Night," I said. "It's always been my favourite, especially sung in German."

Stan chimed in enthusiastically, "I can't believe that your entire congregation sang the 'Hallelujah Chorus' from Handel's *Messiah*. And sang it very well, I might add, with all the different parts... I was astounded."

Back at home, I switched on the gas fireplace and lit the candles along the wooden mantel, creating an atmosphere that felt like a big, cozy hug. The CD player on the bookshelf filled the room with the festive melodies of the Boney M. Christmas album.

In the opposite corner, a real Douglas Fir glowed with lights and displayed a cherished collection of sentimental ornaments gathered over the years. Among them were popsicle stick reindeer with googly eyes, hand-painted snowmen, and glittery cardboard stars—the proud creations of the boys. Beneath the branches lay a pile of carefully wrapped Christmas presents.

We began with the stockings. They eagerly unwrapped the tiny treasures inside, eyes lighting up with excitement as they discovered fun little novelties or chocolate coins.

Then, one by one, they opened their gifts. Stan had bought each of the boys a red mailbox piggy bank, a miniature version of the real mailbox at the post office. He smiled proudly at their giddy reactions, adding, "There's a few coins in each one to get you started."

I gave Stan a big coffee table book about the history of pianos and a new cardigan with pockets, just like the one he had, but in navy blue.

The highlight of the evening, though, was the gift that Mark received from my sister Mary: Tickle Me Elmo, the wildly popular plush toy from *Sesame Street*.

Everyone thought it was cute, but nobody expected Stan to ask, "Could I have a go?"

Mark handed him his new red Elmo. When Stan gave Elmo's tummy a squeeze and the toy let out its infectious laugh, he burst into uncontrollable laughter. We all started laughing along with him. He squeezed it again, and as Elmo vibrated and giggled, Stan's laughter grew so intense that tears streamed down his cheeks. I had never seen him so happy.

Chapter Six

It was a cold January morning when, after dropping the boys off at school, I sat down with the local newspaper. As I unfolded its crisp pages, my eyes landed on Emil Geering's obituary. Only four weeks had passed since the concert. I carefully cut it out, pinned it to the fridge, then went to my harp. I hadn't known the man well, but it seemed fitting to create music with my hands on the very instrument he had crafted with his.

When I visited Liz the next day, I tried not to study her pale skin or the deepening circles under her eyes. I knew she didn't like it when people constantly asked her how she was feeling, especially if there was pity in their voices. So, upon seeing that her beautiful, thick blonde hair was now all gone, I went for the practical approach.

"How do you feel about getting a wig?"

"I thought I would get used to these headscarves, but I can't stand them." Her voice carried both vulnerability and humour. "I always used to say, 'you only feel as good as your hair looks.'"

"I remember you saying that." I nodded, understanding that part of her identity probably felt lost. She always carried herself with a confident radiance. "Your hair always looked good."

"I think I'll feel more like myself if I get a wig. Do you have time to come with me?"

"Definitely. Do you want to go later this week?"

"Does Thursday work?"

"Sure, if we go while Mark is at kindergarten."

With that out of the way, Liz lay back on the couch and pulled a throw blanket over herself for warmth. "How's your neighbour doing?"

"Good. We found out we both have the same birthday!"

"Both on January eleventh? What a coincidence."

"Yeah, we went out for lunch to celebrate—it was nice. He told me about Lulu, a woman from England who wrote him a sympathy card after Vera passed. They've been writing back and forth ever since."

"Is her name really Lulu?" Liz mustered a faint smirk, but I noticed her eyelids starting to droop.

"No," I shook my head. "Her name is Louisa, but Stan likes nicknames. Anyway, he told me that nearly fifty years ago, on a night when both their spouses were sick, they attended a grand ball in London, where they shared a kiss. He said it felt so natural that he didn't think of it as cheating."

Liz had closed her eyes but still raised her eyebrows in reaction to the story.

"He's like a teenager in love," I said, but Liz had already fallen asleep.

During the next round of chemotherapy at the cancer clinic, Liz and I didn't talk about our kids, and I didn't talk about Stan. We didn't talk much at all, not because there was nothing to say, but because words seemed too small for the oppressive heaviness of it all. The sterile scent of the hospital lingered as I pushed her wheelchair down the hall toward the elevator. Liz sat, thin and pale, with her head bowed.

When we entered the elevator, she broke the silence. "I think someday, in the future, people are going to be shocked that anyone had to endure chemotherapy treatments."

"Yeah, it's crazy when you think about it—how could something so toxic be the only cure? I wish there were a better solution," I said as we headed toward the car.

"Someone told me about a faith healer coming to the Pentecostal church in Langley. I'm thinking about going. Would you come with me?"

I knew she was desperate for any glimmer of hope while in the overwhelming grip of cancer. "Yes, of course I'll come. When is it?"

"Wednesday at three in the afternoon."

"I'll arrange for the boys to go to Elsie's place after school and pick you up at two thirty."

We peered into the sanctuary from the foyer. At the front of the church, a small group huddled closely, and at least a dozen more were seated in the pews, their heads bowed. The usher stepped toward us, gestured down the aisle, and quietly said that Liz would be next.

As the group before us departed, we stepped forward to take our place in front of the faith healer. She was a middle-aged woman wearing plain black pants and a floral blouse, resembling any passerby you might see walking down the street.

The healer asked Liz to kneel. She dipped her index finger into a small bowl of oil and used it to make the sign of the cross on Liz's forehead. Then she lifted her hands and invoked the power of the Holy Spirit, saying, "Release the language of heaven, surrender to God's presence."

With an authoritative tone, she instructed Liz. "Allow yourself to speak in tongues."

This practice was not part of our faith tradition, but Liz, with eyes closed, started praying earnestly.

The woman didn't seem satisfied. "Try harder. Let go of your inhibitions. Open yourself to the Holy Spirit."

Liz continued to pray. I glanced up at the faith healer and noticed her furrowed brow and clenched jaw. Gently, I put my hand on Liz's arm, offering silent reassurance.

People from the pews gathered around, laying their hands on Liz's shoulders as the woman brought her ear closer to Liz's mouth. Recognizing that she was still speaking English, she bellowed, "You must have faith!" Her impassioned cry filled the room, commanding attention and causing the crowd to raise their voices with passion. I couldn't understand anything they were saying and assumed they were all speaking in tongues.

I was anxious to get out of there. The way that woman implied that Liz's faith wasn't strong enough really bothered me. After what felt like an eternity, the healer dismissed us and we walked out of the building, into the bright light of day.

When we got to the car, I said, "That was a bit weird, don't you think?"

"Yeah, I didn't expect so much pressure to speak in tongues. It really turned me off." I noticed Liz's defeated expression.

"You were great just being yourself. I don't believe they have any more faith than you do."

"I didn't know what to expect, but it wasn't that," she said, looking down.

When we got back to Liz's place, she invited me in. "Do you have time for tea?"

"Sure, I can stay for a few minutes," I replied. "Do you want me to make the tea?"

"No, I can do it."

With her blonde wig on, Liz looked almost like her old self. She was a dedicated elementary school teacher but had taken the year off. As she prepared the tea, she talked enthusiastically about her sons, both of whom were not only exceptionally athletic but also musically talented and thriving academically.

Liz took two mugs out of the cupboard while the herbal tea was steeping. Her movements were slow but graceful. She expressed how much she depended on her husband. "He's been my rock through all of this. I know he's tired, but he keeps going, never complaining." She looked at me with a soft smile. "He even started to build a wheelchair ramp at the back of the house."

"That's great," I said, watching her carefully pour the tea.

We carried our cups to the kitchen table. After a brief pause, I asked, "Do you miss teaching?"

"I loved working with the kids and the staff at the school." She looked out the window, her fingers tightening around the handle of the mug. "But I don't miss being so busy."

She sighed in a way that held longing and gratitude all mixed into one. "The hardest part has been not being there for my boys. Not being able to sit in the stands and cheer them on at their games or even just drive them to practices and other events. I miss that."

"I can imagine," I said with a heavy heart. I found myself thinking about how much I took for granted without even realizing it. It made me want to value those small everyday moments more often.

Her expression shifted and her voice softened as she leaned in slightly toward me. "One thing I've really noticed since having cancer is how much everyone rushes around from one thing to the next." She stared at me with a pensive gaze, willing me to understand. "I wish people could learn to slow down and... *just be.*"

On the drive home, I couldn't shake her words, spoken with such a depth of understanding. My route home was so familiar that as my body went through the motions, my eyes wandered from the road to the endless farmland around me, a patchwork of crops and pastures. My mind followed suit, drifting into contemplation about what it would look like to *just be*. Was I doing too much? Or was I allowing myself to get lost in distractions?

Chapter Seven

Weeks tumbled by with birthday parties, dentist appointments, committee meetings, and time spent with Liz. At
home, I could barely keep up with the demands of food preparation
and laundry. George was away for a whole week on a business trip
and then at a conference in Whistler the weekend after that. A few
snow flurries had come and gone, dusting the ground just enough
to leave a brief reminder of winter's presence before disappearing.

Late one afternoon, I walked over to Stan's place. Peeking
through the glass of his front window, I saw him sitting in his old
recliner, a blanket draped over his legs. His face lit up when he
saw me, and with a casual wave of his arm, he motioned for me to
come in. As I let myself in, the warmth of his home felt welcoming. I removed my shoes and looked over at Stan.

He crossed his arms and looked away from me as he said, "I've
been feeling a bit neglected lately. I haven't seen you in almost
two weeks."

"I've been busy with the boys, with Liz—"

"I know, I know," he cut the air with his hand, "but *I* also need
some time with you."

I glanced at his clock. I needed to start dinner soon. "I was
thinking, since it's supposed to be a sunny day tomorrow, how

about we go on a special outing? We'll take the SkyTrain and then the SeaBus to North Vancouver and have lunch at Lonsdale Quay."

He mulled over the idea, a grin spreading across his face as he responded, "That sounds good. I've never been on the SkyTrain before, or the SeaBus for that matter. I usually finish my morning ablutions by nine thirty, then I still need time for tea and biscuits, so you can pick me up at ten."

I tilted my head. "Ablutions?"

Stan nodded, counting on his fingers, "Washing, brushing teeth, shaving, that sort of thing. You know, ablutions."

"I've never heard that term before," I giggled. "Okay, see you at ten tomorrow morning."

That night, I lay in bed thinking about Stan and Liz. They couldn't be more different from one another. Liz continued to exude such positivity, despite battling cancer, while Stan seemed entrenched in self-centredness, despite being reasonably healthy. It was interesting how their characters and enduring personalities were shaped by all the things that had happened to them over their lifetimes—not to mention the impact of family and culture. The complexity of the matter, however, was too much to delve into at such a late hour, and I soon drifted off to sleep.

In the morning, I had just enough time to drop off the boys and put the ingredients for a hearty chili into the slow cooker for dinner later. Stan was unusually upbeat as we set off for the day.

He stared at the passing scenery from the SkyTrain and then the SeaBus windows and chatted the whole ride in. Lunch went by without complaint, and he seemed content to wander around the market for an extended period. When fatigue set in, we took the SeaBus back downtown and then meandered toward the SkyTrain station.

"You know, Anne," Stan kicked a small rock off the platform, "I haven't had this much fun in a long time."

A rare smile formed in the wrinkles around his mouth, and I couldn't help but grin back. We stepped onto the train and settled into the seats, silently beginning the trip back to the Park and Ride where I had left the van. Stan had once again chosen a window seat and angled his body to watch the world go by.

Several stations later, a well-dressed young man, probably in his late twenties, with a sleek modern haircut, turned around in his seat to look at me.

"Excuse me, sorry to bother you, but I was wondering if you were someone important?" He scanned my face as if to help trigger recognition. I thought I detected a slight accent but couldn't place it.

"Ummm, no?" My laugh sounded loud in the quiet train. "Unless you consider a mother of four boys important."

The young man, looking a bit embarrassed, turned his whole body around to face me as he explained, "Oh, I thought you looked like a reporter, like someone who would be on TV."

I felt a slight blush rising. "No, but thanks for the compliment."

Over the speaker, the upcoming station was announced. It was our stop. Stan and I gathered our things and disembarked.

On the walk from the station to the van, I noticed deep creases developing between Stan's eyes, his mouth now forming a deliberate frown. I waited until we were seated in the van before saying anything.

"What happened?" I slid the keys into the ignition but didn't start the vehicle. Instead, I looked over at Stan. "You were having such a good time."

He folded his arms and appeared to be pouting. "You shouldn't talk to strangers."

"Really? That guy on the SkyTrain?" I shook my head, feeling a bit exasperated. "He asked me a question and I answered it."

Stan didn't say anything, so I started the van. We were both quiet on the drive home. I could feel myself getting impatient with Stan's mood swings, but as I drove down the highway, my mother's voice echoed in my mind: "*Lass ihm.*"

Her words stirred a memory, taking me back to a peaceful Sunday afternoon when I was still a preteen. My sister Mary and I were seated in the kitchen nook, playing a board game, surrounded by windows that overlooked a vast expanse of farmland with the majestic Mount Baker visible in the distance.

A couple from church had stopped by to have coffee with my parents. My dad was in the living room, engaged in conversation with the man, while in the kitchen, the woman stood at the counter, lamenting about various aspects of her life. My mom quietly brewed coffee and arranged a tray of her homemade baked goods, her movements calm and deliberate.

The woman crossed her arms and glanced around the kitchen. "Your cabinets are so ugly," she'd said. "They're too plain." Her voice was edged with disdain, "They need to be updated."

Mary and I glanced up at our mother, perfectly composed in her blue dress, her permed hair framing her gentle face, and her glasses resting delicately on her nose. She smiled warmly, continued with her preparations, and responded with how much she liked the simplicity of the plain cabinets.

Then the woman turned her critique on us, saying our teeth were crooked and that we should get braces. Mom appeared unfazed by the insults.

After the guests departed, Mary implored, "How can you stand it? She constantly criticizes everything. No wonder people don't like inviting her over."

Mom simply answered, "*Lass ihr.*"

German was the language we all spoke at home, so I understood she meant: let her be the way she is. But I still didn't understand how that excused the woman's lack of manners.

In our basement bedroom, Mary's bed was parallel to mine, separated only by a white nightstand and a simple white lamp. That evening, nestled under homemade blankets, handcrafted by our mother, we talked late into the night. I looked up to her, even though she was just twenty months older than me. When we discussed the encounter with the rude lady, Mary summed it up in a way that seemed beyond her years, "I think it's not what people say, but how we react that matters."

As I turned the van onto our street, Stan drew in his breath, gearing up to have the final say. With an authoritative tone, he pronounced, "I think you are very naive, Anne. You need to learn that it's better never to trust anyone."

I chose to respond in a lighthearted manner, "Well, if I'd had that attitude, I wouldn't have gotten to know you, would I?"

I pulled the van into his driveway. He said nothing in response and got out without looking at me. As I parked the van in my driveway and walked into my home, I found myself thinking, "What a character… Bless his heart."

Chapter Eight

Afternoon sunlight filtered through the windows, casting a soft glow over Liz's tired features. I helped her put on her crocheted slippers, covered her with a blanket, and placed the eye pillow gently over her eyes. Then I settled onto my own mat as we spent the next peaceful hour at relaxation therapy.

At the end of the session, after tidying up the blankets and pillows, I noticed that Liz seemed quieter than usual. During the drive home, she appeared small in the passenger seat. When I looked over, she caught my gaze and breathed in deeply.

"I know I'm going to die soon." Liz's voice was steady and calm, but her eyes were tearing up. "I'm ready to accept it. All I want now is a peaceful journey."

I struggled to hold back my tears, blinking them away to keep my vision clear. My voice caught in my throat as I tried to respond. "I have so much respect for you." A tear rolled down my cheek. "Your attitude is amazing."

We drove the rest of the way in silence. When we got to Liz's house, I helped her in, supporting her up the stairs. We moved slowly as I guided her to the couch. "Do you need anything before I go?"

"I think I'll just sleep until the boys get home," her voice was barely a whisper.

I leaned down and gave her a hug—gentle but lingering. She gave me a small nod, her eyes soft with gratitude.

Her words stayed with me, and the moment I arrived home I went straight to my harp, letting my emotions flow from my heart to my fingertips. From that deep well of sadness, a melody began to flow. I named the song "Peaceful Journey" and played it for the boys that night as they drifted off to sleep.

Shortly after Easter, I visited Liz as she lay on the couch, too weak to move. After a little time spent chatting, she held up a folded piece of paper, her hand trembling from the effort. "Often, I wake up at four in the morning and can't sleep, so I listen to the birds. I wrote this poem one of those mornings. I thought you might like a copy."

I took the page and tenderly held her pale hand for a moment. "Thank you, that's very special." Her hand was cool, a stark reminder that the vibrancy was slowly slipping away from my dear friend. "I'll leave you to have your nap and see you soon."

Before I left, she managed a faint smile and said, "Remember... *just be.*"

When I got home from picking up the boys, I walked over to the piano and carefully placed her handwritten words on the music stand above the keys.

The next day, with the house silent while the boys were at school, I found myself drawn back to the piano. Sitting there, I stared at the words, my fingers instinctively gliding across the keys as if searching for the melody hidden within them.

Faith is like a bird that sings to the dawn while it's still dark
I believe in You, my God
I will keep singing through the darkness in my life.
I cannot see it now, but I know the dawn will come.
I cannot find the right tune of joy,
Still, I will sing a song of trust to You.
When I see the soft glow of a new day coming on the horizon,
I will know once again that You are my God
Who carries me in loving arms,
Lifts me on eagle's wings,
And speaks quietness and comfort
To my innermost being.

Inspired by her words, I composed a melody and called it "Song of Trust." During my next visit with Liz, I sang it to her as she lay on the couch. She listened with a quiet, contented expression. By the time I finished, a single tear rolled down her cheek, and I struggled to hold back my emotions. There was a tenderness in the moment, a peaceful calm radiating around her.

Our family attended the annual church camp retreat on the first weekend of May. The serene forest surroundings immediately created an atmosphere of rest and reflection. The air was crisp and cool but held a subtle warmth, a promise that spring would soon give way to summer.

The boys always looked forward to these weekends and felt comfortable interacting with everyone at the retreat. There were intergenerational baseball games, hikes in the woods, and shared meals together in the lodge. Saturday night was always a highlight, full of energy, with entertaining skits and games that had everyone joining in the fun.

After Sunday lunch, we were loading up the car, getting ready to leave, when a friend approached me. Her expression was serious. "We just found out," she said softly, "Liz passed away early this morning."

I had tried to prepare myself for this moment, but nothing can truly prepare you for the finality of those words. She was gone. My eyes welled up, and as I walked toward George, the tears flowed freely. We held each other tightly for a while, then George suggested, "Let's go for a walk down the nature trail."

We walked hand in hand through the woods, silent, cherishing one another a bit more deeply. The sun filtered through the canopy, casting dappled light along the meandering path. Finally, I broke the silence, my voice wavering with emotion. "I'm going to miss her so much."

George squeezed my hand as I continued. "She knew me." I said, dabbing my tears. "Not only like a friend in the church community, but she saw my soul." I stepped over a branch, my feet pressing into the earth with more care than usual, as if each step carried the weight of my thoughts. "We could talk about anything. I'll miss that."

As we emerged from the trail into the open field, we saw other couples walking slowly, their heads bent in quiet conversation. Liz had touched so many lives. Everyone loved her.

Those who hadn't left for home slowly gathered in the lodge, hugging, sharing memories of Liz and crying together.

During the two-hour drive back to our house, we processed the news with our sons. Liz's boys, only slightly older than ours, had always been kind and friendly, creating a bond that made the loss feel even heavier. A quiet sadness filled the van. Our boys, still too young to fully grasp the depth of it all, shed their own tears, mourning not just for Liz but for her sons who had just lost their mother.

There were over three hundred people at Liz's funeral. Her husband requested that I play piano, and that "Song of Trust" be included in the service. As I accompanied the singer, my throat tightened with emotion, remembering Liz and how this song reflected her willingness to embrace the entirety of her journey.

I sat at the front by the piano with a box of tissues beside me. During the eulogy, I lifted my gaze and looked at the crowd, a sea of tear-streaked faces. There was a quiet, collective grief in the room, a shared understanding that we had lost someone very special to all of us.

I felt oddly numb, as though I had detached myself just enough to keep going, to keep playing piano without breaking down in tears. When it was time for the final hymn, my fingers moved across the keys as if I was on autopilot. The congregation's voices filled the sanctuary, and as the last notes faded, I exhaled, relieved that I had somehow managed to hold myself together.

After the funeral, I stopped in at Stan's. I didn't make it past his doormat before my tears started to fall. I could feel my face contorting with anguish and put my hands over my eyes, letting my sorrow wash over me without holding back. Stan walked over, wrapped his long arms around me, and held me as I sobbed. There was comfort in being in the presence of someone I didn't have to explain myself to because he also knew the deep ache of grief.

A few days later, as George and I crawled into bed, exhausted, I said, "We should try to find a way to spend more time together.

Maybe a weekly date night? We could ask Trevor to watch the boys for a few hours. Maybe walk into town for sushi or something?"

"That's a great idea."

Trevor was a teen from church who had a natural connection with the boys. They looked up to him in a way that felt effortless, almost like he was a big brother. We'd asked him to babysit occasionally in the past, and I was sure he would agree to come regularly. He was one of the few people I knew capable of managing our four rambunctious sons.

George was typically quite reserved, so I was happy when he shared his thoughts. "As I was driving home from work today, I was thinking about how short life is... Liz was so young. You just never know what's going to happen next."

"It's true. We need to savour every moment. That's what Liz said so often."

We lay in comfortable silence for a few minutes until sleep began to tug at our eyelids.

"Good night," I said. "I love you."

"I love you too."

Chapter Nine

Morning light spilled through the blinds as my alarm clock rang, nudging me out of bed and into the rhythm of another day. After getting the boys off to school, I inhaled a deep breath of fresh air and started my walk into town to grab a few groceries and pick up the mail.

As I strolled down the street, my attention was drawn to the vibrant hues of the tulips adorning the yards of my neighbours. Liz had always been especially fond of tulips. We had recently begun the tradition of taking a day trip to the Tulip Festival each spring.

The soft whir of bicycle tires against the pavement caught my ear, and I watched a young woman glide by, her face full of ease and purpose. As I neared the park, I noticed a mother beside a stroller soothing her crying infant. She balanced a coffee in one hand, and in the other, a leash looped around her wrist keeping a small dog close.

As I walked past the cemetery, the memory of that day came rushing back—the solemn gathering of family and friends, the quiet sobs, and the heavy stillness as Liz's casket was gently lowered into the earth. That was almost two weeks ago, but the image was so vivid, I reached into my pocket for a tissue, wiping away the tears that had welled up at the thought.

At the post office, people popped in and out, exchanging small talk as they grabbed their letters and parcels. I heard the faint clang of construction as I walked to the grocery store. Someone in the distance was probably building a new house.

In every direction I turned, the quaint town of Fort Langley was enjoying a typical spring day. Despite feeling suspended by grief, there was something comforting about knowing that the world continued to spin.

I noticed posters around town for the annual May Day Parade, which would transform our quiet village into a bustling hub of bright colours and cheerful noises. I was grateful to have a few more days before this festive energy would make its way through the centre of my heavy heart.

I located our folding lawn chairs in the far corner of the garage and asked the boys to help set them up in front of the hedges by the road. At least two dozen people from church were planning to attend the parade. Liz's family had always been part of the group that came, and their absence this year would be deeply felt. I had also invited Stan to join us.

After our potluck picnic lunch, we all settled into our lawn chairs and blankets to enjoy the parade. Marching bands and floats, each boasting unique themes and sizes, trundled by. Performers waved and occasionally tossed handfuls of candy or squirted water from their water guns in our direction, while my boys waved their arms, asking for more. Even Stan seemed to hold a steady smile until a clown narrowly missed his head with a spritz intended for the boys.

The parade ended with a procession of antique and collector cars. Droves of people were already walking behind them toward the park at the end of our road where the May Day festivities would continue into the evening.

"You know, Anne, this is the first time I've ever watched the parade."

I gave Stan a quizzical look and said a little incredulously, "How is that possible? It goes by our houses every year!"

Stan sighed and looked at the ground. "I know." He pushed down a clump of grass with the heel of his shoe and then looked back at me. "But I feel as if I'm waking up from a long sleep. I've even noticed that I have more energy than I used to."

I grinned and stood up, folding my chair. "That's great."

Stan walked back to his house looking lighter on his feet than he had in some time. At his driveway, he turned around and shouted, "Thanks for the invitation."

I gave him a wave.

Before I even reached the door, I could hear music coming from Stan's home. I didn't bother knocking and just let myself in. He peered up from the record player as I entered, the scratchy sound of an old vinyl record filling the room.

"It's Glen Miller," Stan yelled over the song. "It's called 'In the Mood.'"

I took off my shoes and stepped onto the thick shag rug, only to be swept up in Stan's arms. He twirled me around the room in rhythm to the retro tune. A combination of delight and uncertainty bubbled up in me in the form of a tentative laugh.

"Don't you know how to swing dance?" Stan asked, his eyes twinkling.

He was effortless and graceful in his moves as he led me, and I tried to follow along while still laughing at being swept up like this. When the song ended, Stan released my hands and turned down the volume. He collapsed into his chair, and I flopped down on the couch.

By way of explanation, I offered, "We weren't really allowed to dance growing up."

"Really? What a shame. Had you been born forty years earlier, you would have been the belle of the ball," he said with a confidence that compelled me to believe him.

"It's not that I personally have anything against it," I added quickly. "There just wasn't any opportunity for dancing in my world." With a slight blush colouring my cheeks, I changed the subject. "Why do you walk with a cane anyway? You obviously don't need one."

He straightened his shirt and adjusted a cuff, composing himself before replying. "I've always thought that a gentleman with a cane commands a certain amount of respect. When I was younger, I looked forward to the day when I would stroll down the street with a cane."

"Huh, I never would have thought of it like that."

"C'mon, let's try some more swing steps."

While preparing dinner that afternoon, my thoughts kept drifting back to dancing. I couldn't deny it—I loved the way it made me feel. There was a sense of freedom to it, a release that makes you forget everything else for a little while.

It brought back memories of one summer during my teenage years when I had saved all my berry-picking money to buy a transistor radio. I would lock my bedroom door, turn on the station everyone at school raved about, and lose myself in the rhythm of an ABBA or Beach Boys song. The exhilaration I had once felt swept over me again while dancing in Stan's living room.

"What do you think about taking ballroom dancing classes at the community centre?" I asked George that evening. I was unsure what he would say, considering the ingrained cultural taboo around dancing that we both grew up with, but he surprised me.

"I've always wanted to learn. Maybe then we can dance with confidence at the next company Christmas party!"

"Are you sure you'll have time? I looked into it, and classes are every Wednesday evening at seven o'clock."

His brow furrowed slightly as he gave it some thought. "I can't really give up another evening, so I guess that would have to be our date night."

"I'm okay with that. I think it will be fun."

And so, with visions of my husband and I expertly twirling around the dance floor by Christmas, I signed us up for a six-week course. However, by the end of the first lesson, George acknowledged that he wasn't naturally gifted at dancing. Despite his slightly bruised ego and my slightly bruised toes, we chose to finish all six weeks of the dance lessons.

I reminded myself that being a good dancer wasn't even on my list when I was seeking a marriage partner in my early twenties. At the age of eighteen, I had already decided that I would only devote my time to men I could envision as lifelong partners. When I worked as a receptionist at a car dealership, hardly a day went by without someone asking me out—to dinner, a movie, or even just for a drive. However, if I did say yes and realized after the first date that there was no potential for a future together, I ended things right away.

After a hundred different dates and a few short-term relationships, my dad started to worry that I was waiting for a knight in shining armour who didn't exist. When I turned twenty-one, he warned me that I was at risk of becoming an old maid. He reminded me of all the good options from church that I'd already passed up, but I wasn't willing to settle. I wanted someone with strength, intelligence and shared values—someone who would also make a great father. Most importantly, I refused to marry anyone I wasn't truly in love with.

The first time I met George was at a rollerskating event organized by several church youth groups. I vividly remember mentally checking off my criteria: we shared a passion for travel, he held my hand with a firm grip, and we came from similar backgrounds. He aspired to be an architect, and I was drawn to his dreamy dark eyes. After our very first date, I knew—he was the man I had been waiting for. Two years later, we were married.

Chapter Ten

I brought Stan a plate of cookies, and he eagerly helped himself as he handed me the latest letter from Lulu. Tucked inside was a photo of her standing in a garden, dressed in a navy blue pantsuit and looking younger than I had imagined. The flirtation between them was charming.

As I finished reading the letter aloud, Stan reached for another cookie and said, "If I had to choose, I'd take pastries and cookies over any other kind of sweet. Baked goods are my weakness. What about you?"

I responded without hesitation. "I love chocolate. When I was young, I would save up all my hard-earned money just to buy a Cadbury Caramilk chocolate bar. It was my absolute favourite. I would savour every bite, one square at a time."

"I think I need a computer desk."

Stan changed subjects so quickly that sometimes it left me wondering whether he heard anything I said, even when he was the one who asked the question.

"That room in the back is the only one left to organize, and the old table in there is wobbly," he continued. He dunked the cookie in his tea before popping it in his mouth. "Will you take me to Staples?" His request was muffled by his chewing.

"Sure, but I won't have time until next week."

"Say, what are you doing for dinner tomorrow?"

"I don't have anything planned yet. George will be working late again."

"How about we go out for burgers? I haven't had a hamburger in fifteen years. I've been craving McDonalds. I'll pay for you and the boys if you take me there."

Despite my initial resistance to indulging in unhealthy fast food, the temptation of a night off from cooking was too strong to resist. Besides, I hadn't had a burger in a long time either, and I knew the boys would love it.

Stan took a bite of his Big Mac. "Mmmm, I forgot how tasty a burger is." Each satisfied moan affirmed my decision to go along with Stan's suggestion to eat at McDonalds.

"I've got something to tell you about Lulu," he said as he slurped root beer through his straw. "I got tired of waiting for her letters, so we've been talking on the phone a lot this past week. But now my phone bills are going to cost a pretty penny."

"Right." I calculated the international call rate in my head as I wiped ketchup from Mark's chin.

"We talked for almost two hours last night, and I suggested she come to Canada for a visit." His eyes sparkled, "She called this morning and already booked her flight. She's arriving at the end of this month!"

"Oh wow! How exciting. I can't wait to meet her!"

At this point, the boys were done devouring their food and already climbing up the slide in the brightly coloured ball pit. When they started hurling the plastic balls at each other, I knew it was time to leave before things got out of hand.

Stan chose the cheapest desk available at the office supply store. It came in a box and needed to be assembled. It was a sizable desk with upper shelves and lower filing drawers. Once we hauled the heavy box into the back room, I opened it and began laying out the pieces.

Stan sat in a chair and started flipping through the instructions. Eventually, he stood up and dropped the pamphlet in front of me. "I'm not good at this sort of thing."

I looked up at him from where I sat in the middle of the floor, surrounded by a mound of hardware. "What sort of thing?"

"Following directions."

He shuffled back into the living room. I hadn't anticipated assembling the desk alone but decided it was probably more efficient this way anyway.

It took four entire visits to get every nut and bolt in place, but my true sense of satisfaction came when I began organizing his papers into the filing drawers.

I didn't mind paperwork—at least not until it started piling up. Managing everything at home involved picking up and sorting the mail, writing cheques and paying bills by mail, making trips to the bank, and keeping our filing cabinet organized. I also assisted George in managing his business finances. Then there were things like the boys' medical and dental records and never-ending school forms, and of course, compiling the papers for tax season. I was always relieved when May came around and the taxes were done.

When I finally finished organizing Stan's office, there were neatly labelled files for every bill and document that used to be haphazardly stacked in a pile, including a big file for all of Lulu's letters. I named the file "Louisa" and decided that I would call her by her proper name from then on. It felt more respectful, and besides, after reading enough of her letters, I had concluded that she seemed more like a Louisa than a Lulu to me. There was a quiet strength and grace in her words that didn't quite match the lighthearted nickname.

I took a proud glance at his new office before heading down the hall toward the living room.

"I'm done," I told him, utterly exhausted.

Stan rose from his leather recliner and met me at the door. "I do appreciate everything you've done for me," he said, handing me a Cadbury Caramilk bar.

"Oh, you didn't have to get me anything." I was shocked that he had listened to, much less remembered, our conversation about my favourite chocolate bar. "Thank you. I haven't had one of these in years."

"You earned it."

I sure did, I reflected silently, *that was a lot of work!* Yet I didn't voice my thoughts because Stan's face held such genuine gratitude. In that moment, my fatigue quickly faded, and all I could do was accept the chocolate bar with a knowing smile.

With less than a week until Louisa's arrival, I stopped by Stan's for a quick visit. When I knocked, there was no response. I rang the doorbell, waiting, but there was still only silence. Worried, I found the door was unlocked, so I let myself in, calling into the darkened home, "Stan?"

He came around the corner with an almost hysterical look in his eyes.

"Don't come near me, I think I have the flu!" He seemed disoriented. There were beads of sweat on his forehead. "I'm feeling a bit dizzy."

"You should lie down!" He didn't look good at all. "I think I should call an ambulance, Stan. Something is definitely wrong."

He was almost in tears. Collapsing onto the sofa, he pleaded, "No, no, please don't. Please don't call an ambulance. Promise me you won't call. It's probably just the flu."

I moved toward him, but he raised his hand in protest. I stood for a moment, observing him lying there, his breath coming in halting exhales. "Please, just go. I don't want you getting sick. Promise me you won't call anyone."

"Okay, but are you sure?"

"Yes, please go. I'll be fine, really."

I left, promising that I wouldn't call an ambulance, but a lingering sense of unease stayed with me.

George had promised me that he would be home in time for dinner that night, so I had decided to prepare one of our family-favourite meals, a roast beef dinner. A rich aroma wafted through the kitchen as I basted it.

Growing up, we had butchered our own cattle and often enjoyed roast beef. I vividly recalled one dinner with my family when my mom remarked that everything on the table had come from our farm—from the meat and vegetables to the milk and homemade butter. Gathering around the dinner table was a sacred time for us, as we were sharing not just a meal but also a lively exchange of stories.

This afternoon, my boys sat around the kitchen table working on their homework assignments. As I peeled potatoes and carrots, my role shifted between addressing their questions and diffusing trivial arguments. All the while, my mind kept circling back to Stan's illness. I couldn't shake my concern for him.

George got home just as the Yorkshire pudding came out of the oven—a golden, pillowy perfection. The boys' favourite part of the meal was dunking it into the rich brown gravy.

That night, as I made my rounds from one bedroom to the next, youngest to oldest, it was clear that all the boys were content.

Our conversations had a comforting rhythm. Maybe their peaceful state had something to do with their dad being home early that night. It certainly was a nice change to have the whole family together at the dinner table.

In the morning, I went over to check on Stan. He greeted me at the door as if nothing had happened.

"You look fine today," I remarked, the surprise and relief apparent in my voice.

"I feel fine," he said. "Must have been something I ate."

"I brought a frame for that picture of Louisa so you can put it on your new desk."

"Wonderful." He walked over to the dining table, picked up the photo, and handed it to me. I carefully slid the picture into place just as Stan mentioned he'd received a letter from his sister, Irene.

"You've never mentioned that you have a sister."

"Irene writes depressing letters occasionally. She's a total recluse, not very healthy, and she has a very negative outlook on life."

I silently acknowledged the familial trend. "What was it like growing up in London?"

"My parents... well, I was just a young boy when my father died. My mother was an opera singer, but she never achieved the fame she hoped for."

I settled into the couch, ready to go on another adventure through his storytelling.

"Did you know that police in London were called *bobbies* and carried billy clubs?" A low laugh escaped him. "And they used a secret rhyming slang with one another which, later, was used by common folk as well."

"I've heard of it, but don't know much about it."

"*Apples and pears* means stairs, and *Barnet Fair* means hair. And instead of saying the whole phrase, people would just say the first word, like, 'I went up the apples,' or 'I got my Barnet cut.'"

"That's fascinating!" I couldn't help but giggle. Sometimes Stan's stories felt like a journey through time, offering a sense of travel without leaving my seat. I loved the feeling of being transported, especially as I hadn't done much travelling at all since George and I had settled down to have children.

"Why haven't you ever gone back to London for a visit?" I asked him.

"I have absolutely no desire to go back. I would rather remember things exactly as they were when I left." It seemed as if that door was closed for further discussion.

He continued. "When we heard about work opportunities in Canada in 1954, we decided to go. As soon as I got a job, Bubbles, Stanley, and I moved into a brand-new house in Edmonton. We thought we were in heaven. And then one day—I'll never forget it—we came to Vancouver on holiday." A broad grin illuminated his face. "We couldn't believe how beautiful it was here! Why stay in Alberta? So, I promptly gave my notice, sold the house, packed up the family, and we moved. Just like that. We settled in Richmond, near the coast, and were delighted to get away from the harsh winters in Edmonton. We never looked back."

Stan explained that his new job was in a lab at the University of British Columbia. He had been a wood technologist and species analyst. Trees were his life. He pointed out his coffee tables, two large slabs of oak in his living room that he had sanded by hand and finished with multiple layers of lacquer.

He was delighted that I was interested in hearing about his career and promptly got up and returned from the spare bedroom with a long stick.

"This is a cross-section of a 483-year-old tree," he instructed proudly. "I counted every ring myself, more than once."

I carefully examined the piece of wood with his markings and numbers on it. "Wow, it must have had a diameter of... what, about seven feet?"

"Yes," he replied, watching as my hand traced the smooth edge of the stick.

"Unfortunately, that," he pointed at a crack close to one end, "happened during our move to Fort Langley, but I carefully glued it back together exactly as it was. When I retired, we drove around a lot, exploring different areas all over the lower mainland. We decided to move to Fort Langley because it was so charming, with its heritage buildings and the farmland surrounding the town. We thought it would be a good place to spend our final years."

"Good choice. We love it here too," I remarked as I stood up to leave.

"Before you go, I have another chocolate bar for you."

When he disappeared into the kitchen to get the bar, I looked again at the photo of Louisa, admiring her wavy dark hair and radiant smile. Stan came back with a Caramilk as I pointed to the picture.

"Are you ready for this? She'll be here in two days!"

"I can't wait," he beamed, handing me the chocolate.

Chapter Eleven

S tan was a nervous wreck on the morning of Louisa's arrival. He shifted in his seat and talked non-stop all the way to the airport. Once we were inside the terminal, he paced back and forth in front of the electronic board, scanning the status of incoming flights.

When the board finally showed that her flight had landed, he said, "What if Lulu doesn't look like the picture? I haven't seen her in donkey's years. What if she sent an old photo or gained a lot of weight since then?"

I stood beside him. "Don't worry, it'll be fine."

"What if that's her?" he pointed to a hunched-over, elderly lady snailing along with her walker. We both burst out laughing.

As our laughter tapered off, Stan began to fidget with the bouquet of flowers he had brought. "I feel like a schoolboy," he giggled, unable to hide his excitement.

Just when I thought Stan's nerves were at their limit, Louisa emerged, dressed in the same outfit she wore in the photo, sweet smile and all. I could see the anticipation on her face as she quickened her pace and walked straight into Stan's open arms. Reunited at last, they held each other in a warm embrace. She was shorter than I had imagined, and I noticed her rising onto her tiptoes as she hugged Stan.

She flung her arms open to hug me as well, and her words came out with a posh British lilt. "It's lovely to meet you, Anne. Stan has told me all about you."

"Nice to meet you too," I replied warmly.

Stan walked alongside her, full of questions about her trip as we made our way through the parking lot. He lifted her suitcases into the back of the van, his face beaming.

On the ride home, conversation flowed easily between Stan and Louisa. They were already finishing each other's sentences and exchanging quiet laughs. Her easygoing nature made her instantly likeable.

When we pulled up to Stan's house, I helped carry the luggage inside, then stepped back toward the door. "I'll leave you to your visit," I said. "But call me if you need anything."

"Nonsense," Stan declared. "You must join us for lunch at the Lamplighter on Tuesday."

I chuckled at his mock sternness. "Okay, sounds good. I'll come by around eleven thirty, so we have time to walk into town together."

Back at home, I went straight to the kitchen, washed my hands, and got to work preparing dinner. I was running a little late, but a glazed meatloaf with mashed potatoes and a medley of vegetables was quick, easy, and the boys loved it.

George arrived home after the boys were in bed. He came into the kitchen, setting his briefcase down near the table. I took the plate I'd saved for him from the fridge, placed it in the microwave, pressed the buttons, and went to the sink to finish scrubbing the last of the pots and pans.

"I think Louisa will be good for Stan," I said. "I hope she sticks around."

The microwave beeped. I dried my hands on the dish towel, took out the steaming plate and set it in front of George. Then I opened the cutlery drawer, grabbed a knife and fork, and passed them to him.

"Maybe Stan will find joy in his life again," he commented.

"I hope so."

George raised an eyebrow, his tone teasing but with a hint of concern. "Maybe then you won't have to commit as much time to him."

"I know," I smiled, wiping down the counter. "Stan can be quite demanding. Even having lunch with them on Tuesday means pushing something else aside. Tim desperately needs a new pair of shoes—he's in the middle of a major growth spurt. And I really need to start practising for the wedding I'm playing harp for next Saturday."

Between bites, George looked up, his head tilting slightly as he listened to me continue.

"And it's my turn to bring baking for coffee time this Sunday." I leaned against the counter. "It feels like there's never enough time."

"You're stretching yourself too thin," George said, scraping his fork across the plate to scoop up the final bite before sliding it toward me.

I picked up his dirty dishes and put them into the dishwasher. "I just find it hard to say no. Everyone seems to need something."

Tuesday arrived in the blink of an eye. Sauntering along the side-walk, Louisa held hands with Stan but directed most of the conversation at me. It felt as if we were already dear friends from long ago merely catching up after some time apart.

We showed Louisa some of the local landmarks as we walked. Stan said, "There, in the cemetery, is the war memorial honouring the veterans." We took a few more steps.

"And that cute little building, called the Little White House," I pointed across the street, "used to be called the Marr House. It was named after Benjamin Marr, the first doctor in the area. I'm pretty sure it was built in 1910. He also planted all these chestnut trees along the road as memorials to Langley men who died during the first world war."

"I didn't know that," Stan said as he stopped to admire the trees.

"It's wonderful," Louisa stared at the old house. "I've never seen so many buildings made of wood. That's not common in England. Most of them are brick where I come from."

A short distance further, we arrived at the Fort Langley Community Hall. It stood in the centre of town, painted a sunny yellow, its historic facade adorned with towering white columns.

"This was built in the early 1930s," I told her.

"Not very old compared to the village I live in. Most buildings are at least five hundred years old, some over a thousand. But I must say, I do like this setting. It's very quaint."

Just down the road, we stepped into the Lamplighter Restaurant—my favourite destination for date nights. George and I had become regulars, and occasionally, Paul—the owner and head chef—would treat us to a complimentary glass of Limoncello as a *digestif.*

Stan, Louisa, and I were met by a friendly server and seated at an antique wooden dining table with a small vase of fresh gerbera daisies in the centre. Louisa flapped open the menu in front of her. "Lunch is usually my main meal of the day. I eat less for dinner."

The corners of Stan's mouth curled upwards. "I like that."

At my house, dinner was the big meal of the day, so I browsed the sandwich options.

Louisa ordered a full salmon dinner accompanied by jasmine rice and seasonal vegetables. Stan ordered the same.

Though my sandwich filled me up, Louisa in her thick British accent kept insisting, "You'll join me for pudding, won't you? Oh yes, you must have a pudding."

It took me a moment to figure out that she meant dessert. We ordered, and the sweet, tangy foam of passion fruit mousse with seasonal fruit hit the spot perfectly.

Later that night, after the boys were in bed, I emptied a basket of clean laundry onto the sofa and turned on the TV, settling on a random show. Methodically, I began the task of organizing each person's garments into neat piles on the coffee table while putting aside a separate stack for the inevitable sock sorting session. George was out at another meeting.

Ever since we'd met, George had dreamed of eventually owning his own business. With the company he was working for restructuring, George and two of his co-workers took the unique opportunity to start their own integrated design and construction company. For months now, they had been meeting to work out the details, and more often than not, the sixth spot at our dinner table sat empty.

When he came home that night, his face was alight with excitement. He wrapped his arms around me in a tight hug, practically vibrating with enthusiasm.

"It's finally happening!"

"Really? When?"

"Officially starting in a few weeks. We already secured our new office space downtown! Everything's falling into place."

"That's exciting!" I listened attentively as he shared the details of the business venture, his words tumbling out in a rush, his joy infectious. I had rarely seen him so happy. His dream was finally becoming a reality.

"It's going to demand hard work and sacrifice." He looked into my eyes. "I hope you understand that."

"Of course. I know how much this means to you, and I'm totally supportive," I said with a smile, though I could already feel my heart sink a little as I realized this wasn't the end of me micro-waving leftovers for him every night.

He kissed me. "It means a lot to me to have your support."

"What about our plans to take the boys to Port Hardy in August?" I wanted to visit my sister Mary, who worked there as a teacher.

"I won't be able to take any time off for a while," he said with an apologetic frown, "so you'll be on your own for that trip."

I wasn't worried about my ability to manage but knowing that the boys would be missing out on quality time with their father saddened me deeply.

I had always been worried about the boys not having their dad around as much as they needed, but as they grew, it felt even more important to make sure they had positive role models in their lives. That's when Trevor started taking on a more active role. The fact that he had his own car made things even easier. He started dropping by whenever his schedule allowed, just to hang out, and often stayed for dinner.

Trevor was incredible with them. He taught them baseball techniques, took them to the park, jumped on the trampoline with them, tossed the football around, and, most importantly, spent time with them. It wasn't just about keeping the boys busy—he genuinely engaged with them, offering that priceless feeling of being seen and valued.

Having Trevor around gave me a chance to catch up on things around the house. The extra time was a rare and welcome gift. The boys adored Trevor—a trusted mentor they looked up to. I was deeply grateful for his presence in their lives.

The air was infused with the sweet fragrance of freshly cut grass. With school out for the summer, the boys filled their days playing with friends or hanging out with Trevor whenever he stopped by. I enrolled them in swimming lessons, which created a bit of structure for a few weeks and added to their fun.

Mornings were leisurely without the usual school rush, and we all felt more relaxed—all except George, whose workload had intensified significantly, making him even more distracted than before.

When August arrived, the nine-hour journey to Port Hardy was filled with endless questions, sibling squabbles, and constant requests for snacks and bathroom breaks. About halfway through the trip, I finally had to pull over. Tim and David's scuffle had escalated from shoves to punches, and now there was blood. I got them out of the van, separated them, and told them we weren't going anywhere until they were ready to shake hands. It took a full twenty minutes for them to cool down enough.

When we finally arrived at Storey's Beach, where Mary met us, it was all worth it. The boys exploded out of the van, unleashing pent-up energy from the long drive like wild horses set free.

With the tide out, the dark grey sand seemed to stretch endlessly before them. I watched my sons run from one clam hole to another, their laughter ringing through the air as they stomped and squealed when water shot up.

Above me, two majestic bald eagles soared before perching on the tops of towering spruce trees. As if flipping a switch, I was suddenly surrounded by an all-encompassing tranquility—a boundless peace that seemed to overflow. It was breathtaking. Tears welled in my eyes as a melody began to stir in my mind.

I became absorbed in the scene, recalling a time when George and I had walked hand in hand on this very same beach. It felt like a lifetime ago.

Shortly after we were married, we devoted two years to volunteering with the Mennonite Central Committee, helping manage a group home in Port Hardy that provided shelter and support for Indigenous children facing difficult situations.

Together, working side by side, we supported children who had endured trauma, abuse, and neglect, each with their own unique needs. At that point, I remember feeling like we had the marriage I had always hoped for. George was great with the kids, whether it was playing baseball or flying a kite at the beach. I could envision our future together so clearly, and eagerly looked forward to starting a family of our own.

We didn't have to wait long. We were both overjoyed when we learned I was expecting. The pregnancy felt natural and easy—my body completely in tune with the experience.

George Matthew was born just before we left Port Hardy. Originally, we intended to name him Matthew George because I thought the name George was too big for a little baby. I vividly remembered the fourteen hours of labour and the moment he had arrived, when the doctor joked, "I can tell who the father is, but are you sure you're the mother?"

I recalled George's broad, genuine smile when I agreed that our son would carry on the tradition, becoming the fifth generation of first-born sons named George.

"Come and eat," Mary called out to the boys as she unpacked her cooler. Their excited shouts and the gentle thud of their hurried feet on the sand brought me back to the present. I walked over to help my sister prepare our picnic, thanking her for taking the time to plan and organize everything for our stay. It already felt like a holiday to me.

Mary had chosen to remain single and had dedicated her life to being the grade one teacher at a local First Nations school. She felt a deep connection to Port Hardy, its community, and its surroundings. It was home for her. Every summer, we made the trip to visit her, and every Christmas, she came to stay with us. The boys adored their aunt and especially loved these trips. Each visit was an adventure, creating memories we could cherish long after we'd departed. Too bad George couldn't join us this time.

Chapter Twelve

We exchanged a knowing glance before beginning the processional, our steps slow and deliberate as I linked my arm with George's.

Nostalgic memories flooded in as I recalled my own walk down the aisle fifteen years earlier. A string quartet had played *Pachelbel's Canon in D* while George, in a navy suit and sporting an '80s moustache, stood at the front of the packed church, waiting for me. The tradition of fathers walking their daughters down the aisle had begun to shift at that time, and I was grateful. I knew walking with my dad would have been far too emotional for me. Besides, I was ready to take that important step alone. The pews had been filled with five hundred people, including extended family from both sides and church members that I'd known all my life. On that balmy August afternoon, everything had gone according to plan.

As George and I neared the end of the aisle on this crisp, clear October day, we parted and took our places as maid of honour and best man. I turned around and looked back down the aisle, feeling a sense of pride as I watched Stan and Louisa begin their processional, her arm locked in his, their faces aglow.

Theirs was a whirlwind courtship to which I'd had a front row seat. Over the past few months, I had taken them on numerous outings and watched their friendship blossom. They'd already had a common history and a deep connection, so I wasn't surprised when they decided to get married.

Louisa had asked me to take her shopping for her wedding outfit. I had admired her British sense of style and her confidence in how she adorned herself at this stage of her life. She looked radiant in the cream suit and matching hat that she'd expertly picked out at the hat shop in Fort Langley.

Stan had insisted on wearing his veteran's jacket with a row of military medals pinned to the breast pocket. As a final touch, I had fastened an orchid boutonniere to his lapel, the soft bloom a quiet echo of Louisa's corsage. Each step they took kept time with Stan's favourite Chopin piece played on the piano: *Nocturne, Opus 9, Number 2.*

While the pastor delivered a short message about love, I looked around, humbled by the various areas where volunteers from my church had generously extended their love. From the abundance of hydrangeas and candles that adorned the front of the sanctuary to the pianist and the pastor who freely shared their time, they had made this event special for my elderly neighbours.

"I now pronounce you husband and wife."

Stan kissed Louisa, eliciting thunderous applause from my sons, soon joined by everyone else in the room. As the recessional played, Stan whisked his bride out through the back doors.

After the reception, the limousine I had arranged as a special surprise pulled up. Stan stammered, "A limo? I can't believe it." He looked genuinely thrilled by this unexpected gift, turning to me to say, "I can't thank you enough for everything you've done."

"You're very welcome." I didn't mention that I had never been in a limo myself, or that this particular one had been a bargain, costing only a little more than a taxi.

Louisa threw her arms around me and gushed, "It was a wonderful day, more than I ever could have hoped for. The food you ordered, the big cake, it was all so lovely."

George Matthew and Tim carried the couple's suitcases to the limo, and a small crowd gathered to wish the newlyweds well and to wave them goodbye as they departed for their honeymoon.

Ten days later, I picked them up at the airport. Their sun-kissed skin glowed, outdone only by the smiles on their faces. All the way home, Stan and Louisa raved about Kauai—the wonderful oceanfront resort I had booked for them, the fabulous weather, and the incredible seafood they had eaten. Eventually, we pulled into their driveway.

"Thanks again for arranging our honeymoon," Louisa said sincerely, giving me a hug. "I can't wait to get the photos developed."

"I'm looking forward to seeing them," I said as I helped them with their luggage, glad they had made it home safely.

The following week flew by in a blur of activity. Tim had karate class on Tuesday, and all four boys had back-to-back dentist appointments the next day. I managed to give them all haircuts and finally caught up on paying the bills. Midweek, I volunteered to chaperone Mark's grade one class on their pumpkin patch field trip, and later that same afternoon, I took the boys to the thrift shop to search for Halloween costumes. George was out of town on business, so I asked Trevor if he could stay with the boys while I went to my committee meeting at church on Thursday night.

When I saw Stan and Louisa again, their printed photos were proudly displayed on the table. The vibrant palms and turquoise waters paled in comparison to the pure joy radiating from the newlyweds' faces. As I browsed through the images, I found a picture of Louisa in a hula skirt with her arms extended to one side, her head tossed back in glee. She looked so youthful.

A subtle pang of jealousy stirred within me. Perhaps it was the idea of a carefree vacation, or maybe their excitement about embarking on a new chapter in life. More likely, it was just my growing sense of wanderlust. Before I could dwell on it, Louisa's voice broke through my thoughts.

"Right. Now that we're settled, I think it's time for some updates around here. Most importantly, we need a fresh coat of paint inside and out. And this ugly green carpet must go. And this couch! Ugh!"

"It's a perfectly good couch! They don't make 'em like they used to, you know," Stan said. He held out his arms, pretending to protect the living room from Louisa. "Anne, tell Louisa it would be a waste of money."

I looked past Stan at the sunken sofa, with its large, faded orange flowers. "I mean, it has seen better days." I tried to sound neutral while being honest at the same time.

"It's settled then. We'll get rid of it straight away!" Louisa playfully tickled Stan to get him to retract his arms. Then she snuggled up close to him. "And what about replacing the fireplace with one of those gas inserts?"

As Louisa continued outlining her list of upgrades and the sheer scale of the project became clear, I reluctantly accepted the role of renovation manager. For the next few weeks, in between grocery shopping, preparing meals, and keeping up with the never-ending laundry at home, I tried to keep my daytime schedule open so I could help Stan and Louisa pick out new furniture, choose carpets, settle on paint colours, and arrange for painters.

Rather than resisting, Stan embraced the plan, even expressing enthusiasm about incorporating a sunroom on the patio. He found a newspaper ad for a company that claimed they could install a patio enclosure with a curved glass roof all in one day.

He called the number and, sure enough, when they arrived a week later, they put up a small sunroom, complete with a new tile floor, all by the end of the day.

I brought over a potted palm to adorn the room and add life to the space. When Louisa entered the sunroom with a cup of tea, she gasped at the plant.

"How beautiful! It reminds me of Hawaii."

Stan wanted his chair in the sunroom, so I wrestled the leather recliner into the corner, despite their protests about its weight. I reassured them that I still had a considerable amount of residual strength from my farm upbringing, which saw me throwing hay bales onto a trailer every summer. Stan settled into his chair and admired the space.

"I'm going to enjoy sitting here. It feels like I'm in the backyard."

Louisa turned toward me, "I've been meaning to ask you, Anne, would you mind taking me clothes shopping again this week?"

I mentally shifted some things around in my schedule before replying, "Sure. I can pick you up at around ten tomorrow morning?"

"Lovely. I'll see you in the morning then."

As I reached the door, Stan yelled his now familiar refrain, "Don't forget your Caramilk bar!"

Chapter Thirteen

The mall was quiet in the late morning, providing the perfect opportunity to ask Louisa more about her life. Stan usually dominated conversations when I visited their home. I asked questions while sliding hangers along the racks.

"I had a wonderful childhood growing up in London. Sometimes my father had to go away on business, but he always came back with sweets for us children. He was a kind man, a good father, and he adored my mother, simply adored her."

We moved toward the back of the store. Occasionally, I held out a sweater or blouse for Louisa to inspect. She picked up a hat and placed it on her head, admiring how it looked in a nearby mirror.

"My family used to go to Cornwall during the summers. I have such fond memories of those vacations—eating ice cream, bathing in the sunshine. My father, he could never stay as long as we could, and I hated seeing him leave. We all loved him dearly." Suddenly, another memory seemed to sour her expression. "I only wish I could have met a man like my father. My first husband was abusive."

"Oh no!" I stepped closer to give her my full attention. "Did you leave him?"

"A few times. I always came back, though. I had nowhere to go and four children to care for." She ran her fingers through her hair, smoothing out the impressions left by the hat, then lowered her voice. "I hate to admit it, but I wasn't very sad when he died of a heart attack. We were separated by then."

I wasn't sure what to say. Louisa continued, almost as if she was talking about someone else's life. "My second husband, he was kind when I met him. It wasn't until later that he became verbally abusive." She pursed her lips while shaking her head side to side. "Oh, he was a nasty man." She practically spat out the word *nasty*.

I couldn't imagine George becoming abusive. Even with his habit of prioritizing work and his occasional emotional aloofness, I never once felt unsafe around him. Quite the opposite, in fact. There was steadfast loyalty in every aspect of his character.

Louisa returned the hat to the shelf, and we walked on.

"When I finally told him I was leaving for good, he took all my photo albums, my possessions—absolutely everything I owned."

I motioned toward the hallway leading to the next clothing store. "Then what happened?"

Louisa paused, the strength in her tone underscoring the depth of her conviction. "I pressed on and just kept going. That was seven years ago. I'm so happy to be away from that man. I should have divorced him much earlier."

We walked a few more steps and her face suddenly lit up. "My goodness, look at that outfit in the window."

With a determined confidence, she strutted into the shop and announced, while pointing her finger, "I want to try on everything that mannequin is wearing."

When Louisa came out of the dressing room, she looked regal.

"What do you think?" she preened, visibly proud of her choice.

"It all looks great on you!" I affirmed.

She bought the pants, top, jacket, socks, shoes, even the necklace that had been displayed. The entire outfit. As we walked out of the store carrying two large bags of new clothes, I couldn't help but ask, "Do you do that often?"

"Yes. If I see something I like, I don't hesitate. I simply must have it. I usually even buy new underwear so that everything I'm wearing is brand new. The full Monty, as we say in England."

We giggled together at that, but I was still having a hard time wrapping my head around justifying such an extravagance for myself. Growing up, my mom often sewed matching dresses for me and my sisters. But being the third sibling in line and getting all the hand-me-downs, this meant that I often had to wear the same dress for about six years. The thought of buying an entirely new outfit from head to toe brought a smile to my face. Maybe someday.

Stan didn't hear us come in, or maybe he chose not to be interrupted. He remained hunched over the piano, enchanted by every note of Franz Liszt's *Liebestraum*. His square-framed glasses threatened to slip from his nose, but it didn't seem to matter because his eyes remained shut. When he played an especially beautiful chord, he slowed right down and tilted his head to take it in more fully, muttering, "Marvellous."

Since meeting Stan, my appreciation for classical music had grown. He talked about Chopin as if they were old friends. He even had a little white bust of the composer atop his piano.

My musical repertoire had been shaped early on—first nurtured in church pews and later deepened through my role as a choir director. Many of the hymns and choral pieces we sang were drawn from scripture and set to classical tunes by renowned composers. For instance, what I knew as *Joyful, Joyful We Adore Thee*, Stan recognized as Beethoven's *Ode To Joy*. But that was the extent of our musical crossover.

I listened to Stan play as Louisa put her new clothes in the bedroom. Although I enjoyed his music, the piano's need for tuning diminished the experience.

As Stan finished, I asked, "When was the last time you had your piano tuned?"

He lowered the lid over the keys but didn't move. "Not too long ago, but it's old and loses its tune quickly." He glanced around nervously to see if Louisa was around. Then, leaning in and lowering his voice as if sharing a secret, he said, "I've been thinking of getting a new one. I've always wanted a grand piano."

From the hallway, Louisa shouted, "That's a great idea, Stan." She came into the room to make her point more passionately. "If you've always wanted a grand piano, then you should have one. Why not? You deserve it after all these years."

I found it endearing how Louisa's effortless generosity toward herself naturally extended to everyone around her.

"It's settled then," Stan declared enthusiastically.

"Great," I chimed in, "We'll go to Heritage Pianos next week!"

On my way out, I grabbed my Caramilk, which had become a regular parting gift that waited for me on a small table beside the door. The accent table's sole function served as the dedicated spot for my chocolate bar.

The spacious piano showroom smelled like polished wood and new leather. I wandered away from Stan and Louisa so they could browse on their own. The Estonia Grand immediately caught my eye, standing out among a row of other impressive pianos. I slid onto its cushioned bench and respectfully placed my fingers on the cool white keys. I spread my hands wide and softly played a song from the endless repertoire in my mind. The bass tones had depth, and the high notes rang sweet and clear. I was swiftly transported to another world, held captive by the enchantment of the notes echoing off the walls around me.

Meanwhile, Stan and Louisa had made their way to the back of the shop where the used section was. I walked through the maze of pianos, following the sound of Stan's melody. As I approached, the salesman was nattering about the affordable price and that this piano only had one previous owner. I watched Stan caress the lustrous oak finish and sensed that he had already made his decision. He played a few chords, which to my ear sounded a bit tinny, but the smile on his face and the adoring way Louisa looked at her happy husband let me know that I was only there to help with transportation, not to offer my opinion.

With the new upgrades in his home, the new sunroom, and now the new piano, Stan's demeanour remained consistently upbeat. He talked about his daily routine as if he'd cracked the code to life.

"Every morning, Louisa brings me tea and cookies in bed, and we stay there until about ten o'clock, reading the newspaper. After my morning ablutions, we move into the sunroom, and I work on the daily crossword. We eat lunch and later go for a walk into town to check the post or buy a few groceries. When we get home, we sit in the sunroom again." He took a sip of sherry. "It gives me enormous pleasure to watch the birds and squirrels in the backyard. And then, when four o'clock comes around, we move into the living room and wait for you." His wide grin suggested that the day he had just described was the epitome of perfection.

Some time ago, after their renovations were complete, Stan and Louisa had begun inviting me over for happy hour at four o'clock—usually just a drop of sherry and a few *crisps*, the British term for chips. It was a whole new experience for me, and I came to cherish those short visits. Popping in for half an hour a couple of times a week allowed me to stay connected without stepping away for long or disrupting the rhythm of my busy days at home.

While I prepared soup for dinner that night, my mind wandered. George's new business was thriving but consuming all his time. Some days, it felt like he wasn't even part of our daily life anymore. He was hardly ever home for dinner, and even when he was, he felt like a distant presence in the house.

Meanwhile, the boys' schedules were becoming more hectic. Every week, I was driving David to violin lessons, rushing Tim to karate, and George Matthew to drum lessons. Tim and David were both in roller hockey and had a tournament coming up on the weekend. At least George would be home for that. Beyond the usual madness of cooking, cleaning and laundry, the holiday season piled on even more. I was involved in planning the Christmas Eve service at church, all the while teaching the youth class on Sunday mornings, playing piano during services and doing Christmas baking wherever I could squeeze it in. I couldn't even imagine a life spent sitting in a sunroom watching squirrels run around, let alone a day spent pursuing my own hobbies and interests. It felt like it had been ages since I'd even played my harp.

The rising bubbles, confirming that the borscht was boiling, brought my attention back to making dinner. I watched the mix of carrots, potatoes, celery, and cabbage as they rose and fell in the rich tomato broth like they knew they belonged. The distinct scent not only evoked comforting memories of my childhood but also seemed to carry with it generations of wisdom.

As I stirred the soup, Liz's words of wisdom surfaced in my mind. *Just be.* A quiet peace swept through me. Was it a reminder to stay present, even in life's busy routines? A reminder to seek inner peace? Whatever those words really meant, I trusted that their significance would gradually be revealed to me.

For now, a huge pot of borscht and the heavenly aroma of freshly baked buns meant that, at the very least, I was fulfilling my role as a good mom and a good wife. And most days, that was what mattered most.

Chapter Fourteen

The chill of winter gave way to the fresh breezes of springtime, bringing a lightness to the air. I finally gave in to the relentless pleading from the boys for another dog. They had been asking for months, wearing me down with their eager faces and promises to look after the dog. I wondered if maybe the problem was that we hadn't had the right breed.

Last summer, while the kids were playing hide-and-seek with a neighbour girl, Bruno had jumped up in excitement and, with his sharp teeth, tore a hole in her new sweater. She ran home in tears, screaming. The boys understood how important it was for everyone to feel safe in our yard, so I had placed an ad in the paper and found an ideal match for Bruno—a truck driver who lived alone on a farm.

I turned my attention to the newspaper in front of me. Flipping through, I came across an ad for a long-haired dachshund in need of a new home because its owners were moving. Maybe this smaller dog would be a better fit for our family than Bruno had been.

A few days later, after a lengthy phone call and then a visit, we picked up Joey, the reddish-brown dog, whose boundless energy at two years old sent him spinning in dizzying circles. When he wasn't being showered with hugs and cuddles, he chased the boys around the house, yapping, hungry for constant attention.

The first time we left him alone in the house for a few hours, we came home to a shocking scene. Newspapers lay shredded across the living room floor, their pages scattered like fallen leaves. Socks and slippers, usually tucked away neatly, were chewed beyond recognition and strewn across every room. In the kitchen, he had somehow managed to get into the trash, spilling and rifling through its contents, leaving a trail of garbage behind. The most heartbreaking sight, however, awaited Tim in his bedroom. His meticulously built Lego castle, a project that had taken him weeks to complete, lay in ruins. As we took in all the destruction, Joey maintained a look of pure, innocent excitement, his tail wagging, clearly proud of his day's work.

I called the previous owner immediately, and she admitted that the dog had never been left alone before. Moreover, she said he had never spent any time in a crate and had always been surrounded by people. I hung up wondering why she hadn't told me all of this before I'd bought him. I began asking Stan and Louisa to dog-sit whenever we were away. They enthusiastically agreed to take him anytime.

Within two weeks, they got so attached, they even asked if Joey could stay for a sleepover. When I went to retrieve Joey after he'd spent the night, he seemed reluctant to leave, and Stan and Louisa couldn't bear to see him go. They hinted at wanting to keep him. After a long goodbye, I brought Joey back to our home and rounded up the boys.

We sat in the family room, all our eyes focused on Joey. David was petting him as I spoke, "We haven't had Joey for very long, and I already feel like maybe he isn't the right dog for our family."

"What do you mean?" George Matthew asked. "We like him."

"I know, but he needs so much attention."

Tim nodded. "And we're too busy and not home enough, right?"

"Exactly." I looked over at David, stroking Joey's long hair and wondered if I was doing the right thing. "Joey gets nervous and anxious when he's alone—he can't handle it. That's why he starts getting into things and wrecking stuff when we're gone. If we put him in a crate, I'm sure he'd be crying all day, and that wouldn't be good for him either."

Mark's eyes widened with sudden clarity. "That's why he likes going to the neighbours."

"You're right. He loves it over there, and Stan and Louisa love having him. They're home all day, every day, and Joey loves that. They give him so much attention."

George Matthew responded, "Then he should be their dog."

"I guess it would be better for him," David said. "He wouldn't get so stressed out then."

"And you could still visit him anytime." I was relieved that the boys were so understanding.

Everyone was silent for a minute. Then I asked, "So, are you all okay if we give Joey to Stan and Louisa?"

"Yeah." Tim was the first to agree.

George Matthew nodded, then Mark. Finally, David spoke, "I think he'll be happier there."

"We might as well bring him over there right now."

"I'll come with you," David volunteered.

I put all Joey's toys and his leash in a bag, and David carried Joey.

Louisa saw us through the front window and opened the door before we even reached it. As soon as we stepped inside and David set Joey down, he ran straight to Stan. Stan's face lit up as he scooped him onto his lap, Joey's tail wagging with excitement.

"The boys and I decided Joey would be better off staying with you."

"I'm so delighted," Louisa gushed. "We would love to keep him!"

"We can't thank you enough," Stan said sincerely. His eyes were sparkling, and even his weathered skin seemed to radiate joy. He looked as happy as he had that Christmas when he played with Tickle Me Elmo.

"I feel as though our little family is complete now," Louisa said, beaming.

"I'm glad." It warmed my heart to see all three of them so happy. "I'll drop in tomorrow," I added, slipping my arm around David's shoulders as we walked back home.

When George came home—late once again—I filled him in on what had happened.

George's lips pressed into a thin, hard line. "Just like that, you made the decision to give Joey to Stan and Louisa?"

"I discussed it with the boys first, and we all agreed he would be better off with them."

His eyes narrowed as if he was holding back anger, "You shouldn't have bought Joey in the first place. Sometimes you rush into things without talking to me first. I could have predicted Joey wasn't the right dog for our family."

"Things have a way of working out, though. You should see how happy Stan and Louisa are."

"That's not the point." I could see tension building in his face and knew I needed to choose my words carefully.

I chose to stay silent.

"Just because the boys wanted another dog, you spontaneously went out and got one."

"We did talk about it. I told you about the ad I found in the newspaper."

"It wasn't a good decision," he concluded. George had a way of making his point and ending conversations on his terms. That was that. He went upstairs to get ready for bed.

I walked around the house, turning off the lights. He was right—buying Joey had been a spontaneous decision—but in my opinion, that didn't make it wrong.

George and I never yelled at each other. Raised in Mennonite homes, we both saw conflict as something to avoid. We tried to keep the peace and discuss things calmly. Growing up, I had learned that it wasn't worth letting disagreements fester or turn into grudges. I also believed that maintaining a peaceful home required being a submissive wife. Combined with George's reluctance to express personal feelings, it meant we rarely clashed. But at times, I wondered if our peaceful home truly reflected inner peace—or if it simply masked a reluctance to have difficult conversations.

Chapter Fifteen

Life carried on at its steady pace, and before long, summer had returned. The moment I stepped into Stan's living room, bright with morning sun, I could tell he was in a cheerful mood.

"I can't believe it's Tuesday already!" he said, "Time goes by so fast. We just seem to go from garbage day to garbage day!"

I chuckled.

"I'm serious, and the older I get, the faster it goes."

Louisa nodded in agreement.

"Then, one day, you look in the mirror and think, who is that wrinkled person looking back at me? I sure don't feel that old on the inside!" He put his fingers around the edges of his face and pulled all the skin back until it was smooth, saying, "Do you think I should get a facelift?"

He looked hilarious, and Louisa and I burst into laughter.

"A facelift!" Louisa repeated and kept chuckling. Once she composed herself, she looked over at me. "You will visit Stan and Joey while I'm in England, won't you?"

"Yes, of course. Don't worry, everything will be fine."

"I'll only be away for two weeks," she said. "I do miss my family terribly and can't wait to see them. I suppose we better get going."

She kissed Stan goodbye, then Joey. I grabbed her suitcases and loaded them into the van.

After dropping Louisa off at the airport, I came back to find Stan and Joey relaxing in the sunroom. The summer heat was thick, and his small rancher felt stifled by the stagnant air.

"Everything went well," I said. "She's off to London."

Stan lounged in his recliner, his unbuttoned shirt hanging loose as he leaned back, his white undershirt visible beneath the open fabric. I saw a small wooden cross resting against his chest and gestured toward it.

"I've never noticed your cross necklace before. Do you always wear it?"

Stan turned it over in his hands. "I made it myself. I never take it off." Dropping it back on his chest, he pulled Joey onto his lap and casually reached for the bag of treats.

"Wouldn't you have liked to go back to England? With Louisa?" I asked.

"No." He took a treat from the bag and waved it in front of Joey's nose. "I'm happy to stay home and look after our little boy."

Joey eagerly nibbled at the treat, looking rounder than he used to, and I wondered just how many treats he'd been getting lately. Stan rubbed the dog's head and set him back on the floor.

"Anne, there's something I've been meaning to say to you for a very long time."

I crossed my hands in my lap, relaxed into the chair, and waited for him to continue.

"First," he cleared his throat, "I need to apologize for how I treated you the day we first met. I was so infuriated walking over to your house, so determined to tell you off. When you opened the door, and I saw your kind, smiling face, I almost stopped dead in my tracks."

I smiled. "But you didn't."

He sighed. "No, I didn't. And I'm very sorry."

I could sense his regret and tried to lighten the mood. "Don't worry about it, Stan, it's all in the past." I waved my hand dismissively.

"No, no." He shook his head, "Really... I don't know what I would have done if you hadn't come into my life."

Stan's face crumpled, the deep lines around his eyes making him look vulnerable. "I probably would have committed suicide, to be honest. I know I would have."

His lower lip trembled slightly. "I had nothing to live for after Vera died." His voice was thin, his tone solemn. Steadying himself, he pulled out his pocket handkerchief and blew his nose. Then he took a deep breath, regaining his composure.

"Secondly, I want to tell you a story." He shifted his posture so that he could face me directly. "As you know, my mother was an opera singer. She would practise for hours on end. There was this song she would sing—*Who is Silvia* it was called. The lyrics are from Shakespeare, the music by Schubert. It was one of her favourite pieces."

I was fully alert as his enthusiasm grew.

"I hated that song throughout my adult life. Absolutely hated it! Do you know why?" Stan's eyes met my shrug.

"Tell me."

"Because Silvia didn't exist. It always made me so mad that there was no such woman." Stan got up to get a little red book by the piano. "Until now."

He handed me the book, already opened to the right page, and gazed into my eyes with the reverence one might have for royalty, "*You* are Silvia," he said, "As I've gotten to know you, it has become clear as day."

He recited the entire piece from memory, while I followed along, reading.

Who is Silvia? what is she,
That all our swains commend her?
Holy, fair, and wise is she;
The heaven such grace did lend her,
That she might admirèd be.

Is she kind as she is fair?
For beauty lives with kindness.
Love doth to her eyes repair,
To help him of his blindness;
And, being helped, inhabits there.

Then to Silvia let us sing,
That Silvia is excelling;
She excels each mortal thing
Upon the dull earth dwelling;
To her let us garlands bring.

As he spoke, my hand instinctively rose to cover my heart. "Thank you, Stan! That's probably the nicest compliment I've ever received in my life."

Stan's face lit up with pride. His eyes shone with a youthful gleam as he gazed into my eyes. "Now I can enjoy that song happily, knowing she—*you*—exist."

Chapter Sixteen

The maple trees throughout town reddened in the crisp October air, their vibrant leaves creating a stunning display of autumn's arrival. Having settled in after the start of yet another busy school year, Stan and Louisa invited me to join them for lunch at the Fort Pub. I was a bit reluctant at first because I had never been to a pub before. I envisioned a dimly lit, grimy place where the worst of society congregated, but Louisa assured me I had it all wrong.

From the moment we left their house, Stan and Louisa's conversation revolved around lively tales of British pubs as they tried to explain to me what to expect, each anecdote adding to the anticipation of arriving at the Fort Pub.

While the lighting inside was dim, there was a warm atmosphere in the room. Most of the available wall space was adorned with a mix of historical and vintage photos. A collection of older gentlemen swapped playing cards in a booth, and a tired-looking waitress floated around with ease among the scattered tables. We sat by the window so that we could see the river.

As Louisa munched on her fish and chips, she continued sharing stories about her recent trip to London. "You really must visit the pubs in England. They truly are the heart of the community. And they do a wonderful Sunday roast beef."

The waitress approached our table and set the bill down saying, "No rush, whenever you're ready."

As he always did on our outings, Stan announced, "This one's on me." He fumbled with his coat pocket. "Oh, I almost forgot... I wanted to show you this," he said, pulling out a grainy photo taken with his Instamatic camera. He held it toward me. "I love this picture. It hangs on the wall at the doctor's office. I'm in there so often, I always stare at it while I'm waiting."

He had mentioned it to me several times—his favourite print— and finally remembered to capture a photo of it. I studied the image closely. A young peasant woman stood by a fence threaded with wild roses.

"She reminds me of you," he said. "Not so much in the way she looks, but there's something about her that exudes the essence of who you are... like Silvia."

"Can I keep this?" I asked.

"Yes, I want you to have it."

I slipped it into my purse, a plan already taking shape in my mind.

With George away on another business trip, I found myself staying up late each night, making progress on all the organizing I'd been putting off in our home office. Long after the boys had gone to bed, I located my magnifying glass and scanned the image Stan had given me, determined to find the artist's name so I could order a copy of the print.

Embracing my inner detective, I studied the signature in the bottom right corner, deciphering each letter with scrutiny. The photo was blurry, so I could barely make it out, but eventually I was confident I had the name correct—Ridgeway Knight.

On the morning of January eleventh, the boys decorated the cake I had baked the night before, as had become our family tradition. I had also instilled the idea that my birthday and Mother's Day were the two days each year that I wanted the luxury of sleeping in a bit longer. When I finally descended the stairs, they belted out their rendition of "Happy Birthday" and presented me with the cake.

I loved how their cake decorating skills became more artistic every year. *Mom* was carefully spelled out in chocolate chips. Around the edges, they'd created a playful border, alternating licorice nibs with bright Smarties. Sprinkles had been liberally scattered over the top, turning the cake into a kaleidoscope of colour. To me, it was a masterpiece, filled with their affection.

Their homemade birthday cards never failed to bring tears to my eyes as well. Unfortunately, my birthday was on a Tuesday this year, so there was no time for lingering. I hugged each of them tightly before dropping them off at school, then returned home to wrap Stan's gift in colourful paper.

Carrying a few pieces of cake in one hand and the gift in the other, I strolled next door, already envisioning Stan's reaction. However, the expression on his face as he opened his birthday present was even better than I'd imagined.

"How on earth...?" Stan's jaw had dropped. He was flabbergasted.

Louisa looked over his shoulder, and her hand flew to her mouth. "Oh, Anne, how did you find this?"

I knew then that it was the perfect gift. "A little computer magic," I said as I mimed tapping on a keyboard. "Happy eightieth birthday, Stan."

Louisa chimed in. "Many happy returns of the day to both of you."

Stan held up the framed print of "Ray of Sunshine" by Daniel Ridgeway Knight. A broad smile stretched across his face as he examined it. "I can't believe it. It's absolutely marvellous." He moved it from wall to wall, envisioning the best place to hang it.

"We can decide where to hang it later," Louisa said, casually putting on her shoes. "I'm looking forward to our lunch at the Lamplighter."

Stan placed the picture carefully in the dining room, then walked over to me and wrapped me in a hug. "Thank you so much," he said softly, adding, "And happy fortieth birthday to you."

The next time I visited, "Ray of Sunshine" was proudly displayed on the dining room wall. Stan pointed at the little lamp that shone down on the peasant girl.

"I drove all over Langley looking for the perfect light to hang above it. What do you think?"

"Looks great," I grinned.

He adjusted the lamp just a centimetre. "I named her Silvia. The girl in the painting."

That made me smile even more broadly. "I'm so glad you like it."

"Like it? I love it!"

The relentless cold of winter dragged on in a continuous cycle of icy winds and grey skies. One evening after dinner, all four boys and I gathered around the kitchen table. Textbooks and art supplies scattered across the surface as they worked on their school projects. I floated between them, offering guidance and encouragement. A bowl of sliced apples sat in the middle, and they snacked on the juicy wedges as the evening wore on, the rhythm of pencils and questions filling the space until it was bedtime.

Although each had his own bedroom, the boys all shared a single bathroom. As they got ready for bed, George Matthew waited patiently for the others to finish, wisely choosing peace over chaos. Meanwhile, Tim and David fought for the toothpaste, eventually knocking the cap to the floor. They elbowed each other as they fought again to be the one standing directly in front of the sink, ignoring Mark as he tried to squeeze between them to rinse his toothbrush. I stepped in, asking Tim to pick up the toothpaste cap and David to hang up the towel that was lying on the floor, urging them along before a real fight could break out.

Once they'd all washed up and gotten their pajamas on, I began my rounds, starting with Mark. He was smiling, as he often did, and informed me that another tooth had begun to feel loose and wiggly. Then he asked if I could tell him the story of "The Three Little Pigs." He scooted over, making room for me to cuddle next to him. After the story, he showered me with hugs and kisses, a sweet display of his natural warmth.

David was in the next room, propped up on his pillow, completely immersed in a library book about planets. We spent time reading the book together, and I could see the wheels turning in his ever-inquisitive mind, fascinated by the workings of the solar system. When I said good night and gave him a hug and kiss, he asked if we could get some of those glow-in-the-dark stars to stick onto his ceiling. I suggested he could use the birthday money from his grandparents to do so, and he readily agreed. I promised we would go shopping for the stars by the end of the week.

Speaking of money, I found Tim in his room counting his savings. From a young age, Tim had a fascination with all things related to money. For his third birthday, he'd asked for "one of those big machines at the bank where you put in a card and money comes out." Having outgrown the red postbox piggy bank that Stan had given him a few years ago, he now used the special money box he'd received from his Aunt Mary. It had three slots: one for spending, one for saving, and one for giving. I noticed the saving section was fuller than the spending, and there was also some in the giving section. Curious, I asked him what he planned to do with the giving portion. He said he wanted to give it to kids who didn't have enough food to eat. I pulled him into a hug, and we talked about the importance of sharing and helping others. I suggested we take some time the next evening to talk about specific charities that would ensure his money would help children in need.

Finally, I walked into George Matthew's bedroom. He was listening to a cassette tape on the tape player he had received for Christmas. He turned down the volume as I sat on the edge of his bed. George Matthew always wanted to know about upcoming plans, eagerly looking forward to events and gatherings. Already, he was excitedly brainstorming ideas for his birthday, still six weeks away. He didn't want to have a big party, just a few friends over and maybe a special cake. After we discussed some of his plans, I kissed him on the forehead, turned out the light, and let him continue listening to his music.

With the boys' evening routine complete, I headed down the stairs toward the laundry room to begin my nightly chores. I thought back to when George Matthew was little and had asked, "Mommy, why do you have to work so hard, and Daddy just gets to draw?" The memory always made me smile. His innocent question had been a reminder of how society often overlooks the countless hours of unseen work a mother puts into her role.

I threw in a load of laundry, then walked into the kitchen and began tidying the table, clearing away dishes and making a stack of each of their homework assignments to put into their backpacks in the morning.

George had called earlier, saying he'd be having dinner with clients and wouldn't make it home until around nine thirty. I was getting the school lunches ready when he walked in. He gave me a hug and asked me how my day was. He was already heading up the stairs when I answered that it had been a good day.

I finished packing up the last lunch and followed him up a short while later. As soon as I walked into the bedroom, I could tell by his breathing that George was already asleep. I joined him in bed, but my eyes simply stared up at the ceiling as I tried to focus on the positive aspects of our relationship. There was far more good than bad. His strong provider instinct was undeniable, and I reminded myself to be patient with him. I rolled over to my side, tucking the blanket around my body, cuddling up in its warmth, only to realize I'd forgotten to put the laundry in the dryer. I got up, grabbed my robe, and made my way down the stairs in bare feet.

I found myself wondering how different things might have been if we had stayed in Port Hardy. I was fairly certain that life would have been simpler, with a slower pace and fewer demands. Thinking back to our time in Port Hardy, I remembered a close friend who often used the phrase "this too shall pass," a mantra that had stayed with me ever since.

Methodically, I shook out each piece of damp clothing before tossing it in the dryer, letting my thoughts wander. I realized my feelings had nothing to do with where we lived—I loved Fort Langley. It wasn't the place. It was something deeper, simmering beneath the surface, tied to the passage of time and how it slipped by unnoticed in the blur of being too busy. Maybe this nameless yearning was something I wasn't ready to face just yet.

After loading the last item, I straightened up, closed the dryer door with a firm push, and turned the dial to start the cycle. The machine hummed to life, and I watched the clothes tumble inside for a moment before heading back up the stairs.

Trying not to wake George, I crawled back into bed, carefully resuming the position I had been in earlier. I closed my eyes and took a deep breath. Amidst the quiet, my mind began to settle, my thoughts stilled, and the familiar phrase echoed. This too shall pass.

Chapter Seventeen

The boys were begging for another dog, which prompted a family meeting. Now that they were fourteen, twelve, ten, and eight, they felt they were finally old enough to handle the responsibility of having a dog.

I initiated family meetings any time there were crucial decisions to be made, important discussions to be had, or disagreements to be resolved. My aim was to create a comfortable space where the boys could express themselves, be heard, and understand the importance of consensus. I wanted them to know that they wouldn't always get their own way in life and that sometimes it was okay to find common ground and make a decision that would be acceptable to the majority.

Our family room was furnished with a mismatched collection of garage sale finds—beige and brown striped couches, a scuffed coffee table, and a slightly crooked floor lamp. Armed with a thick library book about dogs, we huddled around the coffee table, flipping through its pages of glossy photos and detailed descriptions.

Each suggestion sparked a lively debate. Would a Saint Bernard be too large and overwhelming, or should we opt for a smaller dog like a spaniel? We weighed the pros and cons of various temperaments, energy levels, and care requirements. After a lengthy discussion, we collectively settled on the golden retriever as the ideal breed for our family. They were naturally friendly, tolerant, loyal, affectionate, intelligent, and trainable.

I made it very clear to the boys that taking care of this dog would be their responsibility, and we created a detailed chore list that included daily feeding and walking, grooming, filling the water bowl, and picking up droppings in the yard.

When George got home from work that night, the boys were waiting for him in the family room, dressed in their pajamas, teeth already brushed. Knowing he would have the final say, they were eager to present the plan we'd put together that day. After reviewing the responsibilities with them, George agreed to give it one more try.

I made George a plate of food, then got the boys settled into their beds while he ate his dinner in front of the TV.

After my rounds, I picked up a few toys that had been left on the family room floor and tossed them into the toy basket before sitting down beside George, working up some courage to bring up what had been on my mind that whole day. "I wonder if the boys wanting a dog is somehow connected to missing you."

"What do you mean?"

"They wouldn't understand why, but it seems possible that there's a void in their life that they're trying to fill. Now that Trevor is off to university, well, you're away so much."

"I don't think that has anything to do with it. Besides, I'm modelling a strong work ethic. It's how I was raised. Anything less than your best effort was considered a failure."

I persisted. "But these are the most important years. You can always make more money, but you can never turn back the clock and get this time back."

"Money isn't my only motivation for working so hard. I actually love my job. I enjoy building things, problem solving, and seeing the projects come to life. It was my dream to have my own business, and this is what it takes."

His comment made me feel more assertive. "I understand that, but this isn't the way I imagined our family life to be. What does it take to raise strong, healthy children?"

"Just because you grew up on a farm, and your dad was always home for dinner, doesn't mean all kids need to have that same experience."

"I'm not comparing you to my dad," I said, "but since you brought it up, he worked really hard too, but he was always available in the evenings."

George sighed and rubbed at his forehead. "I can't have this conversation right now. It's been a long day."

Knowing the conversation was over, I calmly picked up his dirty dishes, walked into the kitchen, put them into the dishwasher, added the detergent, closed the door, and started the cycle. I turned on the tap to rinse the dishcloth, letting my hands linger in the warm water to soothe my frustration. After wringing out the cloth and wiping away the last crumbs from the counter, I shifted my focus to the calendar and created a list of tasks for the next day.

We went to bed, not mad at each other, but quieter than usual. Sometimes we needed a bit of time to process. I had a feeling that the topic wouldn't be revisited unless I could bring myself to mention it again. George kissed me good night and fell asleep in less than a minute.

I couldn't pinpoint the exact moment I'd begun to sense the growing distance between us. It must have been a gradual change that intensified after he started his business, but it echoed loudly now. I used to think we shared similar dreams and perspectives, but the stark contrast between his deep commitment to work and my yearning for a simpler lifestyle with more family time tugged at my heart like the relentless surge of the sea.

Stan gazed out the window, his voice firm yet reflective, "I'm not a religious man, but every spring when I see that soft, new, bright-green growth at the tip of each branch, it's the closest thing I've ever felt to what I believe would be called a spiritual experience."

I looked out, admiring the branches that were almost touching the sunroom, admitting, "I can't believe I've never taken the time to really look at the tips in the spring." I marvelled silently at their vibrant beauty.

"That's the fir tree we planted when Stanley died," Stan said, motioning toward the tree by the window. "We buried his ashes underneath. I put Vera's ashes there as well, and I suppose I would like my ashes put there when I die." His mood became introspective as he lowered his gaze. "Death comes too soon, you know. You probably feel young now and don't think much about it, but we all have to go sometime." He paused. "And that time comes much too quickly."

Louisa reached over and squeezed her husband's hand. "It's not time for us yet, my dear."

Stan gulped down the rest of his tea. "I got the results of my echocardiogram. My doctor said it showed that I'd had a minor stroke sometime within the last few years, but I don't remember anything unusual."

"Hmmm..." I thought back. "What about that day you felt sick and wouldn't let me call an ambulance? I bet that was it."

"I forgot all about that." His eyes drifted off into the distance, clouded with a faraway look as he delved into his memories.

"A minor stroke! How scary." Louisa tut-tutted as she put the empty cups on a tray and carried them into the kitchen.

Stan nodded slowly. "I suppose you're right. Fancy that."

When she returned, I said, "Louisa, for your birthday tomorrow, I thought we could go to White Rock Beach for lunch. I know how much you love the ocean."

"That would be lovely. Doesn't that sound lovely, Stan?"

"Yes, it's a wonderful idea."

"Great." Recognizing that this would be a good time to leave, I rose from my chair. "I'll pick you up at around eleven tomorrow morning then."

He nodded at me. "Don't forget your Caramilk bar."

The cool breeze from the Pacific Ocean carried the fresh scent of saltwater and seaweed. Seagulls were gliding overhead as we made our way to the Boathouse Restaurant at White Rock Beach. After enjoying a delightful seafood lunch, I presented Louisa with a gold heart necklace for her birthday.

"It's lovely!" she gasped, her eyes wide with surprise.

I gently helped her fasten it around her neck. "It's from my whole family." I said softly. "Happy birthday!"

We walked the promenade, slowly making our way down the pier to admire the sailboats. The breeze swept through my hair, and I turned my face to the spring sun as I asked her, "How does it feel to be eighty years old?"

She joined me at the railing. "I still feel young and alive. I've even been thinking about getting my driver's licence. Eventually, Stan won't be able to drive anymore, and I prefer to be independent."

We both looked back at Stan, who was leaning over the edge, studying the crab fishermen below. He slowly turned and started walking toward us. His once-confident stride had transformed into a cautious shuffle.

Louisa smiled and inhaled the sea air. "Could you help me learn to drive? I don't think Stan will have the patience for it."

"Did you have a driver's licence in England?"

"No, but I drove a motor scooter when I was young. I don't suppose it would be all that different."

I zipped my coat higher and tucked my hands into my pockets. "Sure. We can stop by the motor vehicle branch on our way home and pick up the learner's book so you can start studying."

As we departed, Louisa touched the necklace around her neck once more. "Thank you ever so much for this lovely day."

Louisa struggled with the written test and failed five times before finally getting her learner's licence. The first time I took her out driving, we headed way down River Road, far from any traffic. After she climbed into the driver's seat, I showed her how to adjust the seat forward and the mirrors down so she could see properly.

"The gas pedal is on the right side, and the brake is on the left. Leave your foot on the brake when you're shifting from park to drive." I talked her through it, pointing to the gear shifter. "Now slowly move your foot from the brake to the gas pedal."

The Jag revved awkwardly under her hesitancy. I scanned our surroundings for any hazards as the car lurched forward. Though we were only at a crawl, Louisa gripped the steering wheel tightly. I reminded her to relax. She managed to do a few wide turns on the country road.

Louisa let out a little chuckle. "Feels like a workout, turning this wheel."

"I know. This car doesn't have power steering."

Stan had recently insisted on buying the old Jaguar solely because it boasted the iconic Jaguar emblem on the front hood. With every creak and groan, I questioned his decision more and more. The lack of suspension became apparent as we traversed bumps on the road.

When we pulled back into their carport, I noticed an oil stain right where the car was parked—a tell-tale sign of a leak that would need to be repaired. I couldn't help but feel that Stan should have known better than to buy a car from a newspaper ad without having it inspected first.

Regardless, Louisa was proud when she got home. "I would say that was a successful first lesson."

"Yes, I'll see you on Thursday for the next one."

After the tenth lesson, we were ready to drive into the city of Langley. I pointed to a large, empty parking lot and coached her as she carefully manoeuvred to park between the lines. There was only one other car in the lot, at the very far end from where we were, so I felt it was safe.

"We haven't done any backing up yet, and that will be part of the test."

Louisa looked at me and bit her lip. "Right."

I talked her through it with a calm voice. "With your foot on the brake, slide the shifter to the *R* position. Good. Now slowly move your foot to the gas pedal and turn your head to watch where you're going."

She tapped the gas, and the car lurched backwards, causing her to depress the pedal even more. We rocketed back, Louisa with a bewildered look on her face, me with eyes wide in shock.

"Brakes! Brakes!" I waved my hands wildly. "Take your foot off the gas pedal!"

She lifted her foot, and the car naturally slowed. Relieved, she pressed hard on what she thought was the brake, but in her frenzy, she had forgotten to switch pedals. We shot back once again, tires screeching as we narrowly missed the parked car by inches.

"Brakes!" I yelled as I grasped at the handle by my door. Louisa finally found the brake, and I quickly shifted the vehicle into park.

We sat in the car for a moment, both of us catching our breath before agreeing to change places. On the way home, I reassured her that there was nothing to worry about and that we would wait a while before attempting to reverse again.

Three weeks later, in a big parking lot with no other cars around, Louisa managed to back up and stop without incident. When we got home, she said, "You'd best come inside. There's a chocolate bar waiting for you."

Entering their house, I glanced at Stan, who promptly pointed to the picture of Silvia. The light above her was turned off.

"You haven't spoken to me in over two weeks!" he bellowed.

I tried to keep my expression neutral, but annoyance simmered just beneath the surface, "Sorry, I'm teaching your wife how to drive."

"Well, you certainly don't need to take her out and leave me by myself every time."

I thought for a minute, trying to understand his point of view, before saying, "I'll try to come in every other time, then?"

"Alright. That would be better."

Breaking the tension, Louisa asked, "How's your new puppy? A golden retriever, is it?"

"Yes, the boys named her Molly. She's a lot more work than I anticipated. Even though the boys are mainly supposed to take care of her, I'm already stepping in a lot."

With compassionate eyes, Louisa said, "Puppies can be a handful at first. It gets easier as they settle in."

As we chatted, Stan got up, walked over to the picture of Silvia, and switched on her light.

Chapter Eighteen

Once Louisa got her driver's licence, I turned my attention back to catching up on the demands at home. Eventually, a rare free day came along, giving me the opportunity to visit the neighbours again.

Louisa greeted me at the door, ushering me inside. As I leaned down to untie my shoes, I could see Stan out of the corner of my eye. He looked grumpy, with his arms crossed over his chest. I also noticed that the light over Silvia was turned off.

"I've got a bone to pick with you."

"Oh?"

"You've been neglecting me," he frowned. "It's been almost two weeks again."

I began summarizing my week, ticking off tasks on my fingers. "George and Tim had orthodontist appointments, Mark and David had roller hockey games, I had to bake and decorate two dozen cupcakes for the school bake sale, I had a refugee committee meeting, I had to take the van in for repairs..."

When I got to the second hand, Stan interrupted. "Alright, alright. I guess those are legitimate reasons." He rose and walked over to the picture, once again illuminating Silvia's serene presence. "I forgive you... this time."

As I watched him walk, I noticed it was taking him more effort than usual. His back was slightly hunched.

"I'll try to drop in on Tuesdays or Fridays, but sometimes it may only be for a few minutes. Does that sound okay?"

He considered my offer and then huffed in defeat. "I guess that'll have to do."

I glanced at the clock. "I have time for lunch right now if you want to go?"

Before he could even answer, Louisa was up, reaching for her coat. "Yes, that would be lovely."

Stan got up and grabbed his wallet from the dining room table. "Denny's? My treat."

I tied my shoelaces. "No way. You know my rule." I refused to eat at a restaurant where the standard of cooking was lower than my own. I felt it was a waste of money, and Stan knew this.

He chuckled at me as if it was only a test. "Lamplighter it is, then."

Over salmon entrees and passion fruit mousse, I told them all about Molly. "She's very smart. We're already taking her to obedience training classes."

Louisa was delighted. "We should see how Molly and Joey get along the next time you come over."

I gave her a polite, noncommittal smile. I didn't want to admit it, but most of the work with Molly was falling to me. I also hadn't anticipated the daily chore of vacuuming up mountains of dog hair.

When Louisa announced that her youngest brother Derek, his wife, and their two daughters would be coming from England for a two-week visit, I offered to pick them up at the airport with my van. They had never been to Canada before, but Louisa mentioned they had been captivated by magazine photos of Victoria, our provincial capital located on Vancouver Island. Fortunately, it was only a day trip away, so I promised to take them there.

After giving them a few days to adjust to the new time zone, I cleared my schedule and arranged for my sister Elsie to pick up the boys after school. I wanted to ensure we had plenty of time, determined for Louisa's guests to leave with a lasting, positive impression of the West Coast.

We departed early in the morning to catch the ten o'clock ferry from Tsawwassen. Stan was noticeably quiet during the drive and had a stern, blank expression on his face. I wasn't sure what had set him off, but as we stepped onto the ferry deck, he made contrary remarks about everything—from where we should sit to the occasional blast of the ferry's horn.

We stood on the deck of the ferry, taking in the stunning view of the Gulf Islands scattered across Active Pass. Everyone seemed to be enjoying the scenery—except for Stan, who had chosen to sit inside, a pout firmly set on his face. We decided to stay out in the crisp sea air, our eyes scanning the horizon for any sign of whales.

I was hoping the guests would spot some orcas during the voyage, but the majestic creatures didn't make an appearance this time. It felt as though even the orcas were keeping their distance from Stan's sour mood.

The announcement came over the loudspeaker for all passengers to return to their vehicles, so we went in, meeting up with Stan again. By the time we loaded back into the van, everyone could tell that Stan was grouchy. Derek tried to keep the mood light by telling jokes.

"Why did the elephant paint his toenails red?" he began, the anticipation of laughter creeping into his voice.

"I don't know," said his twenty-something daughter, sounding bored.

"So he could hide in a cherry tree. Have you ever seen an elephant in a cherry tree? No? That proves it works!"

Derek was the only one who burst out laughing. His daughters rolled their eyes. Louisa gave a little chuckle just to make him feel better. I giggled from behind the wheel, mostly because Derek's laughter was contagious.

Then he said, "I have another one. Did you hear about the arborist who asked for tweezers, a telescope, and a jam jar to get the elephant out of the tree?"

Getting no response, he continued excitedly, despite the lack of enthusiasm from the back half of the van, "He held the telescope backwards, picked up the elephant with the tweezers, and put him in the jam jar."

Derek cracked up again as if he'd just heard the joke himself for the first time, but looking around, he saw that everyone else had a puzzled look on their face.

"He wanted to put the elephant in the jam jar," he explained, "so he had to look through the telescope backwards to make him small enough, and then he picked him up with the tweezers and put him in the jam jar."

Derek struggled to get through the explanation, laughing so hard he could barely get the words out. His repetitive emphasis on the words *jam jar*, accentuated by his thick British accent, was funnier to me than the joke itself and had me laughing out loud.

I glanced in the rear-view mirror and caught a glimpse of Derek's face, laughter spilling out as tears rolled down his cheeks. I looked over at Stan. He was staring straight ahead, glowering. Derek's daughters appeared disengaged, while Margaret stared blankly out the window, her face devoid of emotion.

When we finally arrived in the downtown core of Victoria, I started looking for a parking spot. "This would be a nice area to have lunch and walk along the inner harbour," I said.

Before anyone else could even respond, Stan barked adamantly, "No, we are not stopping! I don't want lunch here. I want to go home."

I pulled into an available handicapped parking spot for a moment and turned around to face Louisa. Leaning toward her, I asked in a lowered voice, "What should we do?"

Stan, having heard me, repeated, "We're going home."

Louisa responded immediately, her voice loud and clear. "Keep driving then. I suppose we must go home."

"Are you sure?" I asked, thinking it was ridiculous that we had come all this way just to turn around and go back home. She nodded.

I purposely drove very slowly past the Parliament Buildings so that our visitors could at least get a brief look at the city's iconic attractions. I could hear the *click-click* of Margaret's camera. I kept driving up Government Street, and as she snapped pictures of the majestic, ivy-covered Empress Hotel through the grimy windows of my old van, I felt terrible.

Realizing that this was as close as they'd come to seeing their Canadian dream come to life, I wondered for a moment what would happen if we ignored Stan and went about our day. But when he was in this kind of mood, no one seemed inclined to challenge him.

As we headed back up the highway toward the ferry, I suggested, "What about Butchart Gardens?"

Stan peered over his glasses and huffed. "It's much too expensive. I just want to go home."

Nobody from the back of the van voiced an opinion, so we made our way to the ferry for our return trip. Everyone was silent on the way home, except Derek, who had more jokes to tell.

Determined to give them a positive experience, I took Derek's family to the Capilano Suspension Bridge a few days later, where they marvelled at the towering trees. We spent another day at Grouse Mountain. The gondola ride offered breathtaking views of the city of Vancouver, and Margaret eagerly snapped pictures, capturing the sparkling coastline below.

Stan's mood remained foul, but at least he cooperated without too much resistance. By the end of the two weeks, the visitors returned to England, happily declaring they had a wonderful time.

The final days of summer blurred into fall, bringing a familiar crispness to the air. Stan's complaints about aging and the aches and pains that came with it were relentless, especially as the colder weather set in.

I could see Louisa was growing weary of Stan's crotchety demands. He rarely moved from his recliner, instead barking orders for her to fetch this or grab that, claiming he was too old and sore to do it himself.

I was sitting in the sunroom with Stan as he worked on the daily crossword puzzle. The sunlight streamed through the windows, catching the edges of his glasses as he scribbled down the letters. Suddenly he bellowed, "Louisa, bring me my dictionary!" His tone was sharp and insistent.

As usual, she complied, then returned to the kitchen. I normally kept my opinions to myself, but at that moment, I felt compelled to speak up.

"Has it ever occurred to you that today—this very moment—is probably the best and healthiest you'll ever feel for the rest of your life?"

Stan stared at me, eyes bugging out of his head. At least I had his full attention. Before he could retort, I continued, "Why not make the most of it? True, you can't do everything you used to, but you can still walk, eat by yourself, and enjoy the outdoors. Why waste precious time complaining?"

Stan muttered, "Optimist," under his breath.

He looked as if he couldn't decide whether to lash out or crumble beneath the weight of my words. I watched several emotions contort his features, but he settled on a straight face and said, "Actually, I've never thought about it like that."

We didn't say much else, but the silence wasn't awkward—it was surprisingly contemplative. When I finally rose to leave, he reminded me to take my chocolate bar, and I felt reassured that all was well between us.

A few days later, I returned for another round of happy hour. Stan stood in the living room looking more carefree. Louisa brought out a bowl of crisps while he reached for the brandy glasses.

With a playful glint in his eye, he lifted the bottle and said, "Would you like some Madeira, m'dear?" He chuckled, setting the glasses down. "I've always wanted to use that line," he admitted, tilting the bottle so I could read the label—Madeira.

"Sure, I've never tried it before."

As I sipped the sweet nectar, I picked up on notes of fruit, nuts, and caramel. I took my usual seat on the couch.

Stan smiled. "You know, Anne, I've been thinking about what you said." He took a sip. "You're absolutely right! Six months ago, I felt much better than I do now, and I was complaining then, even though I would be happy now to feel the way I did then." His face suddenly lit up. "And six months from now, I'll probably say the same thing."

"Exactly," I smiled, happy to see that his shift in thinking was perking him up.

He swatted the air playfully as he said, "How did you get so wise? I'm twice your age, but you're probably the wisest person I've ever met."

A blush crept onto my face. "I think it's just common sense."

Stan shrugged. "Well, maybe common sense isn't so common anymore."

Chapter Nineteen

George pulled into our driveway towing a used, sixteen-foot, blue-and-white Campion motorboat. He had found it in the Buy and Sell newspaper. It was quite old, but the motor was in good shape and the price was right. Most importantly, it had just enough seats for the six of us. We had discussed buying a boat before, and while I didn't mind the idea, I couldn't ignore the added maintenance or how it cluttered up the driveway. Still, the decision had been made.

"We should explore some of the lakes in northern BC this summer," George suggested that night.

I shot him a grin. "I'll start looking for accommodations."

The thrill of planning a trip was one of my greatest passions. The research not only expanded my knowledge of new places but also filled me with the excitement of having something to look forward to.

The previous summer, we had gone on a family camping trip to the Kootenays, and I was eaten alive by mosquitoes. So this time, at Horse Lake and then again in Kelowna, I insisted on renting a cottage with screens on the windows and a full kitchen. I still had to deal with numerous mosquito bites, but it was a step up from setting up and taking down a tent.

As our family drove through the picturesque Okanagan Valley, beautiful vineyards and orchards stretched out along the roadside. Trees were heavy with ripe peaches, enticing us to pull over at one of the family-run orchards. We bought a big box of peaches for canning and a smaller basket of ripe, juicy ones to snack on as we drove. I was glad we had a roll of paper towels in the van.

Back at home, I felt a deep satisfaction as I admired the neat rows of jars filled with my canned peaches. I had also reserved just enough to make two peach pies, one of them for Stan and Louisa. I had been away for almost three weeks and knew this would lift Stan's spirits.

"Welcome home," Louisa smiled as she opened the door. "Oh, look at that, Stan, she brought us a pie."

"Wonderful. We sure missed you." It was good to see Stan smiling. "Come here and I'll show you a trick we taught Joey while you were away."

I walked over as Stan took Joey from his lap and placed him on the floor. Then he said, "Roll over," and demonstrated the motion with his hand.

Joey just sat there and tilted his head, unsure of what he was supposed to do. I started giggling. Undeterred, Stan repeated the command. "Roll over. Come on, Joey, you just did it earlier. Honestly."

I looked at Joey, wondering if it was possible for him to roll over with all that extra weight around his middle. Stan tried again. "Roll over, Joey... Oh, I give up."

Louisa said, "What about sitting up?"

She walked over like she wanted to prove that Joey really was smart. With a treat in one hand, she gently coaxed Joey to sit up by lifting the treat higher than he could reach. Joey looked at the treat with anticipation, wagging his tail and making soft noises. Finally, he managed to shift his weight and lift his long torso, balancing on his hind legs. She gave him the treat as they both gushed over him.

"Well done, Joey, good boy!"

Stan was laughing out loud. "He brings us so much joy. I can't imagine life without him."

Louisa picked Joey up and let him lick her face. Then she spoke in a baby voice. "Oh yes, we love you, our lovely little boy."

Observing Louisa's overflowing affection for their dog confirmed that I wasn't a real dog person.

"We taught Molly some tricks too," I said. "She can hold a treat on her nose and stay still until we say, 'eat it,' and then she tosses it in the air and catches it in her mouth."

Louisa chuckled before asking, "And how are the boys managing with their chore list?"

I sighed. "Not very well. I still end up doing most of it. The other day, I took Molly to the vet, and he told me that I should be brushing her teeth and cleaning her ears every day. There's no way I have time for that."

"Do you think you'll keep her?"

It was a valid question that I knew I had been avoiding. "It's a difficult decision. I'm torn between wanting to do what's best for Molly and the reality of our busy lives."

George walked in the door just as the boys and I finished our dinner. I got up to reheat some food for him.

"Guess what I got today?" He held up a black rectangle in his hand.

The boys stared with wide eyes as he explained, "It's called a BlackBerry."

"Whoa!"

"Cool."

I took a closer look. "That's crazy! It even has a little keyboard."

"It's the future of communication," George went on. "It's a phone, but you can even send emails with it! It will be great for work. All the managing partners got one."

"It's impressive!" I could see how excited he was, yet I wondered if this new technology would consume him even more, now that it allowed him to take his work wherever he went.

As I tucked the boys in for the night, making my rounds, Tim hesitated at the end of our talk and said, "Mom, I think I'm getting too old for hugs and kisses."

"You are?"

"Yeah. I mean, I'm thirteen now."

"That's true. I can't believe you're a teenager already." I felt a mix of pride and a twinge of sadness. I knew this day had to come at some point. As I stood there thinking about how to keep the connection between us strong while still respecting his feelings, an idea came to me.

"Just a sec," I said, leaving the room and heading to my bedroom. I grabbed a bottle of body lotion and walked back into Tim's room. "How about a foot massage instead?"

"Sure," he said, looking a little skeptical because he had never had one before.

Standing at the end of his bed, I lifted the blanket just enough to expose his feet. I squeezed some lotion into my hand, warming it between my palms. As I started working the lotion into his skin, I couldn't help but think about how quickly the boys were growing up and how life was always changing in subtle ways.

"Doesn't that feel relaxing?"

"Yeah." He had a big grin on his face. I tucked the blanket around his feet as he shifted onto his side, curling slightly into the warmth. He mumbled a sleepy "thanks" as I turned off the light.

George Matthew preferred to stick to the old routine, but it wasn't long before the younger boys were asking for foot massages too. On occasion, I pampered them by first using a warm washcloth to clean their feet and then applying a special foot cream, which made the process feel even more like a luxurious treat.

A shift in our nightly ritual had begun, but I was grateful that, regardless of how I gave them one-on-one attention, our connection and the opportunity to talk openly about the day endured.

Chapter Twenty

Every Thursday night, we hosted small get-togethers at our house for those members of our church congregation who lived nearest to us. A woman named Janice, her husband Richard, and their two young daughters had been introduced to our church through a mutual friend. Since they had recently moved into a house on the street parallel to ours, I struck up a friendship with Janice. On her days off from her job as a psychiatric nurse, Janice and I regularly went on walks together.

One day, we arrived at our meeting point nearly simultaneously, and I waved as we approached each other. She was wearing jeans and an elegant, knitted cardigan. Her shoulder-length brown hair framed her welcoming face.

"Let's walk through the cemetery," I suggested. It had been quite some time since I'd been able to visit Liz's gravestone. As we approached it, I shared a brief version of my friend's life and death with Janice. We paused for a moment of silence, and then Janice asked out loud, "She died on May third? That's my birthday."

"Really?"

Our eyes met, acknowledging the coincidence. Our friendship had formed effortlessly. Much like with Liz, we could freely discuss anything and everything with mutual respect.

"What do you think about the Joseph Campbell series?" she asked as we meandered back onto the sidewalk. Our Thursday night group had decided to watch and discuss Joseph Campbell's documentary *The Power of Myth*.

"It's fascinating. I like the way he finds connections between different cultures and uncovers deeper truths in their stories."

"I'm enjoying it too," Janice agreed. "I admire that he dedicated most of his life to travelling and researching myths and how they influence and shape our understanding of the world."

"It sure has led to some interesting discussions. I know more and more people from church who are questioning the black-and-white views they were raised with. I used to think that real faith meant trusting without questioning. It took me years to understand that truth and mystery can coexist."

We turned left just past the Fort Pub and continued walking down the scenic trail that followed the river—one of our favourite places to walk.

Janice said, "I didn't grow up in a religious home, so my views have always been based on science."

"Why did you start coming to our church then?"

"Richard and I were interested in the community aspect of it. I really believe it's important to have social connections. Even if we don't have the same faith, we're all human beings."

"That makes sense. My beliefs are slowly shifting. I'm not rejecting them—I'm still grounded in the core values of love, peace, and compassion. But once I began to see things differently, everything took on new meaning."

"Instead of rigid dogmas, I think there's beauty in diversity, and each individual's spiritual journey is unique and valuable," Janice replied.

"That's one of the reasons I love travelling—it helps me broaden my understanding of the world. There's a richness in learning about other cultures, tasting different foods, exploring historical places... It gets me out of my comfort zone. I think it's important."

"It's very important," Janice agreed as we slowed our pace before turning around. "Do you have time to go for lunch?"

"Sure. Let's go to the Little White House for high tea."

"Mmmm, I love their Crème de la Earl Grey," she said.

As we walked toward the Community Hall, a gentle breeze carried the laughter and screams of children playing on the front lawn. The mothers of the children sat on a bench nearby, deep in conversation. I looked at them for a moment, and something occurred to me.

"In a way, you and I are an example of what Joseph Campbell talked about. Even though we come from completely different backgrounds, we've found common ground." I glanced again at the mothers on the bench as we walked by. "Sharing our stories brings us closer, no matter who we are or where we come from."

Janice nodded in agreement. "It's the universal human connection. It transcends everything when we set aside the differences that so often keep us apart."

I came home from grocery shopping feeling cheerful, the rustle of bags filling the air as I set them on the counter. But as I looked around, the sunlight streaming through the windows revealed clumps of Molly's golden fur drifting across the floor like tiny tumbleweeds.

She padded over, her tail wagging furiously with excitement. After unpacking the groceries, I gave her a quick pat on the head before grabbing the vacuum cleaner once again, her curious nose already nudging at the nozzle.

The hair was always everywhere—on my clothes, embedded in the furniture, coating the floors. I had run out of patience. It was time.

When the boys came home from school, I gathered them for another family meeting. With a heavy sigh, I began.

"You guys haven't been keeping your end of the deal." I held up the blank chore list. "I gave you six months and so many reminders to fill this up with your check marks, but it hasn't happened."

"We're too busy," Tim said, sprawled across the loveseat with his lanky frame clad in his favourite skateboarding hoodie, his head propped comfortably on one hand.

"You're right. Our family is too busy to have a dog, and it's not fair to Molly."

The boys looked down. They knew it was the truth. I tried to be gentle.

"I said that I would put an ad in the paper if you couldn't take on the responsibilities, so the ad will go in tomorrow. It's going to be hard to let her go, but I don't know what else to do." I looked at David sitting on the carpet next to Molly.

"Can you give us another six months?" he pleaded.

"I don't think that's going to make a difference. I'm sorry." Part of me wanted to give in, but I knew I couldn't keep going the way things were.

I tried to explain, "When I was growing up on the farm, dogs were always kept outside, running freely in the fields. I was willing to give an inside dog a try for you guys, but if I end up doing all the work, it's too much. I like dogs, but with the dog hair everywhere and the smell when she's been out in the rain... I guess I'm just not an inside dog person."

The mood in the room grew heavy as the gravity of the situation sank in.

"I know we all love Molly, but she'll be happier in a home where she gets more care and attention. We've tried a few times now, but I really don't think a dog fits well with our family."

In silent acknowledgement, the boys exchanged glances, recognizing that this chapter of their time with Molly was coming to an end. A solemn nod from each of them conveyed a mix of understanding and regret as they processed the weight of their collective lapse in responsibility and its impact on Molly's future.

I got an immediate response to Molly's ad from a single, middle-aged woman who told me she was looking for a golden retriever companion. The instant she walked into our house, she established a connection with the dog. I watched, captivated by their interaction.

She knelt beside Molly, her eyes as warm as the dog's golden coat. She extended her hand ever so gently, and Molly, sensing her kindred spirit, nuzzled against her. The woman spoke to the dog with genuine affection and took a new chew toy out of her bag.

"This is exactly the dog I've been looking for," she exclaimed. "Here's a picture of the room in my house that would be Molly's bedroom. It even has a dog door going directly to the fenced backyard."

I stared at the photo. It looked just like a child's bedroom. Molly would have her own bed, toys, and access to the outdoors whenever she wanted. It couldn't have been a better situation for her.

As the woman spoke, she showered Molly with affectionate strokes. "I'm going to get pet medical insurance so that every need she has in her life will be looked after."

"It's clear to me that you would provide a great home for Molly."

"I would, I really would. I'd like to pay in cash and take her with me today."

"Oh?" This caught me off guard. I wasn't expecting Molly to go so quickly.

She nodded her head slowly as she spoke, "I think it would be best for all of us. Give me your address and I'll keep you updated with pictures."

"Okay," I agreed hesitantly, knowing the boys wouldn't get a chance to say goodbye. But on reflection, I decided that maybe it would be easier this way. Before I could think about it too much more, the transaction had already taken place, and the woman left with Molly, her leash, and all remnants of the dog's presence. An unexpected surge of emptiness hit me as they drove away, and I sobbed for a full hour before the boys returned from school.

We sat in the family room as I told the boys about Molly's new home. We all had tears in our eyes. I could tell that Mark and David needed a hug, and I motioned for Tim and George Matthew to join in. Our group hug brought some comfort, but it would take some time to get used to Molly's absence. However, I was certain that she was better off spending the rest of her life with a dog lover.

On my way to Stan and Louisa's, I thought about how much progress they had made. They seemed to have found a good rhythm, needing less and less of my support. I still helped occasionally—running errands or taking Stan to appointments—but overall, Louisa took charge of their daily routine.

Even before I stepped into the house, a sharp, unmistakable fishy aroma hit me, "You had kippers today, didn't you?"

Stan looked surprised. "How did you know?"

"I remember the smell from last time."

It was one of Stan's favourite meals. They were so excited when they discovered Black Pudding, a new store in Langley that sold some of their favourite British treats.

"You really have to go to England sometime." There was nostalgia etched on Stan's face. "You must try the Devonshire cream. Oh, real fresh Devonshire cream is thick and buttery. You can't find anything like it here."

Louisa smiled. "I prefer clotted cream myself. It's rich and velvety, and it's a bit sweeter than Devonshire cream."

"They both sound delicious."

Stan snapped out of his trance. "I was wondering if your boys could cut my grass for some extra pocket money. I simply can't do it myself anymore."

"I'm sure they would. Maybe George Matthew and Tim could take turns. We're planning a family trip to Europe in June so they're already saving as much money as they can."

"Where in Europe are you going?" Louisa asked.

"We'll fly into Rome, then go south all the way to Bari, only because I got a great deal on a two-bedroom timeshare there, then up to Tuscany and Venice, then to Salzburg and Vienna in Austria, then Prague, because we know someone there. Then we'll see a few towns in Germany and fly home from Munich. We'll be gone for a month!"

Stan replied, "With all your boys? That sounds exhausting!"

"Well, they're growing up so fast, and I've always wanted to do a big family trip. I've got everything booked and ready: passports, flights, accommodations, and a rental van to get around."

Louisa smiled, "Will the boys be missing school?"

"Only the last two weeks. Their teachers all agreed they'll learn more in Europe than they would in the classroom during that time."

Stan adjusted his glasses. "Well, I hope you have a wonderful holiday."

"I'm excited. This will be my first time in Europe!"

Chapter Twenty-One

Experiencing more of the world during our month-long European adventure had only deepened my hunger for exploration. But George had already used up all his vacation days, leaving us with weekend getaways as our only option. That ruled out air travel and long road trips. As for camping—we'd done enough of that.

I searched online for vacation home rentals, but everything was too far away or far too expensive. I spent days researching and scrolling through the internet until I came across a site featuring recreation properties for sale in BC. One of the properties, on Harrison Lake, indicated that it could be rented while it was up for sale. Harrison Lake wasn't far away at all, and the price per night was extremely reasonable.

Having grown up in the Fraser Valley, I had often visited Harrison Hot Springs with my family, spending a Sunday afternoon in the public pool filled with hot mineral water, but it had never occurred to me there might be cabins on the lake. This felt worth pursuing, so I contacted the seller for more information.

They emailed back almost immediately. Since the property was boat access only, we were instructed to pack our own food and potable water. Bedding, kitchen amenities, and firewood were

provided. There were lots of trails for hiking, it was kid friendly...
It all sounded great. Maybe George's idea to buy a boat hadn't been
so crazy after all. I inquired about the dates that would work for
our family.

Once again, my email notification chimed quickly with a
response. The dates were open, so I booked it right away. George
was happy to let me handle the decisions when it came to planning
trips and booking accommodations, admitting that he didn't have
the time or the interest to deal with such details.

When George got home from work, I filled him in on the plans
I had made for the following weekend. He found the destination
intriguing and was especially excited about the chance to take the
boat out on the water.

On Friday night, the kids and I waited on the driveway, our
anticipation growing with each passing minute. As usual, George
was late getting home. Out of boredom, Tim and David started
throwing a football back and forth. Mark was slumped against the
full cooler, and George Matthew helped me put the last of the
bags into the boat. Finally, when George had arrived and readied
himself, we set off for Harrison Lake.

It was nearly dark by the time we lowered the boat into the
water. I held onto the rope while George parked the trailer, and
then we finally launched.

The old Campion, loaded with coolers and bags, had a hard
time planing, which required us all to lean into the front end of
the boat while George pushed the throttle to full speed, urging the
boat to go faster.

The only directions we had were to stay on the right side of the
lake until we neared the very end of Cascade Bay. I had studied the
map before we left, but by the time we reached the bay, the moon

had dipped behind the trees. We could barely tell where the lake ended and the land began.

Then, like a beacon of hope, a flashlight waved up ahead. Its beam carved a glimmering path across the water, leading us straight to a dock. A portly, older man with silver hair caught the front edge of the boat.

"*Grüß dich*," his German accent carried through the night air. "Hello, welcome." With one hand, he wound the boat's rope around a cleat.

George hopped out first, extending his hand. "I'm George."

The man gave him a firm handshake. "Dieter."

George reached back as I passed out our things, and he pointed at the kids as he called them out. "That's George Matthew, Tim, David, and Mark. And my wife, Anne."

With our bags and coolers on the wharf, we all grabbed something while Dieter double-checked the ropes.

"Let me show you the way up." He pointed his flashlight in the direction we were supposed to go.

By up, he meant up a winding path into the forest. He led us past his own cabin, where the kitchen light gave us a glimpse of the inside. Dieter's wife, curled on the couch with a book, offered a wave.

The trees thickened as we climbed. We saw a wooden box with pipes protruding out of it, and Dieter explained that it held the water pump.

"Is that so the toilet will flush?" David asked. Not surprisingly, he was up front with Dieter, fearless in the dark and ever curious.

The old man laughed. "No toilets here. You're going to have to use the outhouse out back. Sometimes we need to give up luxury for a little bit of peace and quiet." He ruffled David's hair.

Focused on my feet, I didn't see the cabin until we climbed the steps to the sundeck. The A-frame blended seamlessly into the forest, hidden by the moonless night. I couldn't wait to see it in the daylight.

Inside, Dieter lit the propane lamp and pointed out where everything was, including extra flashlights. He wished us a good night before disappearing into the dark.

The place felt old and outdated, but I found it charming. A glass oil lamp on the bookshelf added a nostalgic touch, and the built-in corner seating for the kitchen table looked uniquely Bavarian. The benches even opened up for extra storage. My favourite feature was the stone wall behind the wood stove. It gave the room a grounded, sheltering feel.

David shouted down from the loft overlooking the main room, "Dibs on this bed." Mark swiftly conquered each rung of the ship's ladder to join him, while Tim pushed impatiently from behind. George Matthew threw his bag in a room below the loft, happy to have a little spot for himself. At sixteen years old, he had mellowed compared to his rambunctious brothers.

In the back room, I ran my hand along the tongue-and-groove cedar. The whole cabin had a refreshing, earthy smell. It took a while to get ready for bed between trips to the outhouse and taking turns brushing our teeth at the small sink, but then a hush settled over the cabin as slumber claimed us one by one.

Surrounded by a profound darkness, George and I found comfort in each other's warmth.

He whispered, "You didn't tell me I wouldn't have any cell-phone reception."

He couldn't see my eyes rolling. "I think that's a positive thing. Maybe we can learn to relax and *just be*."

The next morning, sunlight peeked through the curtains, and for a moment, I forgot where I was. The smell of hand-knitted blankets and cedar was unfamiliar, but cozy and inviting. I rolled over to snuggle with George.

Creaks in the boards above signalled that the boys were waking up. As I got out of bed, I wrapped one of the extra blankets around my shoulders and walked out, opening the glass sliding door that covered the front wall. I stepped into the fresh air, inhaling with my whole body.

To the south, deep blue water extended far into the distance, framed by densely forested hills. The sun and wind played across the surface of the water, forming small white peaks that danced like nature's Morse code, fleetingly conveying their message before vanishing.

To the north, the bay gathered into a collection of logs, and I wondered if the boys would climb along the rocky shore to explore them. Wisps of cloud caught the morning light, while the snow-capped Mount Breakenridge kept its watchful eye.

The cabin itself was obviously well loved. It was painted brown and featured classic Bavarian details, including scalloped edges on the bright orange trim boards that ran the length of the A-frame's front. Not my personal taste, but it looked quaint nestled among the trees.

Mark joined me on the deck, slipping his hand through the diamond-shaped cutouts in the railing. The railing cap, a hefty two-by-eight, was painted bright orange to match the trim.

After a big brunch, we all put bathing suits on and ventured down to the water's edge. I dipped my foot in the lake and quickly concluded that it was too cold for me. Tim, David, and Mark, however, plunged in without hesitation. Then George dove in.

When he popped up, he said, "Come on! It's so refreshing. Not as cold as I thought it would be."

I laughed and shook my head. George Matthew decided to join them while I sat on a beach towel enjoying the rocking motion of the dock every time someone jumped in, the warmth of the sun on my face.

From up on the ledge, Dieter called down to me. "How about you two take these for a spin?"

He came down carrying a full-length kayak in each hand, cautiously making his way toward the dock. George jumped up to help. I glanced at the kids.

"Don't worry about the boys. Helga and I will keep an eye on them."

With the boats on the dock, he pulled a life vest from each and handed them to me and George. "If you paddle around the east side, you can get to the other bay."

I waved to Dieter's wife, Helga, who had come down to sit on the stairs by the water. I had confidence in the elderly couple. There was something about their warmth, generosity, and calm reliability that made me trust them right away.

Dieter coached me on how to position my weight while getting into the kayak. George held the boat steady for me. Once I was in, it was as if I was one with the lake. Paddling was smooth and effortless, and I glided on the surface like a bird in flight. George caught up quickly, having kayaked quite a bit in his youth.

We paddled around the bend to the other side. There were fewer cabins in that bay, and the water was quite shallow near the end. Marsh weeds rose from the murky depths, trailing along the surface. The weeds hooked onto my paddles, dragging them back, and I called to George to wait up while I untangled myself.

He came over with the intention to rescue me, but I was already free by then. Instead, he said, "This was a great idea."

"Kayaking?"

"Coming here." He rested his paddle on his boat. "You were right. Our family needed this. I know I did. Thanks for booking it."

"You're welcome." I felt a warm pride, glad that he appreciated my efforts. "It feels good to spend time in nature," I said as we watched a group of ducks swim by.

The simplicity of leisurely floating in kayaks, listening to birds while exploring the shore, was truly exhilarating. Amidst it all, we were thrilled to spot a majestic blue heron.

I broke our silence eventually. "We should probably head back. I don't want to take advantage of their generosity for too long."

Twenty minutes later, we pulled the kayaks up at Dieter and Helga's dock and carefully carried them to the spot Dieter indicated. He had already started their campfire.

"Come down after dinner and join us," he said.

"Okay, we'll see you later."

We walked single file down the path, following the smell of smoke, straight to the blazing fire. Plastic chairs were set up in a semicircle, enough for all of us to gather around.

Helga said, "I hope you have room for Bavarian smokies."

She showed the boys the best way to put the chunks of sausage on roasting sticks, so they didn't fall off. She also taught them how to keep rotating them so they wouldn't burn.

Dieter poured George and me a glass of wine. When he first mentioned that it was homemade, I was a bit hesitant. However, his full-bodied red surpassed most store-bought wines I'd tasted.

We listened to Dieter's tales of lake life. It felt nostalgic, like simpler times.

After a while, he stood to pour another round, but my glass wasn't empty yet, so I covered it with my hand, shaking my head when he looked at me. I rarely drank more than a single glass of wine.

Helga asked, "You live in Fort Langley?"

"Yes," I said. "George grew up in Vancouver, and I grew up on a farm in Abbotsford, so Fort Langley was sort of our compromise. We lived in Walnut Grove for a few years, but when I discovered Fort Langley, I knew right away that's where I wanted to raise our family."

"*Wir können auch Deutsch sprechen.*" George said, letting them know that we could speak German as well.

"Really?" Helga sounded surprised.

George explained, "German-speaking Mennonites fled from Ukraine to Germany during the war. They were being persecuted by the Russians. From there, Anne's parents went to Canada, while mine went to South America for a few years, then to Canada."

"There are a lot of Mennonites living in the Fraser Valley," I said. "I grew up going to a church where the whole service was in German. I still speak German to my parents." I glanced at Dieter and smiled as his face lit up with a broad grin. The common language we shared seemed to forge an instant connection between us.

George swirled his glass. "How long have you had the cabin here?"

Dieter tossed a log into the fire. "I built the A-frame in 1969. Hauling the materials up was the hardest part."

George looked at the water. "Up the lake?"

"No, up the hill!" Dieter laughed. "But yes, we built a raft, tied up all the cedar, and spent a whole day slowly towing it up the lake with our boat. It was a calm day in September. On a different weekend we carried all the wood up the hill."

Helga disappeared into the cabin, returning with a photo album and a stash of marshmallows for the kids. She handed over the book as her husband talked and pointed at various photos.

"This was a few years later, but there's our son Klaus and I up on the roof, installing the chimney. And here's Peter, our other son, helping me with the floor."

Dieter suddenly leaned over to move David's stick, but it was a moment too late as the marshmallow combusted into flames. David gasped, but Helga just handed him a new one.

"We're only selling the A-frame because our friends decided to sell this one to us," he gestured to the cabin behind him. "It's closer to the water, a bit roomier, and with no hill to climb in our old age."

Helga added, "We're renting out the A-frame first because we want to find the right neighbours."

Dieter shook his head, "We don't want a bunch of hooligans partying it up next door."

I could hear the boys snickering at the word *hooligans*, and I couldn't help but giggle a bit myself. They were done with their marshmallows, and I could sense they were worn out from a day of swimming and running around.

"You know," Dieter said, turning to them, "there's a big waterfall down the lake. Maybe you can convince your dad to take the boat there tomorrow."

A curious murmur rippled through. "Can we? Can we, Dad?"

Their buzzing excitement made George smile. "Why don't you go get a good night's rest, and we can talk about it tomorrow."

The boys took the flashlight and headed up the hill. I called out, "We'll be up in a few minutes." The darkness didn't answer back, but the flashlight bobbed a few times in acknowledgement.

George asked more questions about the area as Dieter began refilling the wine glasses again. I surprised myself by allowing mine to be topped up as well. This older couple was so sweet, it seemed like the polite thing to do.

"Ever since we discovered this place, we've been in love with it," Dieter said as he poured the wine. "We knew we wanted to spend as much time here as possible. I never minded having to work hard all week, because I knew I could come here and recharge my batteries every weekend."

"We decided to retire early, and have no regrets," Helga added.

"I can see why you love it." I reached over to pat George's knee. "Even George is getting used to the lack of cell service."

We all shared a chuckle and a slow sip of wine.

Helga tipped the rest of the second bottle into George's glass. "Why don't you come back next weekend, recharge again?"

I glanced at George. Maybe it was the wine, but a glimmer of hope lit up my smile. Sensing my energy, he turned to Dieter and asked, "No one else has booked the place?"

Dieter finished his wine. "No, not yet."

"We'll see you next weekend then," I beamed.

Rising from his chair, Dieter filled a green watering can at the lake, then let the stream pour over the small flames of the campfire. A long hiss emanated from the dying coals. As the glow of the fire died, Helga's flashlight clicked on, and I felt like I'd just woken up from a dream.

The next morning, on our trip back down the lake, I spotted what looked like the top of the waterfall Dieter had told us about. George steered the boat toward the communal dock, pulling up slowly. Tim and David jumped out with the ropes. We were getting good at this.

From the shore, the waterfall couldn't be seen, and the empty beach looked unassuming. Mark pointed to a small wooden sign by the path entrance, its painted letters faded by the elements. He read out loud, "Rainbow Falls."

Tim and David ran ahead, and the rest of us walked, single file, following a well-worn deer path. The forest floor was lush with ferns and moss, and the trail meandered in a series of twists and turns, avoiding giant cedars and rockfall, forging a path that nature dictated. With each step, anticipation surged as the sound of the waterfall grew louder.

The path led to an opening where a raging creek roared past us. Its waters churned and frothed over the rocks as it flowed toward the lake. A gentle mist rose from the cascading waterfall, displaying all the colours of the rainbow where it caught the sunlight.

"Do you see that?" I said as I pointed to the mist.

"Oh yeah," Tim stopped to look. "I bet that's why it's called Rainbow Falls."

From the heavens, it seemed, the water tumbled down the mountainside with a thunderous roar, collecting into a serene pool below.

We climbed around the edge of the creek toward the waterfall. George suggested it was a good spot for a photo and motioned for us to position ourselves in front of a big rock with the falls behind us.

I took off my shoes and socks, motioning for the boys to do the same. I heard their gasps as we stepped into the cold, flowing water. Slowly, we gathered into a huddle, careful not to slip on the rocks. When we were finally in position, George yelled, over the roar of the waterfall, "Okay, say cheeeese."

Once we'd successfully taken a few pictures, David started gathering rocks and piling them up into a tower. We all joined in. David said he had just learned about this in school and that it was called an *inukshuk*, a landmark made by Inuit people in the Arctic.

To me, it felt more like we were constructing an altar to acknowledge a sacred place. The sheer beauty of this natural setting, shared with my family, evoked such a deep reverence in me that it nearly brought me to tears.

Chapter Twenty-Two

Harrison Lake was all I could think about that week. I was glad we had accepted Dieter and Helga's offer to return. When Friday arrived, the boys packed their bags at record speed. This time, George even got home on time, and we made it up to the cabin before the sun had set.

The next morning, we were all eager to explore. We followed the narrow path behind the cabin as birds flitted from branches overhead. Every rustle and whisper held a hint of mystery.

George Matthew was the first to spot the other bay. We emerged from the forest and wandered out to the shore. George pointed out where we had kayaked the weekend before. I looked around, taking it all in. This was exactly the kind of family time I had been longing for.

The boys ran along the logs, which turned and shifted under their sneakered feet. I called for them to be careful and not get their shoes wet. As I watched, I thought it looked like fun, so I joined them.

It took balance and coordination to navigate our way over the shallow water. Bounding across the floating logs reminded me of my childhood. We worked hard on the farm, but there were also days filled with carefree fun and exploration. I felt like a kid again, lost in the thrill of the moment.

Back at the cabin, we congratulated each other on our new log rolling skills as we lined up four sets of shoes to let them dry in the sun. Admittedly, one pair was mine, as George Matthew had managed to keep his dry.

After dinner, Dieter and Helga invited us down to their fire again. Just like the weekend before, they provided marshmallows and plenty of wine. Tim carefully roasted his marshmallow to a flawless golden puff. Whenever someone admired his expertise, he beamed with pride, generously offering them the perfectly roasted treat before starting on another one.

Dieter tended to the fire in a way that didn't disturb the ongoing roasting. With a long driftwood stick, he masterfully shifted the coals. Whenever the smoke blew in his direction, he stated loud and clear, "I love white rabbits."

David, who heard him say it twice within a few minutes, asked why he did so.

"It keeps the smoke from bothering you," Dieter said matter-of-factly. "Try it yourself."

It didn't take long for the wind to shift, and a column of smoke clouded David's face.

"I love white rabbits!" His eyes started to water, but he didn't move, and sure enough, the smoke faded, drifting the opposite way. "It worked! Did you see that?"

The other boys were laughing.

"Sure did," I smiled, savouring another sip of wine.

"Do you live up here year-round?" George asked Dieter.

Dieter shook his head. "The cabin isn't insulated, so it's too cold in the winter. That's when we travel."

Helga nodded. "We're here from Easter to Thanksgiving except for regular trips to pick up groceries."

"We have a condo in Abbotsford." Dieter added. "The most expensive laundromat you can find, at least in the summer."

"And to pick up our mail," Helga added.

Once it was a bit darker, the boys went back up to the cabin to play cards, but George and I stayed around the fire. It was nice that the boys could entertain themselves now that they were a bit older.

I removed my sweater, casually draping it over the armrest. I thought I would need the extra layer, but the night air held the last of the day's heat, and the summer breeze blew softly.

"I had no idea there were cabins on this lake," George said. "When we were dating, we came to the town of Harrison a few times. Looking at the lake from that vantage point, all you see is Echo Island and mountains in the background."

"We actually got engaged at the Harrison Hot Springs Hotel," I added.

"Really?" Helga looked at me. "Tell me more."

"We weren't staying at the hotel, but George made reservations at the Copper Room restaurant for New Year's Day. He only had a few more days before he had to head back to the University of Manitoba to finish his degree."

George continued. "I told the waiter that, before dessert, we wanted to go for a little walk on the resort grounds."

"And just behind the restaurant, there was a little playground. I said to George, 'Oh look, I love merry-go-rounds,' and I hopped on. George gave it a good push to get it spinning, then he jumped on, got down on one knee, held out a little box, and asked me to marry him."

"And you obviously said yes," Helga smiled.

I only giggled in response.

In his thick Bavarian accent, Dieter suddenly said, "I think you are the right people to buy the cabin." The word *right* came out extra strong because of the way he rolled his *R*s.

I studied George's face at the unexpected statement. He quickly declined. "It would be nice, but with our large mortgage and any extra money going into my new business, we can't do it."

Dieter tried again. "What if we lower the price? Being able to trust my neighbours is worth a lot to me, and this would be perfect for your boys."

Helga looked serious. "We don't want partying people beside us. We already turned down an offer well over our asking price just for that reason."

A hopeful twinge stirred within me. "It's very tempting," I said. I didn't want to shut the door on this opportunity yet.

"I think it's meant to be," Dieter said. "Why don't you come again next weekend? One more time. See if it changes your mind."

What he didn't know was how much I already loved the place. And there was also something special about Dieter. With his round face, thick eyebrows, and big smile that caused his eyes to squint, he had such a magnetic charm. When Dieter spoke, everyone listened. His words carried the weight of importance and wisdom.

George didn't hesitate. "We'd love to come back one more time."

The following Sunday, after another fantastic weekend, Dieter dropped the price of the cabin again—twenty percent below what he was originally asking. I mentally recalculated our budget, trying to see if we could make it work.

George, however, remained firm, explaining that we wouldn't qualify for another mortgage from the bank.

Undeterred, Dieter urged us to seriously consider his offer and extended another invitation to return.

Chapter Twenty-Three

Over tea, I shared the details of the cabin with Stan and Louisa—its location and the rustic charm of the A-frame—curious to hear their thoughts.

Louisa, with her usual positive outlook, was fiercely supportive. "I think you should buy the cabin. It would be brilliant for your family."

Stan, on the other hand, wasn't in favour. "The place probably doesn't even have running water."

"It does," I corrected him. "It gets pumped up from the lake to a keg positioned on the roof, then the water flows down by gravity." I felt myself defending the cabin and the lifestyle it provided, realizing my mind was already made up.

Stan went on. "You won't visit us as much if you buy a cabin." I saw him glance up at Silvia. Her light was off.

"We would mainly be there on weekends, so I could still visit you during the week. Plus, it gets shut down in the winter, so I'd still be here from November to March."

Stan folded his arms across his chest. "Seems like a lot of money for something you would only use half the year."

I simply said, "I think experiences like that are priceless, and it feels like a once in a lifetime opportunity."

Stan softened. "You really think it's a good idea? You're already too busy!"

"Exactly." I set my empty teacup down, staring him right in the face. "My whole family is too busy. That's why it's so important that we create quality time together."

I turned to Louisa. "I can already picture George and the boys chopping wood, all of us having dinners around the campfire. And you wouldn't believe the variety of birds that perch on the deck railings. I'd love to learn all their names."

I could see in Louisa's eyes that she shared my vision. Even Stan's frown had transformed into a hesitant smile. As I prepared to leave, he reminded me, as always, to grab my Caramilk on the way out.

The chocolate bars were piling up at my house, so I started storing them in the freezer. It became a simple pleasure to savour a single frozen piece, relishing the moment the caramel centre slowly melted on my tongue. Sometimes I shared the Caramilks with my boys as a reward when they got all their chores done without a reminder.

When George arrived home from work that night, he found me at the kitchen table, eating one of my frozen chocolate bars, surrounded by papers and a detailed spreadsheet. He pointed to the top of the nearest one.

"Pros and cons? Really?"

I nodded, handing him a piece of chocolate. "I want to make sure we've really thought this through. It's such an amazing opportunity!" I looked down at my list, the pros side so much longer than the cons. "What do you think?"

He looked overwhelmed. "I haven't really thought about it."

This was a typical response from him. Over the years, I had come to realize that his mind revolved around work. Whatever project he took on consumed him, leaving little energy for anything else.

George reviewed the numbers I was crunching. "I just don't think we can afford it right now."

"We may never get another opportunity like this." I shuffled the pages around me, still wanting to discuss my main points. "What about spending quality time together as a family?"

He picked up the papers and slid them to the side. "We can do that here too."

"Yeah, but we don't. I have a very strong feeling that this investment would make a big difference for us."

Instead of answering, he changed the subject. "Before I forget, I need a haircut."

Taking a deep breath to calm my mounting frustration, I looked at him. The mere thought of giving him yet another haircut already felt draining. "I've been cutting your hair every three weeks for twenty years."

"I know. You do a great job."

"Well, I don't want to do it anymore. I do all the boys' hair too. I'm tired of being the family barber on top of everything else."

"But I like the way you cut it."

"It has become a never-ending, thankless chore, and I'm the one left cleaning up the mess afterward. We saved all that money over the years—I think you can afford to get your hair cut by a professional now."

He hesitated before responding. "I guess so, if you feel that strongly about it." There was a plea in his eyes as he asked, "Just one more time?"

"Fine. But that's it."

I had a hard time saying no.

On Thursday, I was sautéing chicken and vegetables for a simple stir-fry accompanied by fragrant rice for dinner. My mind was preoccupied with the grocery list and menu I needed to plan for the lake. George Matthew stepped into the kitchen, asking if his friend Lyell could join us for the weekend. Without hesitation, I said yes.

The boys were getting good at loading the boat, having now done it four weekends in a row. Lyell, too, showed enthusiasm and a willingness to help. I observed the way he easily interacted with the rest of the boys. Despite his slight build, he had surprising strength. I had packed more than enough food and appreciated the extra pair of hands in carrying everything up the hill once we'd arrived.

The cabin was starting to feel very familiar. Lyell didn't mind sleeping on the sofa bed, knowing that all the other beds were already claimed.

We scarcely saw the boys all day on Saturday. They wanted to show Lyell everything they had discovered over the past few weeks and only came back to the cabin when they were hungry. Dieter allowed the boys to borrow his pedal boat, which they eagerly used to reach the small island situated in the middle of the bay.

After dinner, Dieter let them shoot an old pellet gun, setting up some tin cans in his backyard for target practice. I couldn't imagine them having a better day.

We ate pancakes for breakfast on Sunday morning. I knew the boys had been hearing bits and pieces of our conversations over the last few weeks, so I wasn't surprised when Tim asked, "Are we going to buy this cabin?"

"We're talking about it," I answered honestly.

Almost simultaneously, they chorused, "That would be awesome!" and "That would be amazing."

George didn't want them to get their hopes up. "We're not sure yet if we can afford it."

The boys nodded understandingly before David piped up, "Do we have time to go swimming once more before we leave today?" He loved the water.

"Yes, just make sure you put your wet towels and bathing suits in a bag when we leave."

We were putting our last bags into the boat when Dieter came down to say goodbye. He lowered the price even more and then presented us with an offer that took my breath away.

"Helga and I decided that we could finance the cabin for you, so you wouldn't have to take another mortgage from the bank."

I was ready to blurt out a yes, feeling like it was too good to be true, but managed to hold back, saying only, "Wow, that's incredible!"

Dieter added, "And if you can't make a payment one time, that's okay. We can work it out."

George remained calm and collected. "I'll contact you by the end of the week with our final decision."

At home, when the kids were in bed, George and I pored over the papers once more. Given this new offer, I double-checked the budget. It would be tight, but I thought we'd be able to swing it. I could sense we were getting very close to an agreement, but George still had some concerns to voice.

"What about church? We've always been part of a church community. You know that's going to change if we're at the cabin every weekend, right?"

"I know. It would be a huge change." For our whole lives, the church had shaped our social connections and spiritual experiences. "I'm not suggesting that we stop all our involvement, but it normally slows down during the summer anyway."

"That's true," he said.

"And it doesn't have to be all or nothing." I leaned over the computer and brought up the picture of Rainbow Falls, our family with their feet in the cold water, the waterfall behind us. "When we were here, feeling the mist and watching the water roar over the cliff, I was filled with an overwhelming sense of awe. It was so spiritual. I felt closer to God there than I do at church most of the time."

George nodded. "I felt the same way when we were kayaking."

A thrill of hope stirred within me. There was something in his eyes—a spark, a glimmer of the man I fell in love with, a recognition that felt both familiar and new.

"So you're leaning toward buying it?" I asked.

"I think so." George paused, being meticulous in his decision-making process. "It's a big decision, but I have to admit, I like the idea."

"Then let's do it! Call Dieter tomorrow!"

George released a long exhale and, seeing my excitement, hugged me and said, "Okay."

There was no turning back now.

Chapter Twenty-Four

O ur entire family was ecstatic about buying the cabin. Even Lyell, who had become a regular at our house, was excited. He had spent countless nights sleeping over and was practically a fixture at the dinner table most days.

After one such dinner, the boys each put their dishes in the dishwasher and ran to the family room while Lyell helped me clear the rest of the table. I seized the opportunity to start a conversation.

"You live in Glenn Valley, right? That's a long way to ride your bike! How long does it take?"

"I can do it in just over an hour," he replied, as if it was no big deal.

"Do you like living there?"

Without hesitation, he firmly said, "No."

I sensed an undertone of sadness in his voice, then looked into his eyes. "Tell me about your home."

"It's not home, it's just where I live. I've been thinking about running away, maybe joining the army."

I felt a surge of protectiveness toward him. "Why?"

"I need to get out of there. The foster parents don't care about us. They're just doing it for the money, and they use us to work on their farm."

"That's terrible. How many foster kids do they have?"

"Usually there's about four or five, but I've been there the longest."

"How did you end up there?"

"My dad died in a car accident when I was seven years old, and my mom is an alcoholic, so we all ended up in care. I have three brothers. My older brother, Mike, was in the same place as me, but he already ran away. I never see my younger brothers 'cause they're in a different foster home."

My heart ached for Lyell. He seemed like such a nice kid, and it felt so wrong for him to be stuck in a place like that.

"I'll drive you home tonight. It's too dark to ride your bike."

As we drove, I pictured him pedalling tirelessly the entire distance, conquering the big hills on his small rusty bike. Some stretches of road didn't have much of a shoulder.

"I can't imagine biking here. This road is dangerous!"

He laughed. "I do it all the time."

"We used to be foster parents," I told him. "We had foster kids when we lived in Walnut Grove until David was born. Then we moved into a small house in Fort Langley."

As dusk settled, we pulled up to the house Lyell lived in. In the fading light, I noticed a scattering of cats and dogs moving about the messy yard.

He offered a polite smile and said, "Thanks for the ride."

"You're welcome. Anytime."

"I wish I could live at your house." He had such hope in his eyes. All I could do was nod and smile. "Me too."

Deep in thought while driving home, I mulled over how to articulate my thoughts to George.

"It's not a good situation for him," I explained once I'd gotten back. "He deserves better. I think we should invite him to live with us. If I set up a meeting with his social worker to see what the options are, would you be okay with that?"

George looked tired, but I could tell he saw the logic in what I was saying. "I agree. We should do what we can to help."

"It makes me cringe to think that he feels his only option is to run away and join the army. We could provide a supportive environment where he could thrive and feel a sense of belonging. He already fits in and gets along with all the boys."

George kissed me good night. "I'm fine with it if you and the boys are."

"Thanks." I was relieved that he trusted me enough to make the decision, recognizing that the impact on his life wouldn't be nearly as profound as it would be on mine. Deep down, I was certain it was the right thing to do.

The next day, I gathered the boys for a family meeting. "What would you think if we invited Lyell to come live with us?"

Tim was the first to respond. "That'd be awesome." His tone was relaxed and confident.

Sitting beside me on the couch, George Matthew added, "He's my friend, so I'm good with it."

"Sure," David said with a shrug. "Lyell's already kind of like a brother," He was lounging in one of Tim's hand-me-down hoodies and fiddling with some pieces of Lego.

Mark, at the age of ten, still looked like a little boy with his baby face and adorable blonde hair peeking out from under the red baseball cap perched on his head. "I like Lyell," he said. "I think it would be cool if he lived here."

"That's great. I wanted to make sure you all agreed before we asked Lyell." Glancing at each of their faces, I noticed that every one of them was smiling. "I'm proud of you guys for accepting another person into our home so easily. So," I said, turning to practicalities, "if Lyell does come to live with us, where should his room be?"

We had an unfinished basement where the boys used to ride their tricycles and, when they got a bit older, played hockey on rainy days. Earlier that year, we had started some renovations and added a guest bedroom down there.

George Matthew said, "I think because I'm the oldest, I should get the new bedroom in the basement. Then Lyell can have my room in the attic."

"Are the rest of you okay with that?" There were nods all around. "Great. At some point, we'll finish the basement and add a rec room for you and your friends to hang out in."

"Awesome," Tim said, and I could tell by the big smile on his face as he shared a look with David that they were already planning video game parties in their heads.

"I'm going to set up a meeting with Lyell's social worker tomorrow. We'll see what happens." To me, it felt completely natural to be taking this step. In fact, it felt like an occasion to celebrate.

"Who wants a frozen Caramilk bar?" I called as I got up and went to the kitchen, pulling a few out of my secret hiding place in the freezer.

The question barely hung in the air before a chorus of four voices erupted, overlapping and stretching into a unified, enthusiastic, "Meeeee!"

Lyell and I walked into the social worker's office and sat down in the chairs facing her desk.

"Hi, Lyell," she said warmly, then looked at me. "And you must be Anne. Lyell has told me all about you and your family."

I gave Lyell a little smile, then got straight to the point. "I'm hoping Lyell can move from his current foster home to ours."

"Unfortunately, we can't legally do that." She noticed our disappointment and shuffled some papers around. "But," she paused for a moment, locating the pamphlet she'd been looking for, pulling it to the front of her pile, "since Lyell is sixteen, he qualifies for the Independent Living program. That means he can choose where he wants to live and would receive an allowance to help him learn how to become independent." She turned to Lyell and asked, "Does that sound like something you would be interested in?"

"Yes, definitely," he beamed. "And I choose to live with this family." We grinned at each other, and I put my arm around his shoulder.

"Okay then. I'll get the paperwork started and let you know when you'll be moving."

Three weeks later, as September fell into the steady rhythm of a new school year, I stood by the window waiting for Lyell to arrive. A car pulled into the driveway, so I stepped outside to get a look at his foster father for the first time. He sat behind the wheel of his car without a hint of expression on his face as he waited for Lyell to gather his things.

Even as Lyell emerged from the vehicle and began walking up the driveway, his foster father didn't even give him a second glance, immediately reversing and driving away. This man, whom Lyell had lived with for almost nine years, just dropped him off. No goodbye, not even a handshake. Observing his callousness left me feeling disgusted.

Lyell didn't look back as the car drove away. He walked up to our door carrying a small box containing a few T-shirts and comic books and nothing else—not even a winter jacket or an extra pair of shoes. As a former foster parent, I knew that all maintenance payments received were meant to be directed toward enhancing the child's well-being. This had obviously not been the case for Lyell, and it saddened me to think about the neglect he had endured, prompting me to make an even deeper commitment to improving his life.

As he reached the door, I wrapped my arms around him, trying not to cry. "Welcome home, Lyell."

Chapter Twenty-Five

In mid-October, George and I made one last trip to the lake to finalize the paperwork for the cabin purchase and have Dieter show us how to winterize it. After signing everything we needed to, Dieter patiently explained how to drain the water and where to add antifreeze to prevent the pipes from bursting during the winter. I couldn't wait until spring, when it would be warm enough to open the cabin—our cabin—for the very first time.

George's business was thriving, and to my surprise, he received a substantial payout in January after an exceptionally successful year. Beaming with pride, he shared the news with me, clearly proud of the hard work that had led to such a reward. The payout provided the perfect opportunity to finally move forward with the basement renovation project we had been talking about for so long.

George was in his element as he drew up the plans. Every detail had been thought through, but it was up to me to coordinate materials and manage the schedule with the various trades. My brother came in his spare time and on weekends to do the plumbing for the bathroom and small kitchenette. I picked up paint samples, bathroom fixtures, and flooring samples. The electricians installed recessed lighting along the ceiling, adding much-needed brightness to the room. A few weeks later, drywallers were busy measuring and cutting. It felt like a never-ending project, and at times I went to Stan and Louisa's just to escape.

"It's not too loud, is it?" I looked through the sunroom windows toward my house. "With the renovation going on?"

Louisa shook her head. "We can't even hear it."

I took a sip of my hot tea. "The extra space will be nice now that we have *five* growing boys. It will be a lot quieter upstairs when their friends are over. I'm looking forward to that."

Louisa nodded along.

Stan's expression was unreadable, somewhere between a frown and a smile. Then he said, "You might as well put a big sign on your front door."

I turned to the old man. "A sign?"

"Yes." With a flourish, he swept his hand from left to right as if crafting an imaginary sign in the air. "Waifs and strays welcome."

I smiled, sighing at his exaggeration. "What can I say? I have a soft spot for kids." I took my cup to the kitchen. I was ready to leave anyway. "I'll try to drop in later this week."

Stan grinned, but I caught a hint of disappointment beneath his teasing. I knew he suspected I'd have even less time for him now.

"Don't forget your chocolate bar on the way out," he shouted.

When we finally completed the basement renovations, we decided to refresh the upstairs family room with new dark green couches, moving the old set downstairs. Our basement quickly became the go-to hangout spot for the boys and their neighbourhood friends after school. They celebrated with a big sleepover the first available weekend.

As I descended the basement steps that evening, I juggled a huge bowl of freshly popped popcorn and a plate full of chocolate chip cookies. Nine boys were downstairs, immersed in the world of Nintendo. The rapid clicking of controllers filled the room, accompanied by bursts of laughter and animated conversation.

David looked up from his controller and offered an enthusiastic "Thanks, Mom," as I set down the snacks for them.

A sense of satisfaction washed over me, affirming that all the effort we had put into the renovation was worth it. With all the masculine energy now concentrated in the basement, the kitchen upstairs became a haven of tranquility.

One evening, Lyell received an unexpected call from a hospital in Vancouver. His brother Mike, the one who had run away from the foster home, had overdosed on drugs. I took Lyell to see him right away.

As we walked into the hospital room, I sensed Lyell's demeanour shifting the moment he saw his brother lying motionless in the bed.

"He's been in a coma for a few days," the nurse explained. "We're not certain if he'll recover. I'm sorry." She left the room to let us be alone with Mike.

Through tearful eyes, Lyell grasped Mike's hand and spoke words of comfort and connection. The heartfelt moment was so touching that I couldn't help but cry. Time seemed to stretch as Lyell and I stood there, my arm around him and his hand holding his brother's.

Lyell turned to me. "It's so hard to see him like this."

I gave Lyell's shoulder a gentle, supportive squeeze.

Suddenly, Mike's eyes fluttered open. A flood of shock and relief surged through us. Lyell stood up to look into his eyes. "Mike, I'm here! Mike, it's me, Lyell."

Mike spoke in a faint whisper. "Lyell?" Weariness lingered in his gaze, with no energy for further conversation.

I brushed away my tears and went into the hallway to find the nurse, who quickly came and checked Mike's vital signs. Her advice was that he needed more rest and more assessments.

I touched Mike's arm and said goodbye. Lyell gave him a hug, and then we departed, grateful we had come to visit.

Weeks went by without hearing from Mike despite being notified that he had been discharged from the hospital shortly after our visit. Then, finally, he called Lyell, and they arranged to meet at a local coffee shop.

When Lyell got home from seeing his brother, I could tell something was wrong.

"How did it go?"

Lyell shrugged, looking down at his feet. "It was really hard. He's not the same person anymore."

"Do you think the drugs have damaged his brain?"

"Definitely. He didn't even remember stuff about growing up. It's like his brain is all jumbled up." A tear formed in the corner of his eye. "He's not the same brother anymore, and I'm going to miss him."

I walked over and gave him a big hug.

His voice tightened. "What if I could have helped him somehow? Before, I mean."

"None of this is your fault. Everyone is responsible for their own choices in life, and every decision comes with consequences. Some will be positive, and others might be challenging and tough, but they're all part of learning and growing."

"Yeah." He paused for a moment. "Do you think I could try to contact my younger brothers sometime? I hope they're doing okay."

"I'll call the social worker in the morning and see if we can figure out where they are."

"Thanks... Mom."

Hearing Lyell call me Mom filled me with warmth. He had a quiet resilience about him, accepting the situation with more grace than I expected.

It took months for him to be able to connect with his younger brothers again, but when he did, he was overjoyed to find that their bond had stayed intact despite the time and challenges they had all faced.

Chapter Twenty-Six

Spring at last made its long-awaited appearance. Lyell and George Matthew had weekend plans with friends, while I arranged for the other three boys to stay at Elsie's place and enjoy some time with their cousins. I thought it would be best if George and I were alone when we opened the cabin for the first time.

George came home from work early on Friday so we wouldn't have to launch the boat in the dark. With our cooler and boxes of supplies loaded, we were on our way. The boat glided gently over the surface of the water, which looked like a glass mirror reflecting the sky. We were both exhausted from a long week, and the serene setting had an immediate calming effect, soothing both body and mind.

Once we arrived, George got the water pump going while I started the fire in the wood stove. I prepared a hearty steak dinner to celebrate the first night in our own cabin. When it got dark, we stood outside on the deck, captivated by the billions of stars in the night sky.

We opened the sofa bed in the living room to be closer to the fire. While George was in the outhouse, I made up the bed with flannel sheets and an extra warm blanket. I crawled into bed first as George turned off the propane lamp.

The glow of the fire created a cozy atmosphere. It didn't take long to fall asleep, although George got up a few times during the night to add more wood to the fire.

In the morning, I prepared a tray of coffee and toast to serve George breakfast in bed.

"Can you believe it? This is *our* cabin!"

"It does seem a bit surreal," he answered, each word sending a white puff of breath into the cold morning air.

"I can't wait to start transforming the place."

We lingered in bed for a while until George said, "I'm going to start by scrubbing off the green algae that accumulated on the deck over winter."

"I'll start in the kitchen."

I pulled knick-knacks off the walls and started wiping out the cupboards, one of which had beautiful stained-glass doors. Dieter had mentioned that Helga made them herself. Another of her stained-glass pieces was a window set into the wall of the hallway. As I continued to clean, I couldn't help but admire all the details that gave this place its unique character.

A few hours later, I went outside to take a break and realized that it was much warmer outside in the sunshine than inside. The old wood stove wasn't very efficient.

Seated on the deck chairs with a small side table between us, we ate lunch, surrounded by the warm, quiet beauty of the bay. Not another soul was in sight, and the only sound was the cheerful chorus of birds.

I reached over to hold George's hand. "It feels right being here."

George turned to me, smiling. "I agree."

Our short time here had already begun to ease his tension. His features softened, his shoulders loosened, and his smile came more naturally. Seeing him this way filled me with quiet hope. I knew change wouldn't happen overnight, but as we packed up to leave on Sunday, I sensed we both felt refreshed and more connected than before.

I walked into Stan and Louisa's sunroom and announced, "I just found out that I'm pregnant." The priceless expressions on their faces gave way when I quickly added, "April Fools!" Raucous laughter spilled from both of them.

"I didn't realize it was April first today," Stan chuckled. "I usually don't even know what day of the week it is, let alone the date on the calendar. You really got me that time."

Still laughing, Louisa went to the kitchen and brought back a tray of tea and biscuits. After setting it down, she began her usual update on what had been going on in their lives since the last time I had visited. "Stan was at the dentist yesterday. He needed a filling done."

"I didn't want to go. I don't care anymore, but"—he pointed accusingly at Louisa—"she made me."

"One must keep up with these things," Louisa insisted.

"I was sitting in the dentist chair, uncomfortable, with my mouth frozen, and the dentist was *singing*." Stan had a look that was a bit hard to read, as if he found the situation mildly funny but annoying at the same time.

I laughed. "I go to the same dentist. I like when he sings. I find it relaxing."

Stan huffed. "I don't need to listen to an aria every time he's working on my teeth."

I chuckled at Stan's surliness as we all enjoyed our tea, and he eventually cracked a smile as well. We sat for a while, watching the branches sway in the breeze outside the sunroom.

"I heard there's a flu going around. Did you get your flu shots this year?" I asked.

"Yes," Louisa said. "I think it's important to get it annually. We got ours in November."

The topic triggered a memory for Stan, who launched into a story about his childhood.

"Did I ever tell you about the time, when I was about ten years old? I was in a convalescent home for six weeks with scarlet fever. Parents weren't even allowed to visit their own children at the convalescent home." He appeared transported back in time as he spoke. "The nurses were absolutely brutal. They would whistle for us to line up, even when we were feeling so sick, and then they would box our ears if we didn't do what they told us to do. I remember getting my ears boxed quite often."

I shuddered at the thought. "That's terrible. I can't imagine any of my boys having to go through that."

"It was a different time back then," Stan said, which spurred him on to start another story about his time in the army. "Did I ever tell you that I was in the 15th Scottish Reconnaissance Regiment..."

My mind drifted to dinner plans and whether I still needed any last-minute groceries. I knew I should be getting home, but it was difficult to interrupt Stan as he went on.

"... You should read the book called *Scottish Lion on Patrol*. It's all about our regiment and would help you understand—"

"Sorry, Stan, I hate to cut you off, but I really need to get going. I will read it someday."

"Oh, okay." He softened. "Take your Caramilk bar on the way out."

As I reached the front door, I called out a 'thank you,' hoping they could hear me from the sunroom.

When I got home, I quickly jotted down the name of the book Stan had recommended, a silent agreement with myself to follow through on my promise.

Spring had quietly become my favourite season, a shift I hadn't fully realized until I started spending time at the cabin. There was something about the way the forest slowly came back to life after winter's stillness—the budding trees, the light breeze carrying the first birdsong. It stirred something within me. Each day brought with it a sense of renewal, as if the earth was waking up, inviting me to notice and appreciate the smallest details of its awakening.

On the first weekend in May, with the older boys away at a youth retreat, George and I headed to the lake with David and Mark. We were enjoying a delicious Saturday morning brunch, when George decided that the boys should be at the Kid's Club Wrap-Up event later that afternoon.

"I think it's important that we're there," he said, his voice tinged with guilt about missing so many church events back home.

Kid's Club was usually held during the week in a school gym, giving the kids from church a chance to socialize and take part in fun activities. The program was mostly run by dads, so I was pleased to see George getting involved as well. This weekend, a special bonfire and wiener roast was planned.

As I washed the dishes, I found myself wishing I could stay at the cabin longer. Then I bundled everyone's dirty laundry into a big plastic tub and gathered the towels.

George turned to me, "I think we could save some time by going there directly instead of going home first."

I slid a few more things into a tote bag, but I was still resisting packing up my stuff.

"What if you take the boys and I don't go?" The idea left my mouth before I'd even fully thought it through.

"What?" George looked confused.

"What if I drop you guys off at the marina," I shrugged, trying to act casual so I didn't give away how much I wanted it to work, "then I spend the night here, and you pick me up at the marina tomorrow afternoon?"

I watched George think it over, and to my absolute surprise, he agreed to my plan. It wasn't until I dropped them off and arrived back at the cabin alone that it really started to sink in. Solitude. It must have been at least twenty years since I'd had the chance to be by myself for any length of time.

As I walked into the cabin, I noticed that the sliding glass door needed a good clean. With no kids to fill it with fingerprints, I thought this would be the perfect time to address it. After cleaning the glass to my satisfaction, I felt compelled, with similar reasoning, to tackle the floors.

I was about to climb up the ship's ladder to wash the second floor when I stopped. This wasn't why I had wanted to stay here. Turning around, I grabbed the mop bucket and flung the murky water out the back door, watching it splash onto the wild salal bushes. Then, wiping my hands on my jeans, I reached for my hiking shoes, slid them on, and tightened the laces, ready to head out.

The forest edge was just ten steps from the back door, and within moments, the cabin had disappeared from view. Surrounded by the vibrant energy of the woods, I felt as alive as the forest itself. My racing thoughts quieted, giving way to a dreamlike curiosity as I took in every detail of the lush growth around me.

Without the boys shouting, I saw a lot more wildlife. A graceful deer moved quietly along the path ahead, unrattled by my presence. The fresh scent of cedar filled the air. A few steps deeper into the forest, a rhythmic tapping, like a steady drumming, broke the silence. My gaze followed the sound upward to a nearby tree. There, a woodpecker busily hammered away, its vivid colours standing out against the bright green backdrop. I stood in awe, a silent observer of nature's symphony.

The sun slowly shifted to the other side of the sky, so I decided to turn around and follow the solitary path back. My heart raced suddenly at the fleeting glimpse of something slithering across my path. I instinctively froze but was relieved when I saw that it was only a harmless garter snake.

Soon, over the crest of the final mossy hill, the cabin came back into sight. I grabbed an armload of wood from the shed in the back and filled the wood stove. I traded my hiking clothes for cozy pajamas and made myself a cup of tea. I couldn't wait to read a book with no distractions.

Curled up in a deck chair, wrapped in a blanket, I was captivated by the scenic beauty of this place we could now call home. Grateful didn't even begin to encapsulate how I felt. I looked up at the fir tree in front of me and noticed the soft, fresh green tips sprouting at the ends of the branches.

I thought back to that time at Stan's, sitting in his sunroom envious of the slower pace of life he was experiencing. Never in my wildest dreams had I envisioned that becoming my reality, especially at this point in my life.

I read my book as the setting sun cast a golden glow across the calm water. When my eyes began to droop, I retired to bed. It didn't take long before I dozed off.

In the morning, after a restful sleep, I opened the curtains to a picture-perfect view. The sunshine drew me onto the deck, where

I savoured my breakfast: fresh fruit with yogurt and homemade granola. Between bites, I closed my eyes, letting the morning light warm my skin and soothe my soul. Birds, each with its unique song, wove a harmonious melody that echoed through the crisp mountain air.

A butterfly danced gracefully beside me for a moment before ascending to the sky. Then it dawned on me. Goosebumps peppered my arms. It was May third, exactly five years since Liz had passed away.

I could hear her voice as if she were right beside me. "*Just be.*"

This peaceful state must have been what she had meant. Every part of me felt weightless away from the demands of daily life. It was as though I could rise above it all, leaving my cares far behind, existing solely in this serene, unburdened moment.

I sat on the quiet deck, letting my thoughts settle. Maybe *just being* didn't even require a tranquil setting, though nature certainly made it easier. The key, I thought, was tapping into a wellspring of life within, a deep source of inner vitality that could sustain me anywhere. It struck me that this was how people often described God—as the ultimate source of being.

I closed my eyes, lifted my face to the sky and breathed deeply. *Just be.* Be silent long enough to hear the trees whisper their message of freedom.

I thought about the practice of prayer and what I once believed it to be, so focused on saying the right words, hands clasped and head bowed. This, however, felt so much more expansive to me. I sank into the stillness, feeling it settle deep within me.

Time passed too quickly. When George picked me up at the marina later that afternoon, I held him tight and long.

"Thank you," I breathed into his chest. The depth of my longing for solitude had caught me by surprise. "I needed that."

Chapter Twenty-Seven

With school ending and summer just beginning, I knew I'd soon be spending more time at the lake. That also meant making an effort to visit Stan and Louisa as often as possible throughout the month of June. It had already been a few weeks since I'd been to their house, and the moment I stepped inside, I noticed the light above Silvia was turned off.

"Sorry, I haven't been over as much. Life has gotten busy again."

Stan grumbled in response, but I was used to his moods when he hadn't seen me for a while. I carried on, knowing he'd warm up eventually. There was no shortage of things to talk about.

"The church is sponsoring a refugee family from Colombia." I said, settling into my usual spot on the couch.

Stan grumped, "Why do you care?"

"Because this family was forced to leave everything behind and flee for their lives," I replied. "Helping them is one small way to make a difference."

Louisa seemed interested. "What does it mean to sponsor them?"

"We're covering their first year of expenses for housing, food, and clothing. That will give them time to learn English, get used to living in a new country, and eventually get jobs."

Stan asked, "Why do you have to get so involved?"

"Well, for one, I'm the chair of the refugee committee, and also, most of the others on the team are working during the day, so I've taken on a bit more."

"Do they speak any English?" Louisa asked as she finished her tea.

"The dad understands a bit. The mom and three kids only speak Spanish, but somehow we manage. We had them over for a barbecue a few days ago. The boys were great at communicating with the kids. I've always loved the Spanish language and would like to learn it. Now I'm even more motivated."

Stan gave me a glare that clearly said I shouldn't even think about adding one more thing to my already full schedule.

I ignored the look and launched into a story. "The other day, when I picked them up to come to our place, Alberto, the dad, was practising his English as we drove. When we pulled into the driveway, he looked at our house and proudly said, 'Home, candy home.'

I started chuckling when I realized he meant to say, 'Home, sweet home.' He laughed when I explained it to him, and now it's a private joke between us."

Louisa let out a soft laugh, repeating, "Home, candy home." I saw the corners of Stan's lips twitch upward.

"How is everything at the lake?" Stan asked, finally ready to engage in conversation.

"Great. A friend gave us an old windsurf board that the boys spend hours on. George Matthew drives the aluminum boat, towing the board, while the other three balance on top of it. They try to push each other off. It's hilarious to watch." I thought back to the weekend, how laughter had rung through the bay.

"How big is your aluminum boat? Stan asked.

"Fourteen feet, I think. Almost everyone in the bay has one for zipping around."

Louisa asked, "What about Lyell?"

"Oh, I forgot to tell you. He got his first job and is working every weekend as a dishwasher at a restaurant."

"Good for him." Stan rose from his recliner, empty teacup in hand, and made his way to the kitchen.

As Louisa and I continued chatting, he reached for his cane and shuffled slowly down the hallway toward the bathroom.

I leaned over and asked Louisa in a low tone, "Is it my imagination, or is Stan walking even slower than usual?"

"Yes, he almost always uses his cane now. It's not just for show anymore."

Louisa was always interested in stories about the cabin, so she asked me to continue.

"One night, Mark found a bat in the eaves. He named him Howard—the same name he gave the lizard he caught last month."

Louisa had a knowing smile, like we were both thinking about the pure and uncomplicated nature of childhood.

After some time, Stan reappeared. I watched him walk into the kitchen with one hand pressed against his lower back. He returned to the living room a few moments later with my chocolate bar in his hand.

"Thank you, Stan." Interpreting the gesture as a sign of approval for the time spent together, I got up to leave. Putting on my shoes, I spotted Silvia basking in the glow of her light and wondered when he had discreetly turned it on.

Dieter emphasized that owning a cabin meant having a constant stream of projects. "You'll find out that the work is endless. There's always something to keep you busy."

"The first project we want to work on is a firepit," George said.

Dieter suggested, "You're always welcome to use ours."

Helga was nodding.

"Somehow, the cabin doesn't feel complete without one of our own, though," George insisted. "We don't want to bother you every time we want to roast marshmallows."

"It's no bother, but I understand. I wanted one when we lived up there too."

The next time all the boys were available to come to the lake, we decided to start the firepit project. George Matthew and Lyell went out in the aluminum boat to collect buckets of gravel from the other bay. George cut down a few trees in the designated area, cutting off the branches but keeping the logs intact to use as makeshift benches. Tim, David, and Mark dragged the branches together in a pile to burn.

After clearing the area, we spread a layer of gravel, creating just enough space for our family to gather comfortably. At the centre, we arranged large rocks in a snug circle, forming the heart of our firepit. To everyone's dismay, by the time we finished the project, it was time to go home. A wiener roast would have to wait until next weekend.

I loved watching my children grow up on the water. Mark and David had made friends with Dieter and Helga's granddaughters, Emily and Andrea, who spent most of their summers at the lake. The four of them spent all their time together that summer, swimming, exploring, and just being kids. I essentially only saw them at mealtimes.

The highlight of every summer was George's two-week break from work. Those days felt like a gift, a chance to pause the relentless march of time and simply enjoy a slower pace of life.

George and I sat on Dieter and Helga's deck, enjoying their hospitality, while the sound of children's laughter drifted from the rope swing at the far end of the bay.

"It's so good for them, spending lots of time outside. No ifs, ands, or buts," Dieter commented.

I agreed. "I've noticed the boys becoming a lot more independent since we started coming here. It's too bad the older ones already have summer jobs, they're missing out."

With a subtle laugh, Dieter said, "That's good for them too."

"True," I smiled. "And they can still be here on their days off."

"Do Lyell and George Matthew have plans now that they've graduated?" Helga asked.

George answered. "Lyell will be starting a plumbing apprenticeship this fall. George Matthew has plans to go to Thailand on a program through the Canadian Mennonite University."

"Sounds interesting," Dieter said as he took a sip of his beer.

George added, "And Tim is such an entrepreneur, he already has all kinds of money-making ventures going."

Dieter smiled, "And the youngest two get to be kids just a little while longer."

"Yup," I said, feeling completely at ease.

As soon as Helga spotted the four of them returning from the rope swing, she slipped into the kitchen, emerging moments later with a platter of her famous doughnuts—golden, shallow-fried, and generously dusted with powdered sugar.

When Emily and Andrea caught sight of her holding the tray, their faces lit up. "Doughnuts!" they called excitedly to the boys.

David and Mark grinned and scrambled out of the water, racing up to the cabin to join the feast. After his first bite, the white sugar clung to Mark's lips and chin, and all four of them doubled over with laughter as even more sugar puffed out of his mouth when he tried to talk.

Dieter and I exchanged a glance, both silently acknowledging the priceless value of these small but precious moments.

Chapter Twenty-Eight

Summer raced toward fall, leaving us with a collection of memories that seemed to have been woven together in the blink of an eye. The lazy afternoons by the water, my pots of blooming flowers and tasty herbs, the carefree laughter of playing games in the evenings—all of it faded, giving way to the subtle, cooler temperatures of autumn. George and I handled the cabin winterization on our own for the first time. As I turned the key to lock the door, I already couldn't wait to return.

Back in Stan and Louisa's sunroom, while the soft afternoon light filtered gently through the trees outside, I filled them in on a decision I had made the previous week.

"I'm going to record my harp music. A friend from church knows a guy who set up a little recording studio in his garage down in Bellingham."

Louisa clasped her hands together. "How lovely. We do enjoy your music."

Stan nodded, "How long is that going to take?"

"I'm not sure, probably at least a month or two."

He looked over at his piano. "Could you play me that Chopin waltz that I love?"

These days, most of the music played in their home came from my hands. Arthritis had stiffened Stan's fingers, stealing the ease with which he once played. It saddened me to think that the piano, once his conduit for expression, now lay just out of reach—his passion restrained by the slow betrayal of his aching joints. As I played, he closed his eyes as though he were immersed in a trance.

When the final notes faded into silence, I let the moment settle before rising from the bench. Passing Stan's old record player, I teased, "If I bring you a CD of my harp music once it's finished, would you even have a way to play it?"

Stan's insulted expression made Louisa laugh. He said, "Of course we have a CD player. We're not living in the stone age."

I gave him a smile. "Well, I should get going. It was great to see you, but as usual, it's time to make dinner before everyone gets home." I walked from the sunroom to the front door, and just as I reached for my chocolate bar, Stan's voice rang out reminding me not to forget it. I shouted a quick "Thank you!"

By December, the CD was finally ready, just in time to make the perfect Christmas gift for everyone in my extended family. I wrapped Stan and Louisa's in festive green paper before delivering it to them.

"*Peaceful Journey*," Louisa said, reading the album title out loud. The title track was the song I had written for Liz. After admiring the cover—an oil painting I had done that depicted a view of the lake from our cabin—Louisa popped it into their portable CD player with built-in speakers.

"It was more work than you thought, wasn't it?" Stan asked.

"Yes, it was an intense few months trying to get it all done."

We chatted while it played in the background. By the time the third track started to play, Stan said, "It all sounds the same to me."

Louisa frowned at her husband. "I find it very relaxing."

I defended my project to Stan. "The point was to record the original songs that were in my head so I wouldn't lose them. I added some familiar tunes in between to make it less boring."

"Well, it's still boring." He turned the volume down. "You'll never make money from this."

"I'm not trying to make money with it. Although," I bragged, "the first box of 250 is almost sold. Mostly to relatives and friends from church, but at least that covers all the expenses."

Stan offered a small, subtle smile. "Why don't we move to the sunroom and have a cup of tea?"

"So sorry, I can't stay."

Louisa followed me to the door. "When will we see you next?"

"I'll drop in briefly on the twenty-fourth. Do you want to come to the Christmas Eve service with us?" I looked toward the dining room where Stan stood staring at the picture of Silvia. Her light was off.

"I don't feel up to it this year," he muttered.

I tipped my chin toward Stan, trying to sound cheerful. "Our birthdays will be here before you know it. Lamplighter for lunch?"

"I'll mark it on the calendar," Louisa promised as she closed the door behind me.

I called out "Merry Christmas" at the last minute. I realized then that I hadn't even taken my coat off while I was there. Maybe that's what had bothered Stan.

Besides getting the CD done, working with the refugee family took up at least two or three days a week. It felt like a part-time job layered onto the usual demands of my own household, and lately, I was constantly rushing to keep up.

After the Christmas season and all the indulgences that went with the festivities, I felt like I needed an outlet for more physical activity. The idea of going to the gym didn't appeal to me at all, not just because I didn't like the smell of gyms, but because it felt too much like being a hamster on a wheel.

One day, I saw a flyer on the post office bulletin board that said "Want a fun way to get in shape after the Christmas Holidays? Join our Women's Belly Dancing Class." I wrote down the phone number and called as soon as I arrived home. The woman told me that classes started on Tuesday evening, and all I needed was comfortable clothing like yoga pants and a T-shirt. The studio was in her home, less than five minutes away.

After the very first class, I knew I had found something I would truly enjoy. There were only six other women in the group, and most of them were beginners too.

Another new world was unfolding before me, and it felt as though a long-lost part of my soul was coming to life. I loved the rhythm of the music, feeling it resonate deep within my bones as my body swayed effortlessly to the exotic movements.

A thin layer of frost clung to the bare branches outside as I stepped into Stan and Louisa's warm home. The birthday lunch we'd celebrated a few weeks earlier had lifted Stan's spirits, so Silvia's light was shining brightly.

Louisa went to get the tea as I seated myself on the couch. Stan said, "There's nothing new going on in our lives, what's happening in yours?"

"Well, George Matthew is back from Thailand. He had a great experience there."

"What was it called again, Outtatown?" he inquired with a blank expression.

"Yes, it's through the Canadian Mennonite University. Students get to spend a few months in Canada and then a few months in a foreign country. He chose Thailand."

"Sounds wonderful," Louisa said as she set the tray down on the coffee table. I noticed the delicate teacups, their vivid rose pattern standing out against the fine porcelain. It was a nice change from the usual mugs.

"This feels fancy," I said, raising an eyebrow.

She smiled softly, tilting the teapot just enough to let the amber liquid flow smoothly into the cups. "Every so often, we must create special moments," she said, handing Stan his cup before filling mine and then her own.

Visiting with Stan and Louisa had become as effortless as sinking into a favourite chair. Before I knew it, hours had slipped by in the comfort of their company.

Hardly anyone knew about my new exercise class, but I decided to share it with Stan and Louisa. They were far more open-minded than most in my conservative circles. "I started taking belly dancing classes and absolutely love it."

"Oh, that sounds like such good fun!" Louisa said, "If I wasn't so old, I would join you."

Stan's face lit up and his eyes twinkled. "Congratulations. How about a drop of sherry to celebrate?" He shuffled over to the china cabinet to get the small glasses.

As he poured the drinks, Louisa asked out of the blue, "If you're ever out and about in Walnut Grove, do you think you could pick up some of that fried chicken for us?"

"Of course."

"Are you sure it's no trouble? Stan and I have been craving fried chicken."

"No trouble at all. I'll pick it up tomorrow before dinner."

"That would be lovely."

"Cheers," Stan raised his glass, waited until we lifted ours, then laughed. "Here's to belly dancing and fried chicken."

Although I hadn't planned to go to Walnut Grove the next day, I made the trip specifically to pick up the chicken for Louisa. As I dropped it off, Louisa asked me to come in for a minute.

"I'm quite concerned. Stan has stopped walking into town with me."

Stan, overhearing his wife, reacted. "My legs aren't what they used to be."

Louisa turned to me. "I've been thinking, maybe we should get a scooter for him, so he can still get out for some fresh air."

"Do you think that's a good idea, Stan?" I asked.

He was already nodding his head before he replied. "Yes, I suppose I'm at that age now. I was also thinking I should get one of those lift chairs. It's getting harder and harder for me to get myself out of my recliner."

"Alright, I'll look into it."

In the weeks that followed, between taking Stan to a few doctor's appointments and my frequent Costco runs, I found the time to pick up a scooter, which happened to be on sale. I wedged it into my van amidst boxes of cereal, gallons of milk, and enough meat to feed an army. Honestly, with five teenage boys, it felt like I was cooking for at least a dozen people every day, yet there were rarely any leftovers.

A few days later, I spotted Stan on his new ride, cruising down our street with Joey panting happily, perched in his lap. Louisa, also panting, walked briskly behind. I laughed out loud, wishing I had a video camera to capture the scene. I honked my horn and waved at them as I passed their priceless procession.

Chapter Twenty-Nine

The air felt thick, carrying the scent of sun-soaked earth. George was chopping kindling at the back of the cabin, and the boys had gone to the waterfall in the aluminum boat. After tidying the deck, hanging up towels, and picking up empty glasses, I leaned against the railing. The still surface of the bay glimmered in the steady August sun. It was calling to me.

A bead of sweat ran down my temple, tickling as it followed the curve of my face. I grabbed a dry beach towel and made my way down to the lake. I parked my flip-flops and towel on the stone steps and entered the refreshing water, gradually going deeper, adjusting to the cool temperature. Once it reached my waist, I surrendered, letting myself fall gently and float just beneath the surface. With eyes closed, I drifted, attuned to the soothing rhythm of my heartbeat resonating in my ears.

Feeling adequately cooled down, I emerged from the water and began wrapping the towel around my waist, when I heard my name being called. Shielding the sun from my eyes, I looked up and started walking toward Dieter's voice.

He waved from his deck. "Come up for a sangria."

As I stepped onto their expansive deck, the cedar boards creaked beneath my feet. He swirled a coral-hued drink in a massive glass with a carefully cut orange slice resting on the rim.

I sat down on the wooden bench, inspecting the fragrant liquid. After my first sip, I was instantly hooked. It was sweet and bubbly, like sparkling fruit punch but better, with undertones of Dieter's bold homemade red. "This is delicious! Thank you."

He smiled broadly just as the screen door slammed shut. Helga emerged from the cabin, carrying a bowl of pretzels.

As she placed the bowl on the wooden table, I admired her impeccably manicured hands and neatly styled short hair, which had a blend of light grey and blonde tones. She had an air of confidence and independence.

"What's on the project list this week?" She knew the rhythm of life as a cabin owner: some work, some play.

The salty pretzels were satisfying after my swim and paired well with the sangria. I munched them in between sentences. "We bought a composting toilet, but we haven't installed it yet, so I don't know if we'll be using it this year. A lot of prep work needs to be done first."

"I know exactly what you mean," Dieter chimed in. "If you need any tools, you know where to find them." He had a workshop behind his cabin filled with supplies and equipment, a place George already knew well.

"What about you?" I asked. "What are you working on?"

"I'm making ropes," he said, handing me one with a neatly crafted loop at the end. As I turned it over in my hands, he took a sip from his tall can of German beer.

The strands were expertly woven together, creating a seamless pattern that spoke of patience and skill. "How do you do that?" I asked, tracing the tight weave. "It looks complicated!"

"Like anything," he said with a shrug, "it's simple once you know how to do it."

He set the beer down and nodded toward my glass. "Can I get you another drink?"

I glanced down. The glass was mostly ice with an orange slice resting on top. I hadn't even realized how quickly I'd finished it. That explained the heat in my cheeks. "Maybe just half."

He took the glass from my hand as Helga nudged the snack bowl toward me, saying, "I'll eat them all if they're beside me."

I rested a hand over my stomach, "So will I."

Dieter came out with two full glasses of sangria. He placed one down for each of us.

"What?" I picked mine up and shot him a curious glance. "I only asked for half."

"I know." His grin was mischievous. "I only filled up the top half."

I was laughing when George came down to join us. Dieter handed him the rope he'd made and said, "You can keep this one. It's always handy to have an extra dock line."

"Thanks."

"Oh, I almost forgot." Dieter got up and went into the cabin. He came out and gave George a black bag. "It's called a bag phone. I got you this one at the flea market. All you need is an antenna and then you can communicate with the outside world."

George's face lit up. "How much do we owe you?"

"Only twenty bucks. I got a good deal and bought myself a new one too." It was clear that Dieter thrived on solving problems. He embraced challenges with commendable enthusiasm.

While I appreciated his thoughtfulness, a twinge of disappointment lingered in my mind. I understood the importance of having a phone for emergencies in such a remote location, but I had relished the simplicity of being unreachable, undisturbed by life's demands. Being at the lake offered a kind of freedom I rarely experienced elsewhere. It helped me set boundaries, say no more easily, and avoid the weight of too many commitments. It also seemed to help George focus more on our family rather than on work.

George was thrilled about the phone, brimming with excitement. I knew it made sense, but I still felt a quiet ache for the simplicity we were about to lose.

It was time to start making dinner, so I finished off my sangria and thanked Dieter and Helga for a delightful afternoon. George and I stood to leave, and as we made our way back to the cabin, I grabbed his arm and giggled, steadying myself on the steep path. "That was definitely more than I'm used to drinking."

He grinned. "Are you tipsy?"

"For the first time in my life!" I admitted. "Maybe just a little."

In September, George needed to take the ferry to Victoria for a work trip. We decided to make a fun weekend out of it. While George was caught up in lengthy meetings, David, Mark, and I wandered the city streets.

On our final day there, I left Mark and David at the hotel and drove to pick up George.

Traffic moved smoothly through the city, and I ended up arriving slightly early. A garage sale sign caught my eye, so I cruised down the advertised side street and found a spot to park.

A large carving immediately caught my attention from across the driveway. It looked like a lizard that was positioned up on a log. As I got closer, I saw that its eyes looked eerily lifelike.

"Do you like him?" A woman's voice startled me. "He comes with the tank, the special light, and some food."

"That thing is alive?" I took a step back, worried it might jump off the log at me.

The homeowner laughed. "It's a bearded dragon. They make very good pets and don't require much maintenance." She reached down and picked up the large lizard, placing it on her chest.

Much less work than a dog, I thought, and at just fifty dollars, I couldn't say no. "I'm sure my youngest son will love it."

With the lizard safely stowed, I drove a short distance down the road, around the corner, and into the parking lot where I waited for George.

He opened the van's rear hatch to put in his briefcase just as I said, "Surprise!"

"What is that?" He tucked his briefcase on the far side of the glass tank.

"A bearded dragon. An early present for Mark's thirteenth birthday."

He got into the passenger's seat and gave me a look. "Somehow, I'm not surprised."

Undaunted, I said, "I just found it at a garage sale. Don't you think he'll like it?"

His mouth curved into a genuine smile. "A twenty-inch lizard? He'll love it."

And love it he did. On the ferry ride back to the mainland, Mark and David took turns harbouring the lizard, now officially named Napoleon, in their jackets as they walked around the boat deck. They caught a few weird glances from strangers, but no one said anything. At home, Mark set up Napoleon's tank on the nightstand right next to his bed.

Days melded together until I finally had a free afternoon to visit Stan and Louisa. I talked Mark into bringing Napoleon over for a few minutes.

Louisa gasped when she opened the door. "Oh, my goodness!"

"This is Napoleon," Mark said, proudly gesturing to the lizard perched on his shoulder.

Stan got up and walked toward the door for closer inspection. "He looks rather striking if you ask me."

Seeing that he was harmless, Louisa reached over and gently patted Napoleon on the head. "He looks like such a scary creature, yet he's so tame. I've never seen anything like it."

Mark and Napoleon headed back home as Louisa shouted after him, "Thanks for bringing him over."

"He's a lot less work than a dog," I said with a laugh. "I just have to go to the pet store once in a while to buy live crickets for him to eat."

"Add it to your to-do list," Stan mumbled under his breath as he sank back into his new lift chair.

Louisa was clearly fascinated by the lizard. "Is that all he eats? Crickets?"

"Crickets and vegetables," I explained. "At least Mark is old enough to take care of everything himself."

As Louisa and I got comfortable on the couch, she added, "Your boys are growing up ever so quickly, aren't they?"

"I know. I can't believe Tim will be taking his driver's test next week."

She joked, "I'm quite certain teaching him to drive was easier for you than teaching me."

I added proudly, "I'm sure he'll pass the test on his first try—just like George Matthew and Lyell did."

Louisa jumped up and disappeared into the kitchen to make some tea. I looked at Stan, wondering how I could draw him out of his quiet demeanor and engage him in a conversation.

"I bought a new harp recently," I said. "It's a smaller one, called a shepherd's harp. My big harp is getting damaged every time I haul it to another wedding. This one is much easier to transport, especially since it came with a case."

Stan offered no response.

In a few minutes, Louisa was back. I sipped my tea too early, and the hot water burned my tongue. I winced and put the cup back down. Stan remained silent, so I tried starting another conversation.

"I've started a new dance class—Gypsy dancing—and I'm loving it. Same teacher, but the music is even more captivating, and the choreography is so much fun. There's something magical about twirling a big wide skirt." I made some arm motions that I had learned.

Louisa sounded wistful. "I wish I could still move like that."

I took another sip of my tea after blowing on it to cool it down. "I also started volunteering at Ten Thousand Villages, the fair-trade shop in the old part of downtown Langley."

Louisa nodded. "I remember you took me there once."

"Don't you ever stop?" Finally breaking his silence, Stan's words came out sternly with a hint of disappointment. "I think you're taking on too much. Besides, we miss you when you don't come around."

"It's only one day a week," I reasoned. I knew I might be spreading myself too thin, but there were so many meaningful causes I felt compelled to support.

"It's a great concept," I continued. "The organization pays a fair wage directly to artists in developing countries so they can feed their families, and the non-profit stores in North America are run by volunteers."

As I outlined the organization's mission, Stan appeared to be on the verge of dozing off in his chair, prompting Louisa to change the subject.

"My son Chris is coming next week. If you'd like to meet him, we're thinking of having lunch at the Lamplighter next Tuesday, on our anniversary."

"Sounds good. I already have the day marked on my calendar, so I know I'm free. I'll make a reservation for noon."

Stan let out a soft snore.

Chris was a pleasant man with a huge smile. Noticing his receding hairline and glasses, it struck me that Louisa seemed too young to have a son of his age. He conveyed a strong love for his mom and had an endearing accent. After our lunch together, I invited Stan, Louisa, and Chris to our house for dinner later in the week.

George and I greeted our guests at the door, taking their coats and ushering them into the kitchen. Chris handed George a bottle of Châteauneuf-du-Pape. I had never seen a bottle like it before. There was charm in its intentionally misshapen silhouette, an artistic touch inviting curiosity about what was inside.

George had recently started appreciating wines more, especially reds. He opened the bottle and poured the wine while I brought the food to the table.

"It's a real treat to enjoy a classic French wine," George acknowledged as he savoured his first sip. Knowing how expensive it was, he turned to Chris and said, "Thank you for bringing it."

"It's been a favourite of mine for many years," Chris said. "It's a wonderful blend from the Rhone region of France."

"It has a nice complexity." I could tell that George was testing out his wine lingo.

"Yes, a very elegant red with a bold character," Chris added.

As always, when Stan wasn't enjoying a conversation, he ended it. "It all tastes the same to me. I prefer sherry, myself."

Chapter Thirty

Being a particularly cold January, the snow drifts made navigation on a scooter impossible, so I picked them up and drove to the Lamplighter for our birthday lunch. Even inside, I felt chilled and didn't take off my coat.

"Happy New Year," our regular waitress, Debbie, greeted us. "Nice to see you again. Will it be the usual today?"

"Yes, please," Stan replied, taking off his jacket. We didn't even bother looking at the menu anymore. All three of us ordered the salmon every time.

Louisa added, "We'll have the usual pudding after the meal as well."

Debbie laughed good-naturedly. "Don't worry, I won't forget about your passionfruit mousse."

As Debbie left, Stan glared at me and asked, "Why are you still wearing your coat? My mother always said, 'If you come inside and don't take off your coat, you won't feel the benefit.'"

Louisa started snickering. "I remember people saying that back in the day! 'You won't feel the benefit,'" she mimicked with finger quotes.

At her dramatization, Stan, too, began to laugh. He saw that I looked confused.

"The benefit," he mocked again, regaining his composure. "You put your coat on before you go out in the cold. If you don't take it off when you're inside, and you're already wearing it when you go back out, you won't feel the full benefit of being warmed by your coat." He laughed harder. Louisa wiped a tear from her eye. Their laughter got me going too.

We celebrated our birthdays by raising our water glasses in a toast and reminiscing about past celebrations. Lunch was delicious, and as usual, Stan insisted on paying the bill.

Our ribs were sore from laughing by the time I pulled into their driveway. They invited me to come inside.

Louisa said, "This has been a perfect afternoon. Many happy returns of the day."

"It feels good not to have to rush home," I said. "With the older boys driving the younger ones to sport practices, I feel like I have a lot more freedom."

"It's about time," Stan remarked, a cheeky grin evident in his tone.

We spent another good hour chatting away. This was the happiest I had seen Stan in a long time.

I came home to the rich smell of chocolate cake. Tim had followed the recipe on the cake-mix box and was just pulling it out of the oven as I stepped into the kitchen. A surge of pride filled me as I watched the boys grow more independent with each passing day.

I'd been gradually getting them to manage their own laundry and teaching them some basic cooking skills. Over time, each of them developed their own specialties. George Matthew had a knack for making deluxe sandwiches and wraps, Tim had mastered sheet pan nachos, and David and Mark had become experts at making crepes, one of their favourite dishes.

The boys decorated my birthday cake while George and I were out for dinner. Even Lyell was home to enjoy the dessert with us.

The room was filled with easy conversation, the clink of forks on plates, and warm laughter. It was one of those rare moments where everything felt perfectly right, just a simple evening made special by the family gathered around the table, enjoying cake and each other's company.

Four days later, an ambulance arrived to take Stan to the hospital. As soon as Louisa called, I hopped in the van to drive her to emergency, and she explained on the way.

"Stan started having more and more trouble breathing, and with his feet so swollen, I didn't know what to do."

After some initial tests, we found out that Stan had fluid in his lungs. The following weeks passed by in a hazy whirlwind. When Stan was finally discharged, I went to the Red Cross to pick up a wheelchair as well as the proper rails and bathroom aids that were recommended to enhance Stan's comfort at home.

Two days later, he was back in the hospital with fluid in his lungs again. It went on like this for several weeks, each stay in the hospital getting longer and longer with less and less time at home in between. Eventually, the doctor delivered the sombre news that Stan's organs were slowly shutting down. There was little hope he would be returning home this time.

Louisa and I hugged in the dim hospital hallway. Stan slept in his room just a few feet away, his heart monitor singing its steady song.

We fell into a rhythm. Louisa was too upset to drive, so I dropped her off at the hospital every morning, then visited Stan every evening when I picked her up. Sometimes she stayed by his side all night.

"I want to be here when he dies," she said, running her hand along her husband's arm. He didn't stir. "I have a feeling it won't be long now." His complexion paled by the day, and she was starting to look haggard herself from lack of sleep.

One day Louisa had her own doctor's appointment, and I assured her that I would stay with Stan and keep him company. He slept on and off. When he was awake, I filled him in on what was happening at home, and sometimes I hummed to him when he dozed off. He looked small and shrivelled in the sterile bed.

"Would you like some water?" I asked, when he woke up again. I picked up the paper cup and held the straw to his parched lips. When he was done sipping, he spoke softly.

"There's something I've been wanting to say to you." His voice was hoarse but determined, and he stared at me with watery eyes. "I love you."

I squeezed his hand. "I love you too."

"No, you don't understand." He struggled with each breath, "I have loved you more," he persisted, "more than I have ever loved anyone in my entire life."

Tears slid from the corners of his eyes. I reached for the box of tissues, gently dabbing at his tears while my own welled up and began to spill over.

Stan closed his eyes with a heavy sigh, as if speaking it aloud had brought him relief. There was nothing I could think of to say, so I took one of his fragile hands in both of mine. I felt a soft, reassuring squeeze from him as I held on tenderly.

We stayed like that for a few quiet moments. Then he drifted off into a peaceful slumber. I looked at the time. I needed to get home. I kissed his forehead and whispered, "Get some rest, Stan. I'll be back tomorrow." I glanced over once more as I slipped out the door.

After dinner, George suggested, "Let's go to a movie. I had a stressful day at work, and you could probably use a break too, with everything going on."

"Sure, Louisa told me she would be staying at the hospital tonight anyway."

Entering the theatre, we chose a mindless comedy and made our way to seats near the middle. The big screen loomed before us with thunderous sound and vibrant visuals, but it didn't feel right being there. Laughter felt out of place after the quiet mood of Stan's hospital room. Then George's cell phone buzzed. It was Louisa's number.

We hurried out to the lobby, and I called her right back. George put his arm around me as Louisa recited the time of death. She mentioned that she was taking a taxi home, and I assured her I would meet her at her house after I stopped in at the hospital. I dropped George off at home and went to the hospital alone.

It was after hours, and the hallway lights had been dimmed. Even the beeping machines seemed quieter as I padded down to Stan's wing. I paused at the door, surprised to see Stan lying back against the pillows as if time had frozen.

I had never seen a corpse before, only bodies in coffins already perfected by the mortician. Someone had tucked the blanket under his arms as if to make him more comfortable, but his too-white skin and gaping mouth didn't look natural at all. I couldn't believe I had just spoken to him earlier that same day. His body looked like a fragile shell without the life that once filled it.

I reached for his hand and was struck by how cold it felt—so different from the warmth it held that afternoon. Then I remembered his last words to me. What had he meant, he loved me more than he had ever loved anyone in his entire life? More than his own mother? More than his wife of almost sixty years? More than Louisa?

I took a tissue from my pocket, wiping my eyes as I brushed off the weight of his words, knowing I would never fully comprehend what he meant.

A presence in the doorway drew my attention.

"Are you family?" the nurse inquired.

"I'm a neighbour," I managed to say, my voice thin and faint, "and a close friend."

"My condolences," she dug around in her pocket, "Could you give this to his wife? She left before I removed it earlier, and I think she'd want to keep it." She held out the handmade wooden cross Stan wore—had worn—around his neck. I took it from her gingerly.

"Yes, I can do that," I said, and carefully tucked it into my pocket. "I'm heading over there right now."

As soon as I got into the car, I let my tears flow freely, thinking I could cry and let it all out before seeing Louisa. But upon entering their house and sensing the profound silence, my emotions surged again. I held out Stan's necklace.

Every crease and wrinkle on Louisa's face seemed to carry the weight of her memories of Stan. We both hugged and cried, finding comfort in our shared sorrow.

"Thanks for bringing Stan's necklace," Louisa managed in between dabs of her nose. "He never took it off, you know, not even in the shower."

We sat on the couch with a box of tissues between us, reminiscing about Stan until well after midnight. When both of our tears had finally slowed, I got up to leave.

"Will you help me plan a memorial service?" she asked as I reached for my coat.

"I thought Stan didn't want a funeral."

"I know," she sighed, "but it would mean a lot to me if we had one."

"Of course. We can talk more about it tomorrow."

Louisa went into the kitchen and returned with a Caramilk bar. As she handed it to me, we both started crying again.

Chapter Thirty-One

A week later, it was April first, but neither I nor Louisa were in the mood for an April Fool's joke. We drove to the airport to pick up Chris, who had come from England to support his mom. Two days later, we held a short memorial service for Stan at the church. The same pastor who had married Stan and Louisa nearly seven years ago was now offering words of comfort.

As the last few notes of the congregational hymn faded away, I walked to the front of the church and pulled out the eulogy I had spent the day before writing. I remained composed throughout the reading until the very end.

"Now Rachel will play Stan's favourite song..." I swallowed hard, fighting back tears, and my voice quivered as I finished, "Chopin's *Nocturne Opus 9 Number 2*."

I made my way back to my seat as the piano started to play, and I wiped my eyes throughout the entire piece. It dawned on me that this song somehow represented the best part of who Stan was. Music had consistently been one of the special bonds in our friendship, and this piece would now live on as a beautiful reminder of him.

In the following days, after Chris returned to England, I offered to pick up Stan's ashes and death certificate from the funeral home.

The half-hour drive back to Fort Langley felt unusually long. I thought about the time Stan received Vera's ashes. How strange it was now to have Stan's ashes resting in a bag on the passenger seat as I drove. Every so often, I glanced over at them, feeling grateful for the friendship we had shared. He was a unique person, so different from anyone else I knew. When Louisa had told me that Stan left his grand piano to me in his will, I was touched. It was his most prized possession.

"Thank you," I whispered out loud, looking at the bag on the passenger seat. Despite all his moods and quirks, I had come to love him for who he was.

I turned down our street, and just like scenes from a movie, memories of Stan and me laughing together replayed in my mind: that Christmas with Tickle Me Elmo, swing dancing on the old green shag carpet in his living room, all the cups of hot and strong and sweet and milky tea, our lunches at the Lamplighter, and the horde of Caramilk chocolate bars... I would miss his sheepish grin and dry sense of humour. I would even miss him using the light over Silvia to let me know when he wanted to spend more time with me. As I pulled into his driveway, I spoke again. "Rest in peace, Stan."

Louisa was at the window as I walked toward the front door carrying Stan's ashes. I gently placed the bag on the small table in the entryway, the table where I used to find my chocolate bars.

"How are you doing?"

Louisa's face was full of strength and sorrow as she mustered an answer. "As well as can be expected, I suppose."

She accepted the envelope containing the death certificate and said, "The service was wonderful and really helped me feel a sense of closure."

"It helped me too." Seeing the same friends who celebrated their wedding come together again for the funeral had filled me with comfort and gratitude.

I noticed her staring at the bag on the table.

"How do you want to do this?" I asked.

"I'm going to put Stan's ashes under that tree in the backyard," she said. She searched my face for a moment before continuing. "I really feel like I need to do this alone."

"Of course. You know where to find me if you change your mind."

I walked away, understanding that this was her way of honouring Stan in the way that he had honoured his own family, and I was at peace with her decision. It's what Stan had wanted.

Chapter Thirty-Two

In August, after the steady stream of family and friends visiting Louisa from England had finally eased, I invited her to come to the lake with me for a day. She was delighted by the idea, her only request being that Joey come along too.

The boat ride from the marina was about twenty minutes up the east side of Harrison Lake. Joey looked a bit nervous, but Louisa appeared to enjoy the stunning views and held him close on her lap. As we approached our dock, the boat's wake rippled across the water, breaking softly against the rocky shore.

After securing the boat, Louisa followed me up the dirt path to the sundeck and gently set Joey down. Joey gave his entire body a vigorous shake, his floppy ears whipping from side to side as if to shed the lingering traces of fear and stress from the boat ride up.

I showed Louisa the inside of the A-frame, then unpacked the small cooler of food I'd brought, making conversation as we went.

"Last weekend, while our family sat around the campfire, we were trying to think of a good name for the cabin."

Louisa didn't hesitate. "As soon as I walked in, I could smell the cedar. I think it should be called Cedar Cottage."

"I like that."

We shared our picnic lunch at the wooden table on the deck, basking in the warm sunlight and the easy comfort of each other's company. Afterward, I brought out the Scrabble board, and we began a game. Joey dozed peacefully at Louisa's feet as we played, his small body rising and falling with each breath.

I carefully placed my Scrabble tiles on the board, then jotted down my score. When I looked up, Louisa's gaze was fixed on the far end of the lake, her expression thoughtful and serene.

"I certainly understand why you love it here!" she said, turning to meet my eyes. "I feel a bit apprehensive about leaving British Columbia, there's so much natural beauty here. And back in England, people don't seem quite as easygoing."

"Why don't you stay?" I offered.

"My family is insisting that I return," she explained. "All of them are trying to talk me into moving home, but this has come to feel like home to me as well."

"I can understand your dilemma. You don't have to decide right away. Take your time. When you're ready, it will all make more sense."

"Yes, I suppose you're right."

Strong winds started blowing up just when it was time for us to head back home. Midway down the lake, a freak storm unfolded, surprising us with its intensity. Rain pelted the canvas top as I kept the boat steady through the choppy waters. Four-foot swells lifted the boat high before plunging it downward with gut-wrenching jolts.

I remained cool and confident on the outside, but inside I was getting a bit worried about being able to dock the boat alone in these windy conditions.

I glanced at the panic-stricken eighty-six-year-old clutching her little dachshund with one hand and gripping the handle beside her seat with the other, hanging on for dear life. I knew we would be fine, and eventually we might even laugh about the wild ride, but at that moment my only concern was getting us safely to the dock.

As I approached the slip, the wind kept catching the bow and spinning it out of alignment. Finally, after a few attempts, I managed to pull in far enough to jump out and lunge for the dock lines, my heart pounding, trying to secure the boat before another gust would pull it away. The dock was slick, and the rain stung my face.

Louisa and Joey waited patiently inside the boat as I secured the ropes. Gradually, the downpour eased. I was drenched but relieved they had stayed dry. I took off my wet jacket and held Louisa's arm to steady her as we walked up the ramp and back to the van. Joey was still visibly shaking.

We were both quiet as I started driving, and then, in her calm British accent, Louisa exclaimed, "My goodness, that was quite an adventure!"

On a crisp October day that would have marked Stan and Louisa's seventh anniversary, I took Louisa to the Lamplighter for lunch. Outside, the leaves swirled in bursts of amber and gold, but inside we sat comfortably at one of our favourite tables, tucked in the corner by the window. We both ordered the salmon with jasmine rice and seasonal vegetables. Louisa glanced around, perhaps recalling the many times the three of us had sat at this very table.

Then she sighed. "I've decided to move back to England after all."

"When?" I asked, my heart sinking just a bit as the waitress brought two glasses of water to the table.

"Soon," she said. "It wasn't an easy decision, but my children told me I must be realistic about my age. I have mixed feelings about it, but I do think it's for the best." She took a few sips of water. "There are so many things I need to do before I leave."

"How can I help?"

"I can't imagine having to part with Joey. And selling the house will be difficult too. Do you know anyone who would want to buy it? I would rather not go through an estate agent."

"Actually, I was just talking to a couple from church last week. They're retired and would love to move to Fort Langley."

"If they're interested, I would like to meet them. It would be simpler to sell it directly." She seemed slightly relieved at the idea.

"I'll call them when I get home."

"Thank you," she said just as the waitress set our plates down in front of us. Louisa picked up her fork. "Coming to the Lamplighter has been a wonderful tradition, hasn't it?"

"It really has. We've had some great times here."

We ate our meals with few words. Louisa's gaze often wandered to the window, her eyes distant, as if lost in memories—or perhaps in the weight of the decisions that lay ahead.

She suddenly perked up, her eyes brightening with her usual cheer. "We must have our pudding one last time," she declared, a smile tugging at her lips.

"Yes, definitely."

"It's my favourite." She looked into my eyes and said, with tenderness, "I can honestly say, these past seven years have been the best years of my whole life."

"Really?"

"I didn't have much luck with husbands, as you know. I loved Stan dearly and miss him an awful lot."

I raised my water glass. Louisa smiled and lifted hers, and we brought them together in a celebratory clink. "Here's to Stan."

I arranged for Walter and Jean to view Louisa's house, and she found them to be a lovely couple. The timing was going to work out perfectly, and after a brief discussion, they quickly reached an agreement on the price.

Every day, without fail, I went next door to assist Louisa. Everything she wasn't taking to England had to be sorted and packed. I made several trips to the Salvation Army with boxes and helped her ship two large suitcases overseas. Yet, the amount of stuff they had accumulated over the years made the job seem endless.

A couple of weeks later, the piano movers arrived. They joked that this was one of the shortest moves they'd ever had to do. After Stan's baby grand had been carefully placed into our living room, I hung the portrait of Silvia on the wall beside it. Then, taking my place on the oak bench, I let the notes of Chopin flow in Stan's honour.

Once the last note faded away, my curiosity was piqued, so I lifted the wooden lid of the piano bench and discovered some very old music books and antique sheet music. On top of the stack was the small red book he had shown me years ago. Flipping to the index, I searched for the song "Who is Silvia" and found the page. There at the top, in Stan's familiar scrawl, were the words, "I know who she is."

My heart skipped a beat. It felt as if Stan had sent me a secret message. The flood of emotions caught me off guard. Memories I thought I'd tucked away resurfaced, and the loss felt as sharp as it had the night he passed away. Yet, amid the sadness, there was also comfort, a sense that part of him still lingered.

The next day, Louisa's house felt hollow, the once lively rooms now scattered with half-packed boxes and bare shelves. Every echo seemed to carry the weight of memories and the deepening ache of her impending departure.

Eventually, Louisa spoke up. "Of all the decisions I've had to make, the most difficult task by far has been finding a new home for Joey."

"Do you think the couple you've been meeting with are a good fit?" I asked.

"I think so. They picked him up last night, and then shortly after, they called asking if they could keep him the whole weekend for a trial run."

"That's great news."

In my mind, this was another check on the checklist, but the shimmer in Louisa's eyes told me exactly how much she was struggling to make the decision. I put my arm around her, and hoping to help her take her mind off things, I suggested, "Let's finish packing up the last pots and pans. I can take another load away today."

By the end of the afternoon, however, it was clear that packing had not helped to ease Louisa's distress. Every time I looked at her, she appeared to be on the verge of tears.

Then, in the middle of wrapping a vase in newspaper, she broke down. "I'm sorry, I don't have any energy left," she confessed. "I can't stop thinking about my dear little boy. The house feels even more lonely without him. I hardly slept last night. But I suppose I must get used to it."

She pressed a hand to her mouth trying to stifle the flood of emotion. I grabbed the tissue box from the counter and handed it to her. She took a deep breath, blew her nose, and slowly began to regain her composure.

"I've been thinking about this all day, and I decided I'm going to call the people and tell them they can keep Joey. I can't bear the thought of seeing him, and then having to part with him all over again." Her tears were flowing freely now. "It will be better for both of us," she sobbed. "Sorry I'm being so emotional."

I sat down beside her. "You've experienced a lot of loss in a short time—Stan, and now moving away and parting with Joey—it's understandable. No need to apologize."

On Louisa's last night, I hosted a farewell dinner for her. A few of the neighbours were invited, along with Louisa's son Peter who had come to escort his mom back to England. The evening was filled with stories and reminiscing. For dessert, I served a chocolate cake that I had decorated just for this occasion. It had a little toy plane flying from one side of the cake, adorned with a Canadian flag, to the other side of the cake, which sported a British flag. In the middle, I'd written "We'll miss you, Louisa."

My alarm went off earlier than usual, and I got ready quickly in the dark house. I started the van and cranked up the heat before pulling into the driveway next door. Louisa and Peter emerged from the house, suitcases in tow. I opened the back hatch and helped pile the bags in as the cold November air revealed every one of our exhaled breaths.

We made mindless chatter on the drive to Vancouver International—as if it were any other day, as if we could delay the inevitable by not acknowledging it.

In the parking garage, Peter unloaded the luggage, and we each grabbed a piece before walking toward the terminal. We saw a mix of weary travellers and excited young families, all bubbling with the anticipation of their departures.

I was genuinely happy for Louisa, but I knew I would miss her. She had come into my life under such unique circumstances, and over time she felt like family. As we kept on walking, I could feel my eyes beginning to water. As soon as Louisa saw me, she started crying and threw her arms around my waist.

"Promise you'll come for a visit."

I hugged her back. "I would love to." I meant it sincerely, but I knew there would be a few obstacles to making it a reality.

Once the bags were checked, we approached security. This was it. This was as far as I could go. Louisa and I hugged for a long time, tears streaming down both our faces. Seven years. It had gone by so quickly, but we'd forged such a deep bond during that time.

Louisa started thanking me for everything, which only made me cry harder. Finally, we pulled apart. Peter uttered one last farewell, and then they showed their boarding passes to the official. As she walked through the door, Louisa looked back one more time, and I offered one last wave goodbye.

Chapter Thirty-Three

January was the quietest month in Fort Langley. The holiday tourists had left, and the sharp chill in the air kept most people indoors. After a month of travelling with my family, it felt good to be home.

Janice waved as I walked toward her. We hugged as if we hadn't seen each other in years, and she immediately asked, "How was the trip?"

"It was fantastic. This is the first time our family has ever been away for Christmas, and I have to say, I loved it. We stayed in a beautiful three-bedroom suite in Portugal for only $299 for the entire week."

"One of your timeshare deals?"

"Yes," I laughed. "I love taking advantage of the off-season rates."

"So how did you spend Christmas?"

"We walked along the beach collecting shells to use as ornaments on a small fake tree I found at a bargain store. It was so simple, with no stress and no gifts. The trip was the gift. It's too bad Lyell couldn't join us. He just moved into an apartment with a friend and was busy with his plumbing apprenticeship."

"That's too bad, but I'm glad the rest of you had a good time. What were some of the highlights besides Christmas?"

"Morocco was the biggest highlight for me. Marrakesh was amazing—so full of life. The markets were bursting with colour, especially the spice stalls. I've never seen so many spices, stacked like mini volcanoes—the smell was intoxicating."

Janice and I crossed the street as I continued. "Waking up to the call to prayer echoing from the minarets took a while to get used to—it happened five times a day. But after a while, I found it quite beautiful. Wandering through the historic medinas, the colourful textiles, and sipping Moroccan mint tea on the rooftop every night—I loved it all."

"What were the people like?"

"They were very friendly and welcoming. We met one man, Muhammed, in Fes, who led us through the maze of ancient narrow streets, sharing history and interesting stories. He told us that it was customary for them to say a sincere goodbye to their family before going to bed every night. Then in the morning, they wake up full of gratitude, surprised to be alive and grateful to have another day."

"Really? It makes you realize how much we take our daily lives for granted."

"For sure. There were so many things I experienced there that made me think differently, and I learned so much about the history and culture. It was fascinating!"

Janice tapped the crosswalk button at the intersection. As we waited for the light to change, I took the opportunity to thank her for the journal she had given me before I'd left.

"I love that quote by Miriam Beard you wrote on the first page of my journal: 'Travel is more than the seeing of sights. It is a change that goes on, deep and permanent, in the ideas of living.'"

"Yeah, that pretty much sums it up, doesn't it?"

I nodded. We walked a bit further and stopped at the post office to pick up our mail. Janice held the door for me. "Sounds like this trip really had an impact on you."

"It definitely did." I opened my post office box to find a letter addressed to me in handwriting that I recognized immediately—Louisa. I carefully slid my finger under the seal, peeling it open with excitement.

Inside was a Christmas card accompanied by a small note with a few handwritten lines. "All is well. I am settled in my new flat in Haverhill, Suffolk. I would like you to come for a visit in May. Love, Louisa."

On the walk home, Janice laughed as I tried to figure out how I'd sell George on the idea of a solo trip to England.

"I'm pretty sure I could find another timeshare deal, and I think we've got enough Air Miles to cover the flight. And it's not until May—there's still time. It's not like I'm leaving right away."

"Why is it such a big deal if you go?" Janice asked.

"Because George and I haven't spent much time apart—except when he's away on business. And he doesn't even know how to make a box of macaroni and cheese."

"Sounds like that's exactly why you *should* go!" she laughed. "I think he's too dependent on you."

"Maybe." I nodded. "But it's partly my fault. I've been catering to him throughout our marriage, and now he expects it will just continue. He's kind of stuck in his ways, and not very willing to change."

"He goes away a lot too, doesn't he?"

"At least half a dozen times a year, all work related of course. He works at least fifty to sixty hours every week. On top of that, he regularly goes to conferences and often has late meetings."

"You've really been raising the boys on your own!"

I nodded. "That's what it feels like. From fall until spring, it's especially challenging."

"So how do you cope?" she asked.

"When things get really bad, I just reframe the situation to keep it more lighthearted."

"How do you do that?"

"I haven't shared this with anyone," I chuckled, "but if we go out on a date, I pretend I'm a single mom having an affair with an architect."

Janice laughed. "That's brilliant."

Chapter Thirty-Four

On Saturday morning, after breakfast, the boys dropped their dirty dishes into the dishwasher and scattered—just as George called, "Outdoor chores start in an hour!" I couldn't help but smile as their groans echoed down the hallway.

While I cleaned the kitchen counter, George remained at the table, sipping his coffee and flipping through the newspaper. Watching him there, relaxed, I figured this might be the perfect moment to bring up my idea.

"I got a card from Louisa," I began, my tone careful. "She invited me to come visit her in May."

George looked up, surprised. "To England?"

"Yeah, she's all settled in now, and I would love to see where she's living."

"What about everything going on here?" His brow furrowed.

"The boys are already so responsible. You really wouldn't have to do much."

He leaned back in his chair. "How long would you be gone?"

"Maybe a week or ten days?" My voice filled with excitement and determination. "I'll make dinners ahead of time, freeze them, and leave a full schedule so everything is organized. I'm sure it will be totally manageable."

"I don't know," he said. "You've never been away that long before."

I waited, putting more dishes into the dishwasher. Out of the corner of my eye, I could tell he was staring at me, studying my face.

"If it's that important to you, I guess we can make it work."

I walked over to him and settled into his lap, wrapping my arms around him. "Thank you," I said softly, giving him a tender kiss. "This *is* really important to me."

For the next few nights, I stayed up after everyone had gone to bed, caught up in the excitement of planning the trip. The thrill of finding good deals kept me going. Once everything was booked, I wrote Louisa a letter with all the details. The months that followed passed in a flurry of activity, but my anticipation never dimmed.

As the plane soared homeward from England, I gazed out the window, lost in thought. The gentle hum of the aircraft became the backdrop to the cherished moments replaying in my memory.

I reminisced about my first night in Louisa's Haverhill flat. We had watched the movie *Casablanca* while eating Thorntons Fabulous Fudge. When the song "As Time Goes By" came on, I had warmly recalled the first time Stan played it for me on his piano. The next day, Louisa's son Chris showed us the majestic architecture of Cambridge. He wove in tales of his time spent working at the university, including a behind-the-scenes glimpse of professors whose servants spent decades polishing centuries-old silverware.

Another day, I met most of Louisa's children and grandchildren at the Red Lion pub, a typical red-brick building that looked exactly like Stan and Louisa had described it. After the meal, they'd all said, "You can't come to England and not try spotted dick!" It didn't sound very appetizing, but they laughed when I breathed a sigh of relief upon seeing that it was just pudding with raisins in it.

I had managed to find an incredible deal on a timeshare in Chelsea that was spacious enough for both of us. It was Louisa's favourite area in London, and I booked the whole week for only two hundred dollars. Louisa proudly became my tour guide as we went to Trafalgar Square, Buckingham Palace, Big Ben, and Westminster Abbey, but my favourite part was just being in London with Louisa, seeing everything through her eyes.

She had grown up in Chelsea. We walked the streets of her old neighbourhood and found her childhood home. Pointing to a window in the basement, she said, "That's where the coal man would deliver coal every week, dumping it into the chute outside. I remember the tremendous racket it made as it landed in the bin below. Did you know that was the only means of heating our house and water in those days?"

As we walked down King's Road, lined with shops and boutiques, I imagined what life might have been like for Stan and Louisa in their younger years.

The flight attendant interrupted my thoughts with her warm smile. "Would you like chicken or pasta?"

"I'll have the pasta, thank you." Somehow I didn't trust meat served on airplanes.

She set the tray down, unveiling a neatly arranged meal with a side of salad and a small dessert. It struck me then how effortless it was, travelling by myself with nobody else to look after. There wasn't even a passenger in the seat beside me on this flight, allowing me even more space and freedom. I knew that solo travel wouldn't always be my preference, but in this current phase of life, it felt like a real treat. When the flight attendant came around offering beverages, I opted for tea.

It reminded me of the day Louisa and I went to the Ritz for tea. "It has always been a dream of mine," she claimed. We were both full of anticipation, sitting in the large, elegant room where the chandeliers glittered, and live musicians played classical music. The ambience was of timeless sophistication. But upon viewing the menu, we quickly reconsidered our indulgence. I calculated the exchange rate between British pounds and Canadian dollars, and it worked out to about a hundred Canadian dollars per person.

Louisa looked at me and said, "That's outrageous! I can't do it." Neither could I, so we got up and walked out, laughing like teenagers as we made our way along the sidewalk. "Oh well," Louisa had said. "At least I got to sit in the Ritz."

I couldn't fall asleep on the flight, so I watched a movie. When it ended, I thought back to the night Louisa and I went to the theatre where she had worked over fifty years earlier. She became nostalgic as we had entered, shocked that it still looked the same. She told me about her job as a cashier and usherette. I could easily picture a younger version of her in my mind.

The flight attendant came by again to collect the trash. With less than an hour until landing, my mind drifted back once again to the experiences I'd had in London. I couldn't wait to tell George and the boys about my unexpected joyride.

Louisa's son, Peter, had invited us along to his friend's opulent home in the most expensive area of London. The grand architecture of the mansion, with a swimming pool on the lowest floor, felt more like a museum than a home. Peter had pointed out the window at a fancy black sports car as he chatted with his friend. I asked if I could take a picture of it to show my sons. Without hesitation, Peter's friend declared, "Better yet, I'll take you for a ride!"

It was a ride I would never forget. The engine revved, accelerating from zero to a hundred in seconds. I had laughed out loud, caught off guard by the exhilarating thrill of being thrust back into my seat by the G-force, flying down the road at breathtaking speed.

That night, I had written in my journal: "Unbelievable! Who would have ever thought that someday a simple Mennonite farm girl would be having tea in a twenty-million-dollar home in London and getting a ride in a Maserati? What a crazy life!"

The plane touched down, marking the end of my solo journey, but I noticed a new kind of anticipation beginning within me—I had truly missed my family. Walking through the airport's security doors and seeing George holding a bouquet of flowers instantly brought tears to my eyes.

When we arrived home, all the boys were waiting to greet me, and my heart swelled with joy. I was deeply grateful for the adventure and the chance to explore a different part of the world. Yet coming home gave me an even deeper appreciation for my life— and the profound sense of belonging I felt here.

Chapter Thirty-Five

B y the end of May, the air had warmed enough to launch the boat again, but this year was different. We had just sold our old boat, which had served us well but was starting to feel too small, too slow, and too outdated for our growing family. In its place, we upgraded to a sleek twenty-one-foot Four Winns complete with a wakeboard tower. Thanks to a cousin of mine, we were able to get it at a wholesale price. The boys could hardly contain their excitement as we prepared for our first outing on the water.

As we cruised up the lake, the journey felt familiar but refreshingly new, the comfort and amenities of our new boat enhancing the experience.

We trod up the dampened moss and breathed in the cedar-soaked atmosphere of the cabin. The boys got to work cleaning up the small birch and alder trees that had fallen during the winter storms.

While I swept pine cones and cedar needles off the deck, I stopped to watch my family. George Matthew and Lyell carried themselves with the steady confidence of young men, a new maturity shaping their faces. Tim had somehow outgrown them both, his eighteen-year-old frame tall and lanky, full of boundless energy. George's chainsaw buzzed as he trimmed branches and cut logs into manageable pieces. Tim, Lyell, and David carried the heavy chunks up to the woodshed to be chopped and stacked. George Matthew and Mark dragged branches into a big pile to be burned.

A quiet sense of pride welled up inside me as I observed them. There were no chore lists on the fridge, no reminders or prodding. The boys had simply fallen into a rhythm, taking ownership of the tasks at hand, working seamlessly together alongside their father. In that moment, I realized just how far we'd come. This was what I had envisioned for our family life. This place had slowed us down and become a catalyst for our family, giving us time and space to reconnect and grow in ways I could never have anticipated.

From one weekend to the next, other cabin owners began to appear, and soon the lake hummed with activity as we all prepared for summer's arrival. A cacophony of chainsaws and generators roared during the day, replaced later by a gentle murmur of late-night fireside conversations that carried across the still bay.

The boys had fun doing their own thing in the evenings, often playing board games with other kids from the surrounding cabins. Once again, George and I found ourselves down at Dieter's fire, glasses of wine in hand. Words flowed easily between us, with topics ranging from travelling to cabin maintenance.

During moments of silence, we took in the crackle of the fire. Dieter pushed another log in, and it roared bright, illuminating our faces in the darkness. Helga used the extra light to top off our wine glasses.

George took a long sip, then spoke to Dieter and Helga. "The business has exceeded our expectations this year. We could pay down some of the debt we owe you."

He hadn't even finished the sentence before Dieter started shaking his head. "We don't want it right now."

I was surprised. "Are you sure? I would feel better if we could pay you."

"Keep it. You'll need it for projects." He gestured around, his hand moving in a directionless circle. "There's always something."

He was right of course. I smiled at George. "You might get your wish after all."

Dieter looked from me to George questioningly.

George explained. "I was thinking of replacing the old dock with a bigger one, especially now that we have a bigger boat."

Dieter's slow nod clearly conveyed his agreement. "It needs to be done. I built that one almost forty years ago, and it has warped over time."

My words felt inadequate, but I said them anyway. "We can't thank you enough for your ongoing generosity."

To prepare for the new dock, we needed to build a larger landing deck. It would support the new aluminum ramp we'd ordered, which would connect the landing to the dock.

Richard and Janice had already been planning to join us at the cabin for the annual Canada Day fireworks, so upon hearing about our new dock plans, Richard readily offered a helping hand.

On the Canada Day long weekend, under the golden afternoon sun, Richard and George worked steadily, mixing and pouring concrete. Meanwhile, the rest of us relaxed on Dieter's patio, perched on a rocky outcropping at the water's edge just in front of his cabin.

We sipped sangria, chatting and occasionally calling out words of encouragement as we watched the hardworking men. The kids were swimming and playing on the floating air mattress securely tied to the dock. David and Mark took turns jumping onto it, sending ripples across the water, while Richard and Janice's girls shrieked and tried to keep their balance.

John and Donna, who often joined us around the campfire in the evenings, owned the cabin next to Dieter and Helga's. It was quite common for neighbours to drop by during happy hour, usually bringing their own drinks—except in my case, since Dieter always made me a sangria.

Drawn by the sound of the laughter that afternoon, John and Donna wandered over to join the fun. Soon, Joan and Bruce came over from across the bay. By the time they moored their aluminum boat at the dock, Dieter was ready for them with two more glasses of sangria in hand.

As Joan greeted us, she asked, "What is he wearing?" pointing down at the working men. "It's July!"

We all pivoted and took in Richard's green and red Christmas T-shirt, hilariously mismatched against the backdrop around him. He noticed us all staring and waved. We burst out laughing.

Janice piped up, defending her husband through her giggles. "He never pays attention to what he throws on in the morning... or packs for that matter. Plus, he doesn't care what anyone thinks of his clothes."

"Cheers to that," Bruce said, raising his glass.

I clinked my glass to Janice's, and we all enjoyed the tart sweetness of our refreshing sangrias. The sun slid easily through the sky, drawing out the day.

When the men were done, they joined us on the patio. Richard introduced himself to everyone, and Helga ribbed him again about the snowman on his festive T-shirt.

Just then, Joan perked up. "Wait, I have a crazy idea."

We all turned our attention to her. "What if we have a Christmas in July party? We could invite the whole bay!"

Donna and Helga lit up with enthusiasm, diving eagerly into party-planning mode as we tossed around ideas. The energy lingered until things naturally wound down and everyone slowly drifted back to their cabins for dinner.

After eating, we piled into the boat and headed to the town of Harrison to watch the fireworks. We anchored among the array of boats that dotted the water. As dusk settled, a procession of boats adorned with lights and Canadian flags passed by in single file, adding to the Canada Day festivities.

With each burst of brilliant light, oohs and aahs spread across the lake from the surrounding boats to the enormous crowd that lined the beach. The kids munched on popcorn as they watched. The colours reflected off the water, creating a stunning visual display as the crowd cheered anew with every bang from above. Exhausted after the day's activities, everyone went straight to bed upon returning to the cabin.

By the end of the month, the Christmas in July party had come to fruition. About sixty-five people boated over to our side of the bay. For many, it was the first time they were meeting some of their neighbours in person, finally putting faces to names they had heard over the years.

We gathered on the gently sloping patch of grass between Dieter and Helga's cabin and John and Donna's. Joan had gone all out with the Christmas decorations—wreaths, twinkling lights and an array of decorative Santas—creating a festive holiday spectacle on the hottest day of that summer.

Everyone who came brought something for the potluck table. Donna contributed her signature chicken wings, a staple at every gathering. My contribution was a double batch of the boys' favourite sugar cookies, shaped like Christmas trees. Helga had hung a colourful, star-shaped piñata from one of the trees and organized a bunch of games, complete with Christmas-themed prizes.

After lunch, I handed out song sheets for a singalong while Dieter ran an extension cord from his generator to my keyboard. Just for fun, I had changed the words of nine familiar Christmas songs to reflect the current season. I started playing an introduction before everyone chimed in enthusiastically.

Bring your chairs to John and Donna's, fa-la-la-la-la, la-la-la-la.
Christmas time is now upon us, fa-la-la-la-la, la-la-la-la.
Don we now our shorts and swimwear, fa-la-la, la-la-la, la-la-la.
Basking in the summer's warm air, fa-la-la-la-la, la-la-la-la.

Some voices cracked, some wobbled out of tune. Occasionally someone started laughing, but the rest held the song. People were wiping sweat from their brows by the time we got to the last song.

I'm dreaming of a hot Christmas,
Just like the one we're having now.
Where the lake is glist'nin'
And children listen
To waves, splashing on the bow.
I'm dreaming of a hot Christmas,
With every water toy I bought.
May your days be spent on a yacht,
And may all your Christmases be hot.

The whole afternoon was filled with laughter, games, and delightful conversation. By the time everyone said goodbye, we all felt a little closer. No longer were we merely cabin owners, but we were a community: a group of people sharing a fun time together in this unique place we all loved.

As the party tapered off and people began to head out, I watched the older couple, Ed and Mary, from the green cabin across the bay. They climbed into their small aluminum boat, and to my amazement, Mary, at the age of eighty, skilfully tilted the engine into the water. She squeezed the primer bulb, yanked on the starter rope several times, then advanced the throttle, and motored off across the bay.

I turned to Helga beside me. "I hope I'll be able to do that when I'm her age."

She laughed. "Me too."

Chapter Thirty-Six

The cabin had become a cherished retreat for our family, though Lyell and George Matthew were now at an age where their free weekends had become increasingly rare.

Tim, David, and Mark joined us for George's annual summer vacation. We hiked through the forest, kayaked, chopped wood, and spent many evenings playing games. Enjoying Dieter and Helga's company was also a highlight that never lost its charm.

George and the boys were out cliff jumping—always an adrenaline-packed experience, but not necessarily one I wanted to partake in. I was happily sitting on Dieter and Helga's deck at four o'clock, sipping sangria.

"Did you know that this lake used to be full of sturgeon?" Helga's eyes sparkled. "I mean, hundreds of them."

Dieter added, "You could look at the water and easily see them swimming. They were huge."

"Once we went snorkelling in the other bay," Helga said, "and it was such an eerie feeling, swimming with giant fish beside you."

"I've only seen pictures," I said. "They look like dinosaur fish to me."

Dieter went inside and came out with an old photo. "This is Peter," he said, handing the framed snapshot to me. It depicted a young man in a kayak, holding a fishing rod, with a six-foot sturgeon breaching beside him, hooked on the line.

I stared at the photograph, flabbergasted. "That's crazy!"

"Dieter and I were in the aluminum boat," Helga explained, "when Peter said he had caught a fish. I was just getting my camera ready to take a picture and out jumped the sturgeon."

"What a great shot! Unbelievable."

We hadn't seen any sturgeon in the lake, so I had to ask, "What happened to them all?"

"We don't know." Dieter shook his head. "One year they were suddenly gone, and they haven't been back since."

We spotted the boat coming back. After they tied it up, I noticed Mark hobbling out, his face in agony. I met him halfway up the ramp, checking for signs of injury.

George helped Mark to a chair on Dieter's deck while David animatedly described Mark's jump from the forty-foot cliff and how he must have landed wrong. Dieter was sure it was just a sprained knee and went inside to get a special tube of *schmerzgel,* a German pain relief cream. I made a mental note to update my first aid kit, relieved that Mark was going to be okay.

Later that night, since Mark needed to keep his leg propped up on a pillow, we decided to play charades in the living room.

Tim looked at his clue, then we flipped the hourglass as he started to act. He mimicked driving a car, then stopped to look around. We shouted out, "Driving, scenery, ummm... road trip!"

He pretended to get out of the car, threw up his hands in frustration, and then kept looking around like he didn't know where he was. Finally, Mark shouted, "Lost!"

Tim had a big grin on his face as he gave Mark a high five and sat back down next to him on the couch. I noticed Mark grimace in pain as he moved, but he still managed a smile while holding the ice pack against his sprained knee.

It was George's turn next. He looked at his card and started the timer. He crouched into a strange position, both his hands up and pointing out. He kept looking side to side.

David guessed first. "Duck?"

George shook his head and continued. His eyes were big, and his head kept turning side to side. We all started laughing, because he looked hilarious, but beneath my laughter my heart was singing. Moments like these when George was willing to let loose and join in were incredibly rare. If they happened at all, it was only during his two-week vacation from work.

We kept guessing. "Scared? Ummm... some kind of animal maybe?"

The timer ran out and we looked at George, puzzled, waiting for him to tell us what he had been trying to convey.

"Crab."

We all erupted in laughter. He hadn't looked anything like a crab. David got up and imitated him, which made us all laugh even harder until I had tears running down my cheeks.

Crawling into bed that night, I reflected on the abundant life surrounding us here. Not just the natural beauty outside, but the life we were living as a family. Over the summers spent at the cabin, the boys had learned that life wasn't only about having fun—it entailed hard work too. Knowing they were learning valuable lessons and interacting with their father was exactly what I had deeply longed for.

As summer faded into September, the version of George who had spent time laughing with us faded with it. The weight of his extra-long days at work seemed to swallow him up. He was managing a major construction project with a demanding client who was difficult to satisfy.

I had seen George busy and worn out before, but the exhaustion sat even deeper now. He rarely smiled anymore. His words were sharp and clipped, spoken with little patience, as if even small conversations were a burden.

A few months later, as winter crept in, a chill settled over the house—not just from the weather, but from the growing distance I felt from George and his unrelenting stress. Although I sympathized with him, I struggled to understand why he had to remain so disconnected—both mentally and emotionally.

One evening, I poured my thoughts onto paper. When he finally got home later that night, I held it out for him to read.

"I wanted to express some of my feelings, and it came out like a short poem," I said quietly.

He blinked his eyes slowly. "Do I have to read it now? I want to get ready for bed."

"Okay, I'll wait."

When he came back into the bedroom, I handed him the piece of paper.

Time passes quickly,

the seasons change,

and so do our sons.

There's a range,

of needs and gifts,

as each day begins.

You work so hard,

day after day,

year after year,

maybe it's time to slow down.

My dear,

Love is worth far more than gold.

To be rich would mean

we together grow old.

He glanced at it, his eyes lingering for a brief moment, then he handed it back to me. Without a word, he crawled into bed and fell asleep.

I lay awake that night, trying hard to be patient, but I felt that George's lack of acknowledgement had only deepened the disconnect between us. I took a deep breath. I never doubted his love for me and the boys—his devotion ran deep. He simply expressed it in the way he knew best—by working hard and providing for us. I took another deep breath. I knew I needed to learn how to *just be,* no matter where I was or what was happening in my life.

Chapter Thirty-Seven

Another refugee family from Colombia had become part of our lives. After a year of sponsorship, their nineteen-year-old son, Javier, had grown restless, quit his job, and moved in with a dubious acquaintance. His worried mother confided in me, concerned about the negative influences and poor living conditions he faced. I met Javier for lunch in town, and after a heartfelt conversation, it became clear he needed time and space to find his path forward.

Following a lengthy discussion with George, we decided to let him move in with us for a while. What started as a short stay extended to almost a full year, with Javier joining us at the lake often during that summer.

Our cabin was bustling on the July long weekend, filled with our five boys, Javier, and my nephew, Aaron. One evening, as George and I sat around Dieter and Helga's campfire, we heard the aluminum boat return and saw all the boys scurrying up to the cabin. Mark came over to deliver the news.

"We found a goose," he exclaimed with youthful enthusiasm. "It had a broken wing, and we saved it. We're going to build a habitat for it so it can get better."

"That's so nice of you," I said. I watched him sprint over to join the other boys. We all chuckled before easing back into our conversation.

A few hours later, Mark came down again. There were no extra chairs, so I patted my knees, and he comfortably sat on my lap. Even though he was already a teenager, I was glad he didn't think he was too cool to sit with his mom.

"How's the goose doing?" I asked.

"We ate it," he confessed.

Startled, we burst into laughter, and Helga followed up with a puzzled, "What?"

Mark grinned. "We realized it wasn't going to heal, so Aaron chopped off its head. Then Javier butchered it. He knew exactly what to do, how to pluck the feathers and everything. Then we barbecued it. They're eating it as we speak."

We could still hear Dieter and Helga's laughter as George and I walked up the hill with Mark. On the deck, just as he had reported, the boys were chewing the last bits of meat off the bones. I couldn't help but smile at their antics. At least I knew they could fend for themselves if they had to.

The next evening on our way to the campfire, George and I spotted Dieter on his concrete patio. We walked over to see his most recent project: a beautiful bench, handmade out of big fragrant slabs of cedar wood.

He proudly lowered himself onto his creation. "I could sit here and stare at the lake all day."

I sat down beside him. "Me too."

"The bench turned out great," George remarked, appreciating the evident skill in how it was put together.

There was a glow in Dieter's cheeks, "When I saw it in one of the national parks up north, I loved it so much, I wrote down all the measurements so I could make one for myself."

George nodded his respect.

Eventually, we made our way back to the campfire. Glasses had already been set out in our places, and Helga filled them as we settled into the white plastic chairs.

"I've been all over the world, and I still think this is the best place to be," Dieter said out loud to no one in particular.

I nodded. "I feel the same way."

After a brief silence, George said, "I've been working on drawings for renovating our cabin."

Helga looked at George. "The company must be doing well."

"It is," George admitted. "But this time Anne has money."

"My parents just sold their house and downsized to an apartment, sharing the profits with me and my siblings," I explained. "Our first priority is to pay you back the money we owe you."

Dieter shook his head. "We don't need it right now. Use it for your renovation."

"Are you sure?" I asked, my brows knitting together in quiet disbelief.

"Your family will only get bigger," Helga added.

"I don't even know where to begin," I said, my voice thick with emotion. "Saying thank you doesn't feel like nearly enough for all you've done for us."

A deep, proud smile spread across Dieter's face, radiating warmth and generosity. Then he turned to George and said, "I would love to see your drawings. I thought about doing an addition once, but it's hard to add onto an A-frame. I'll come up tomorrow to check out your plans."

With work finally easing up a bit, George had more time to focus on the cabin renovation project. We started on-site immediately that summer. George meticulously outlined the footing locations using marker spray paint. During the week, while George and the older boys were at work, Mark and I took on the job, wielding pickaxes and shovels to dig large holes to the precise dimensions.

The sun was hot, and the mosquitoes were relentless that year. But cooling off in the lake gave us the energy and motivation to keep digging through the rocky soil. With all the boys' help on the weekends, we hauled up bags and bags of concrete. In just over a month, the pad footings were prepared and poured.

Lumber was delivered by skiff and stacked in a pile on the low bank in front of John and Donna's cabin. Every sheet of plywood and every two-by-four was carried up the hill by the boys, their cousin Aaron, Javier, and any other friends who were available to help. In one weekend, they hauled ten thousand board feet of lumber.

With our brother-in-law Henry's expertise, framing the addition got underway. George's plan was to expand the main floor by opening the walls and adding extensions that would wrap around the existing A-frame. That would give us a master bedroom facing the lake, two bedrooms in the back, and two extra bedrooms upstairs. We had to remove the roof shingles so the new timbers could be tied in.

It was a big project, and the constant cleanup was overwhelming at times. Sawdust and nails were scattered everywhere, both inside and out. Always clever, Dieter had a quick solution. He sent Mark around the property with a strong magnet that he had duct-taped to a stick. By evening, Mark had collected an entire bucket of nails. After I swept up the piles of sawdust, things were manageable once again.

On the last Friday in August, after the workers had left, we finished tidying up outside just as large droplets started falling from the sky. By the time we ran inside to the safety of the cabin, a torrential rain was pouring down.

There was water seeping through the ceiling and walls inside, not only in one area but in about thirty places. As the drips turned into streams, we worried about the damage to the tongue-and-groove cedar. Fortunately, George had some massive tarps, so we spent the next hour battling the elements to put them up.

While George and I anchored the base, David and Mark climbed the roof, pulling ropes to haul the tarps into position. Soaked and shivering, we finally headed back inside, hoping the tarps would protect our hard work. The rain continued for days, but thankfully our makeshift roof was a success.

In October, the beams for the sunroom were barged up. Our boys, along with four others, came after their day jobs to help carry the beams up the hill. They were so heavy that it took all nine strong young men to lift each one.

While lugging one of the beams up the steep slope, one of the boys at the front stumbled, causing the beam to drop heavily at the back. The impact left both Aaron and David with deep gashes on their shoulders. Despite their injuries, they all persisted, labouring until midnight before going home totally exhausted.

After Thanksgiving, most of the cabin owners had already winterized and packed up for the season, but George and I continued making the trip every weekend. There was so much work to be done, even as the temperatures steadily dropped with each passing day.

Dieter and Helga, with many travel plans over the winter, graciously offered us their cabin as a refuge during our renovations. I briefly considered declining, but the persistent dampness and mouse droppings in our exposed cabin quickly changed my mind. Grateful for their generosity, we humbly accepted their offer once again.

The first night in Dieter and Helga's cozy cabin, with the fire's warmth and the faint howl of the wind outside, left no doubt in my mind—we had made the right decision. November brought rain nearly every day and it wasn't until early December that the windows and doors were finally installed.

March ushered in the long-anticipated spring, hinting at the return of sunny days. At last, the metal roof on the cabin was completed.

We temporarily put a mattress on the floor in one of the upstairs bedrooms, but there was still a lot of scaffolding set up inside for the next phase of the renovations. One dark night, I walked head-long into a protruding two-by-four and got a big goose egg on my forehead. Frustrated, I pleaded with George in the morning.

"This renovation is going to take forever if we try to do it all ourselves."

"I know," George agreed. "I heard about a guy named Erik Lacey who has a good reputation for building in remote areas around the lake. I'll contact him and see if he's available."

Erik came up to assess the extent of the project. As soon as we met him, we knew he would be a good fit. He understood our vision right away. I could picture exactly how it would look when he talked about "beefing up" the original beams in the living room, wrapping them with cedar cladding. We were eager for him to get started.

Dieter and Helga returned just before Easter. As we gathered around the table on their deck, Helga brought out the wooden bowl brimming with colourful Easter eggs and chocolates. It was then that I noticed she had a slight limp.

Before I could ask, she exclaimed, "We had the worst holiday ever!"

"What happened?" George asked.

"We were on a dive trip in Turks and Caicos," Helga began. "The weather wasn't great, and the waves were getting high. I was sliding off the bench in the boat, so I decided to move. Just as I stood up, we hit a big wave, and I flew up and crashed down on my heels. A sharp pain shot up my leg."

"Oh no!" I sympathized.

Dieter said, "We went directly to the only doctor in the area. He was an old army doctor with ancient equipment."

"The doctor told me my ankle was shattered. He gave me a shot of morphine, put a cast on it, and said I needed to go home right away to have surgery."

Dieter slowly shook his head. "We were so glad we had insurance through the dive company. They covered everything."

"To make a long story short, we flew home, I had to get three pins put in, and I had to stay off my feet for six weeks."

"That sounds terrible!" I said.

"Dieter was a champ." Helga gave him a sweet smile. "He took care of me the whole time."

A pleased look crossed Dieter's face as he pushed the wooden bowl of chocolate toward me. "So that was our winter. What about you?"

I grabbed another handful of Cadbury Mini Eggs. "On top of the renovations," I told them, "I agreed to be part of a leadership team at church for six months while our pastor is on sabbatical. It's a much bigger commitment than I thought it would be, with endless phone calls and meetings."

"We've been a bit overwhelmed," George said, "to put it mildly."

"You still have some of your stuff stored in our back room," Helga noted.

"Yes, I'm so sorry—I'll get it out of there this weekend." I had planned to clean it up before they returned. I felt uneasy ever since we stayed in their cabin over the winter. I never wanted to take their generosity for granted.

"That would be great," Helga said. "The renovation is taking longer than you thought, isn't it?"

"Definitely," George said.

"That's always the way it goes," Dieter stated. "We've done it enough times to know that no matter how much time and money you think it will take, it's always going to be more in the end."

"Letting us use your cabin made a huge difference," I said. "Thanks again."

"Glad it worked out." Dieter's warm smile helped to ease my conflicted feelings. I was truly thankful to have such amazing neighbours.

While cleaning up an area behind the cabin, I turned to George, "I was thinking, I really need to be able to cook for a crowd. Maybe we can salvage some of the old cabinets to create a temporary kitchen on one side of the woodshed?"

"Great idea," he said. I could see the wheels turning in his head. "If we put Dieter's old gravity-fed water system up in the tree, we could even hook up water for the sink. It should work."

"Perfect! Let's do it next weekend."

Lyell had almost completed his apprenticeship and agreed to do the plumbing for the outdoor kitchen. As Lyell focused on installing the old kitchen sink, Dieter wandered over to inspect our progress, his hands resting on his hips as he took it all in. After a moment, he leaned in, reminding me to stuff any holes bigger than a dime with aluminum foil to keep the mice out.

As the summer went on, I served the stream of working trades-men and visiting guests delicious meals from my provisional kitchen. George joked that the electricians were probably stretch-ing out their work hours just to keep enjoying my home-cooking.

One of their favourite lunches was my signature chicken sand-wich: a buttery croissant sliced in half and layered with Boursin cheese and sweet fig jam. It featured tender grilled chicken breast topped with rich, melted Brie cheese and finished with caramel-ized balsamic onions, thinly sliced pears, and crisp fresh greens—a perfect balance of savoury, sweet, and tangy flavours.

My brother handled the plumbing work during our cabin reno-vation, and my parents pitched in by helping with site clean-up several weekends in a row. Tim and David pulled nails from the old cedar boards that had been removed, and George and I ran the boards through the planer to be repurposed. Throughout that summer, everyone who came got involved.

During the week, whenever we were home, I was constantly gathering samples of flooring, tiles, cabinets and countertops. The project kept us extremely busy, and working with George brought a shared sense of purpose and accomplishment. We made a great team when our focus remained solely on getting work done.

We needed help hauling bulky items to the cabin, and the timing couldn't have worked out better. That fall, Tim was enrolled in the Outtatown program and stationed in BC. While the program would take him to South Africa after Christmas, he was home in November and brought along some of his new friends to lend a hand.

Among those he invited was Sarah, a young woman he'd recently started dating. It became evident how serious he was about her when he asked if she could ride along with me in the cube van I had rented. I needed to get our kitchen cabinets, countertops, and boxes of tiles and hardwood flooring to the main dock in Harrison. Tim thought it would be a good opportunity for me to meet Sarah, and I gladly agreed, eager to get to know her better.

Sarah's thick blond hair and captivating blue eyes were undoubtedly part of what initially had drawn my son to her. After some casual conversation about her family in Ontario and how she was enjoying the Outtatown program, I gathered that Sarah had a kind heart and had been raised with strong values.

About an hour into our drive, I felt comfortable enough to ask, "So, what do you like best about Tim?"

She responded shyly after a moment, "Everything."

I loved her innocence and felt an instant kinship with my future daughter-in-law.

We met the barge at the main dock. Tim and his friends were waiting for us there, ready to unload the truck. As they carried every item onto the barge, I noticed Tim's curious glances in my direction, trying to get a read on what I thought about his new girlfriend. When I offered him a reassuring thumbs up, a wide grin stretched across his entire face.

Chapter Thirty-Eight

T hat winter, subtle changes began weaving into the fabric of our daily lives. George Matthew embarked on a three-month volunteer opportunity with an organization in Austria. Lyell secured a stable plumbing job and moved into an apartment with a friend. Tim was off on his adventure in South Africa, leaving the house unusually quiet with only two boys at home—at least until May.

At the cabin, Lyell helped my brother install the plumbing fixtures and pressurize the water system. It was a relief to finally have hot and cold running water. They installed the new toilets, and I gladly closed the outhouse door for the last time. With every day that passed, I saw more and more changes.

One morning, I stood in our new sunroom, now occupying the space where the old deck had been, gazing out at the tranquil lake. It was hard to believe that, after two years of hard work, our vision had become a reality.

I walked out onto the new deck, now perched near the cliff's edge, extending beyond the spot where our firepit used to be. I couldn't wait to host family barbecues in this breathtaking space.

Erik Lacey and his crew were almost done. When they finished trimming the windows, I eagerly wiped the last layer of dust from the ledges. Erik had crafted bookshelves and stairs using live-edge cedar, seamlessly blending the essence of the outdoors into our living space. I was pleased that we were able to incorporate Helga's original stained-glass pieces into the design as well.

I finally got to peel the protective paper off the floors. I did it slowly, admiring the honey-toned finish of the maple hardwood underneath. A beautiful, peeled-branch railing in the loft and a maple butcher block island in the kitchen completed the West Coast feel we both loved.

Although the inside was finally done, Erik's crew still had exterior work to finish. For two years, our family had collected as many flat rocks as we could. The crew used the larger ones to build cascading steps down the hill toward the lake, and the smaller ones to form a rock wall on the lower part of the cabin.

By the end of June, I could finally start relaxing. We brought our old wooden beds from home, and I covered the mattresses with new sheets and vintage quilts. I finished stocking the pantry and filling the cupboards, and for the first time in a long time, I took a book off my new shelf to read. As much as I had loved creating this home, it was a relief to finally ease the pace and unwind.

Occasionally, I felt a twinge of guilt at being able to retreat to such a beautiful place. I knew it was a privilege few would ever have the fortune to enjoy. Yet, in those moments, gratitude filled my heart and eclipsed any lingering guilt. We created a place that had become the embodiment of home to me. A place where I found a sense of belonging, surrounded by kindred spirits and the unparalleled beauty of nature.

George and I spent every weekend at the cabin. I loved the way Dieter would casually update us on the week's events as we gathered around the fire. Bringing us up to speed became a ritual.

"Mark Stevens floated his propane tank down the lake on Tuesday, filled it up, and floated it back again. It took the whole day."

His remarks were often followed by an easy silence, until he thought of something else to say.

"I saw an owl. He landed on the flagpole."

We sat in stillness again, staring into the flames. In the distance, the faint drone of a plane caught our attention, prompting us to glance skyward and spot its blinking lights.

Dieter said, "That's Air Canada flight number 206 flying from Calgary to Vancouver."

I started laughing. "It amazes me how you always know exactly what's going on, whether it's in the water or up in the sky."

Helga laughed too. "That's Dieter."

George took his vacation days in the height of summer, and the August weather was perfect. We inflated two air mattresses and floated near our dock, basking in the warmth of the sun's rays.

"Yeah, it's a tough life, but somebody's got to do it."

I opened my eyes and saw Dieter on his bench, his low chuckle bubbling like water over stones.

Helga walked to the edge of the patio and peered down at us. "You both look very relaxed."

George shielded his eyes, squinting into the sun. "Yup. All I need now is a cold beer."

Dieter turned and went into his cabin. A few moments later, his granddaughter, Emily, swam over to us with a homemade floating beer holder. She tied the string to George's mattress and swam back, giggling.

Dieter called down again. "See the bell on the back? Ring that when your beer is empty, and Emily will bring you a new one."

George laughed as he pulled back the tab on the can, releasing a sharp hiss as the seal broke, "This is amazing."

Seeing George so calm and relaxed was a welcome sight. Even though he didn't ring the bell, Emily swam out to bring him another beer when she saw he had finished the first one. She took away the empty can, obviously proud to be her Opa's accomplice, joyfully contributing to the fun.

That evening, as we walked down our stone path, we were still laughing about Dieter's contraption. George thanked Emily before she ran up to our cabin to join the boys in a game of cards.

We settled into the chairs around the fire. After some casual chatter about the day, a long silence followed before Dieter turned to us, his voice growing more serious. "We are so glad we have good neighbours. You are family now."

Helga bobbed her head gently in agreement. "I would put my hands in the fire for your boys."

I looked at her, wide-eyed, not understanding.

"It's a German saying that means we care a lot," she explained.

"I would put my hands in the fire for any one of you," Dieter professed, looking at me.

Tears welled up in my eyes, and I brushed them away, offering Dieter a grateful smile. I was touched by the sincerity of their words and the thought of the sacrifice. Dieter and Helga were family to us as well. I wanted to say that I would also put my hands in the fire for them, but I was too choked up to express my feelings verbally just then. Instead, we sat together in silent companionship, the kind we often shared when words weren't enough. The crackling fire echoed in the night, accompanied by the distant croaks of frogs.

George was the first to speak again, and it didn't surprise me that he shifted the conversation away from emotional topics to something more comfortable for him.

"How did you find out about this place anyway? I overheard Donna say they used to call this the 'German side' of the bay."

Helga's eyes lit up at the memory. "Years ago, I had a hairdressing shop in Vancouver. One of my customers was German too. She said she knew someone who spoke the same dialect as Dieter and me, and that we should meet them. So, we went to the Alpen Club restaurant in Vancouver, where we met Elmer and Kay for the first time."

Dieter poured us all some more wine and added, "They weren't actually Bavarian, they were Shwäbisch, which is a totally different dialect, but we became good friends with them anyhow."

Helga said, "They talked about a lake where they were building a cabin and invited us to come with them to see it."

"It was Easter Monday, 1969 when we came here for the first time," Dieter said, with his exceptional ability to recall dates. I loved the way he and Helga effortlessly tag-teamed when sharing a story.

"They kept everything rough," Helga added. "Plywood floors and handmade furniture sort of thrown together. But Elmer was a foreman at the mill, so he had the benefit of picking choice lumber. The beams had no knots in them, and the walls and ceilings were all tongue-and-groove cedar."

She took a sip of her wine. "At that time, you could only get leased land, and they ended up also leasing the property next to them. We were getting together with them quite often in those days. Our kids were almost the same age as theirs, so they played well together. We talked about the lake a lot."

Dieter chimed in. "And then one day Elmer said, 'Why don't you build a cabin beside ours? We reserved that property so we could control who our neighbours are.' Funny how people do that, isn't it?" He winked at me.

Helga kept the story on track, her hands moving animatedly as she spoke, "The neighbours on the other side of them were Kay's sister and brother-in-law. The people in the cabin next to Kay's sister were also German. All the men worked together at the mill."

Dieter took over. "We were skiing a lot at Grouse Mountain in those days, and I really liked the A-frames I saw there. So I decided to build one. I figured out the measurements, and Elmer supplied the lumber. The whole cabin cost us $3,000. We put up the A-frame in one weekend and then it didn't take long to nail on the boards."

"A weekend?" It had taken us a whole crew and two years to renovate the cabin.

George mirrored my thoughts. "That's impressive!"

As we left on the last Sunday night of George's vacation, Dieter came to help us untie the boat and say goodbye, as he often did. Knowing George was returning to the frenzy of work in the city, he teased him as we took off.

"Work hard! Someone has to pay for my pension."

Chapter Thirty-Nine

Another winter went by, and soon it was time to prepare for the summer season. Cleaning and planning menus for guests became my focus. With no nearby grocery stores, careful organization was key. Everything had to come by boat, and I needed to ensure there was enough food for three full meals a day.

George's business partners and their wives came first, followed by my book club's annual retreat the next weekend. When we weren't hosting others, our kids joined us whenever they could. Summers always unfolded this way, one weekend after another, and I wouldn't have wanted it any other way.

After Tim and Sarah returned from their Outtatown Africa program, Sarah had moved into our basement. Her parents travelled from Ontario to visit and see where their daughter was spending all her time. We invited them to the lake, and they instantly fell in love with the place.

While George, Tim, Sarah, and her dad went fishing, her mom and I enjoyed a quiet afternoon relaxing on the deck.

"Sarah tells me it can get pretty hectic out here during the summertime."

"That's for sure. George's side of the family was here last weekend—twenty-two of us in total. Some camped in tents, and

George Matthew slept in the boat." I laughed then as if I were about to tell a joke. "How many cousins can you fit in a hot tub?"

She chuckled. "I don't know, how many?"

"Fourteen!"

"No way!"

"Yup, every one of Tim's cousins were in at the same time. I was amazed the deck could support all that weight."

When the others had returned from fishing, I served a simple dinner of buns, farmer sausage, potato salad, and a large tray of sliced watermelon for dessert.

Sarah's mom helped me with the dishes. "Where did you get this beautiful plate?" she asked, pointing to the big platter full of fruits and vegetables on the butcher block island.

"George and I went to Cabo San Lucas last winter. There's a cute little artists' town called Todos Santos. I found it in a pottery shop there."

"I love the colours," she said, as she ran her finger along the edge of the blue-and-yellow plate.

"Eventually, we hope to do what Dieter and Helga do: spend spring to fall at the lake and travel during the winter."

"That would be nice," she said with a hint of playful envy. "Are you going anywhere this winter?"

"It's only for ten days, but I've already got it all booked. Our family is going to Hawaii to celebrate the new year and my fiftieth birthday."

"Oh, right, Sarah mentioned that. She's really loving her life here in BC. Once we retire, we'd like to spend more time out this way as well."

"That would be great."

She smiled. "If we could live in a place like this, we would move here in a heartbeat."

"Yeah, if George ever retires, I would love to live here too."

I had said it lightheartedly, but she laughed, understanding the truth of my words.

Another six months drifted by, and just like that, the world was poised for renewal. It had been an unusually mild winter, allowing us to reopen the cabin by mid-February. Dieter and Helga arrived in March, and as we gathered around the table on their deck, I couldn't hold back my excitement, "Tim and Sarah are engaged!"

"That's wonderful," Helga exclaimed.

Dieter poured the wine. "When did that happen?"

"On New Year's Eve in Hawaii. Tim had it all planned. The boys had fun lighting off fireworks at the beach to celebrate."

George chimed in. "The whole trip was a lot of fun."

"It was amazing!" I gushed. "Relaxing under palm trees and swimming with turtles."

"That reminds me," Dieter munched on a pretzel, "did we ever tell you about the time we swam with the jellyfish?"

Helga's eyes lit up. "It was incredible! The place was called Jellyfish Lake. We were snorkelling and literally surrounded by thousands of jellyfish. It was absolutely beautiful."

"And they don't sting, because freshwater jellyfish are different," Dieter added.

George grabbed a few pretzels. "Interesting."

"They were sort of a golden colour but still transparent, so you could see inside them when they moved. It was magical," Helga remarked, as if in a trance.

After a few minutes of silence, I said, "Speaking of travelling, do you remember me telling you about my neighbour Louisa?"

Helga nodded, "The one who moved back to England?"

"Yeah. Her son called me a few weeks ago and invited me to her ninetieth birthday party. He thought it would be a nice surprise for her if I came."

"So you're going?" Dieter asked.

"Of course she's going," George laughed. "Any opportunity to travel and she goes."

"Well, why shouldn't she?" Helga responded.

"Because there's a lot going on," George stated, a hint of disapproval creeping into his voice.

"There's always a lot going on," Helga laughed. "If you wait until there's nothing going on, you'll never go anywhere. Besides, the boys are all grown up now."

"Exactly!" I valued her constant support, as it eased any lingering guilt and gave me the confidence to list the details that supported her point. "Mark is graduating in a few months, George Matthew is a bus driver, Lyell is a fully qualified plumber, Tim already started his own business, David is at university... They don't need me anymore. And it's only for a week."

"You'll be fine," Helga teased George. "Your wife probably leaves you meals that she prepared ahead of time anyway."

"Yes, she does," he sheepishly confessed before giving me a smile.

"Life is short," I said. "Relationships and experiences are important to me."

Dieter said, "You won't ever regret travelling. I agree you should go whenever you can. No ifs, ands, or buts."

I agreed with Dieter.

I looked forward to seeing Louisa again, but for me, travel was about more than just visiting people and places. It was an expression of freedom, curiosity, and self-discovery. I loved the thrill of the unknown, the connection to new cultures, and the break from routine. But it went even deeper. Travel served as a reminder of how little we truly need. Living out of a small suitcase stripped away the excess and made me feel fully alive.

Chapter Forty

It turned out there was no reason for me to feel any guilt. Half of the meals I made ahead of time were still in the freezer when I returned from England. George had been so busy with work that he'd barely been home except to sleep. As we cruised down the highway toward the lake for the weekend, I finally had a chance to share more about my trip.

"You remember Peter, Louisa's son? He and his wife picked me up at the airport, and it was a long drive from there to Haverhill. He was using this old GPS that kept sending us down random back roads. You should have seen him—red-faced, gripping the steering wheel so tightly, completely frustrated. At one point, we ended up in a town called Helions Bumpstead. He kept repeating the name in his thick accent, 'Helions Bumpstead? What on earth are we doing in Helions Bumpstead!' I laughed so hard when he said, 'Imagine naming a town Helions Bumpstead! Someone asks you where you're from and you say, I live in Helions Bumpstead! It's ludicrous!!'"

"I can imagine you laughing at that," George chuckled as he turned off the highway. "Was Louisa surprised when she saw you?"

"She was in total shock. We hugged each other, and she said, 'Oh my goodness, you came all this way?'"

George flicked on his turn signal, taking the exit to Harrison Hot Springs. Lost in my memories, I hadn't even noticed how far we'd driven.

I recalled the lively music that filled the Village Hall as family and friends mingled in honour of her birthday. Seated along the edge with a plate of hors d'oeuvres and a glass of wine, I watched Louisa on the dance floor. She moved gracefully, guided by her son Chris. I hoped to be that agile when I was ninety. It was a joy to watch her being celebrated by her loved ones.

"I thought it was a bit strange that nobody was giving a tribute or saying anything about Louisa at the party," I pondered out loud to George as he stopped at the only stop light in the town of Harrison Hot Springs.

"Like speeches?"

"Yeah. I asked Louisa's daughter about it, and she said that nothing was planned."

"That is kind of strange for a ninetieth celebration."

"So I went up to the DJ and asked if I could say something."

"You did?"

"Well, I thought somebody should. He stopped the music and handed me a microphone. I almost lost my nerve when everything went quiet. I said, 'Hello, I'm Anne from Canada. Louisa was my neighbour for seven years. She's one of the bravest women I've ever met.' A few people around the room nodded. Then I said something like, 'At the age of seventy-nine, she moved halfway around the world to get married, and at the at the age of eighty-one, she got her driver's licence. Teaching her how to drive in reverse was one of the scariest moments of my life!'"

George laughed. "Did you tell the story?"

"Yes, and a few more. Everyone laughed. Then, at the end, I held up my glass and said, 'Here's to you Louisa, a wonderful friend and an inspiration to us all. Happy ninetieth birthday!'" I could still hear the applause, the cheering, and the clinking glasses echoing in my mind.

"It's good that you said something." George smiled. "Is she happy where she's living?"

"Happy enough, I guess. She did tell me that she wished she would have stayed in Fort Langley for a few more years. She talked a lot about how much happier she was here, aside from having her family closer now. She mentioned so many things she missed about Fort Langley—even Judy at the grocery store."

George laughed. "Judy's great. She knows everyone in town."

When the lake came into view, the sight evoked a feeling of peace within me. But by the time we loaded everything into the boat, got to the cabin, docked, and carried it all up, I collapsed onto the sofa, exhausted. "I still feel a bit jet lagged."

George replied, "Tomorrow I'll fire up the hot tub. That will feel good."

He went on to share his latest office updates with me, and then his voice filled with excitement as he said, "Oh, I put the order in for the ATVs we talked about getting. We can pick them up in about three weeks."

"I'm sure you'll get a lot of use out of them. With all the old logging roads winding through the mountains, the boys will have endless opportunities for exploration and adventure."

The next day, as I sank into the hot water, it was—as usual—a bit of a shock to the system at first, but then came the moment when the soothing warmth melted away all traces of my exhaustion. I looked up at the billions of stars. We could clearly see the Big Dipper and Cassiopeia.

George pointed and said, "Wow, you can even see the Milky Way tonight."

"All I need now is to hear an owl," I joked. Sure enough, as if on cue, two owls started their mating calls. "Amazing," I whispered.

We were silent for a few moments, taking in the night, when George suddenly said, "I really missed you, but I'm glad you had a good time."

We held hands under the water. The haunting sound of the owls continued, serving as a soothing backdrop to the peaceful evening. I savoured the simple joy of being in the moment, together with George, under the vast, starlit sky.

Helga initiated a friendly wager among the neighbours, challenging everyone to guess the water level during the spring runoff in June. Beside their dock stood a pole marked with lines showing past high-water levels, each labelled with the year in white paint. Dieter was usually the winner of these bets, but this year, George won. Helga handed him his prize: a container full of dimes worth five dollars.

As we sat around the campfire recalling last year's high water, George commented on the highest mark. "In 1972, the water would have come up to your deck!"

Dieter answered, "That's right. I looked it up and that's half a metre lower than it was in 1948."

While we all marvelled at the thought of such high water, Dieter remembered something that happened at the lake that week. "Have you seen that big raven around?"

"Yeah," I nodded. I often heard his wings flapping—that deep whooshing sound as he flew by.

"Well, the neighbours at the end of our bay had pork chops thawing on their deck, and the next thing they knew, the raven came, and all the pork chops were gone. They came outside just in time to see him fly off with the last one."

We all chuckled, but he wasn't done with his story. "Then one day, Helga made too many spaghetti noodles, so I decided to put them out to see what would happen." He smiled. "The raven came... and flew off with spaghetti hanging out of his mouth."

We all laughed at the way Dieter told the story, showing with his hands how the noodles were dangling from the raven's beak. I could totally picture it.

"I named the raven Tommy," he added. "Did you know they can live up to fifty years?"

"I didn't know that." Dieter's endless supply of facts always amazed me.

After a few minutes of silence, Helga redirected the conversation. "Have you heard from your friend in England?"

"I just got a call from her son last week. She had a stroke."

"Oh no, is she okay?" A look of genuine concern crossed Helga's face.

"She's still in the hospital, but she'll probably need to be in a wheelchair from now on. It's hard to believe. Just a few months ago she was dancing at her birthday party."

Dieter's eyes conveyed warmth and kindness. "You never know what's going to happen next."

"I wrote her a letter right away, but I have no idea if she'll be able to write back. At least she'll know I'm thinking of her."

Helga responded, "The same thing happened to a woman in the complex where we live, but she's managing. Somehow, life goes on."

After a moment, George steered the conversation back to business. "Lyell is coming up next weekend to do the plumbing for our outdoor shower. Do you need him to do anything else while he's here?"

Dieter jumped at the opportunity. "I've been wanting to replace my water line to the pump. I've patched it up too many times over the years."

"Let me know what length you'll need. I'm sure he won't mind." Helga smiled. "What a nice guy, that Lyell of yours."

"He's such a hard worker," I nodded, "and an excellent plumber."

As George and Dieter continued their conversation, Helga asked, "How are Tim and Sarah's wedding plans coming?"

"Good. We looked at a lot of venues but finally booked the Fraser River Lodge. It's a beautiful setting beside the river with a fantastic view of Mount Cheam."

Helga smiled, "I'm looking forward to it."

By October, Dieter and Helga had already set off on their travels, and a few weeks later, it was time for us to start the annual task of winterizing once again. As George and I worked side by side in the crisp autumn air, we reminisced about how full that summer had been. Tim and Sarah's wedding, in particular, was a highlight. The day couldn't have turned out more perfectly, and we were over-joyed to officially welcome a daughter into the family.

Climbing into the soothing ambience of the hot tub, George said, "Last chance to enjoy this before I drain it for the winter."

With only the occasional hoot of an owl for distraction, it was becoming the ideal place for me to broach sensitive topics with George. We sank into the warmth as I ventured to say, "So, you know that yoga class I've been going to?"

"The one Janice told you about in Fort Langley?"

"Yeah, I'm really enjoying it. I met a woman in class named Abby. We clicked instantly, and now she's trying to talk me into going to the yoga retreat organized by our instructor. The accommodations are for two people per room, and since neither of us know the other women very well, we thought we could share a room."

"Where's the retreat going to be?" he asked hesitantly.

"Costa Rica."

"What?! That's a long way to go for a retreat."

"I know, but I've always wanted to go there. I would learn so much. Rather than just once a week, we would be doing yoga twice a day. The lodge is off-grid on the Osa Peninsula. It's surrounded by tropical rainforest, and you know how much I love tropical climates."

Under the moonlight, I could see the contemplative expression on his face as he processed the information. I didn't expect a response so soon, but he said, "If you really want to go, then you should. I guess I can manage for one week."

"Really?" It was great to see George in such an agreeable mood. "One idea I had is that you could come meet me after the retreat, and then we could explore more of Costa Rica together. Maybe for a week or two?"

"I like that option."

"She needs to know the numbers soon." I could feel my excitement growing but tried not to get my hopes up. I was struck by how much easier it was to talk to George at the lake compared to at home. "You're okay if I sign up?"

"Sure."

I dove across the hot tub and wrapped my arms around his neck. It meant so much to me, having his support.

Chapter Forty-One

Winter's harshness was softened by the warm memories of our time in Costa Rica, a comforting glow against the season's chill. Spring swept in with its usual rush, pulling us along with its relentless pace. Then, at last, we retreated to the lake, where we could slow down and catch our breath once more.

The gentle lapping of waves marked the beginning of another peaceful summer day, where time slowed to match the lazy drift of clouds overhead. It was just before four o'clock, and George and I were reading on our deck, when I thought I heard a little bell ring. Unsure if I'd imagined it, I kept reading. But when it rang again, I looked at George to see if he had heard it too.

"Do you think Dieter is ringing for us to come down?" I asked as I stood up to go check. The stone steps were cool against my bare feet, and George followed behind me. Dieter grinned broadly, Bavarian bell in hand, as we arrived on his deck.

Back in January, I received an email from Dieter that said, "Happy birthday. Your present will be a summer full of sangria." As I took a seat at the table, Dieter announced that this would be the beginning of my birthday present.

Sitting on their deck always felt easy. Every aspect exuded an undeniable charm, from the Bavarian sign over the front door to the hanging planter overflowing with flowers in the corner. Dieter and Helga's presence added a warmth that was truly unique, creating an atmosphere that couldn't be replicated.

I noticed a stack of diving magazines at one end of the table. Diving was a frequent topic of conversation around their campfire. I picked one up and started flipping through it just as Dieter came out of the cabin carrying a large wine glass full of sangria.

The orange slice perched on the rim like a bow on a perfectly wrapped gift. It wasn't just a drink—it was a gesture, a reminder that the smallest acts, when given with such thoughtfulness, can hold the weight of love and connection. His kind, gentle face radiated sincerity, and his eyes sparkled as he handed it to me.

My face lit up in appreciation. "Thank you, Dieter."

George, taking note of the magazine in my hand, asked, "How long have you two been diving?"

"In the last twenty years, we've each done over four hundred dives," he said with pride.

"That's impressive," George said, grabbing one of the magazines for himself.

Dieter picked up another one, flipping the pages to show us some pictures. "This is in Palau in Micronesia. It was the most incredible dive we've ever done. Absolutely incredible. You wouldn't believe the colours of the coral reefs."

"And the water was so clear," Helga added. "We saw hundreds of different kinds of fish."

Dieter's voice was filled with wonder as he recounted the mesmerizing beauty. "And another one of the best spots was in Yap. We swam with giant manta rays all around us."

George and I stared at the beautiful underwater photos in the magazine. The manta rays looked like graceful giants gliding effortlessly through the water, their enormous wings spanning majestically.

"These pictures are no exaggeration," Helga said. "It was just like that."

"We've been to many different places," Dieter said, "and spent lots of time diving in Cozumel, which is beautiful too, but Palau and Yap were my favourites, no ifs, ands, or buts."

"Oh," Helga exclaimed, suddenly remembering something, "I forgot to tell you about what happened here during the week."

We put the magazines down to listen to her.

"There was a baby seal stuck in the shallows right here between us and John and Donna's. It wouldn't leave for days, so Donna called the SPCA, and then she put the seal in one of those little kiddie pools and brought it down to the marina where the animal rescue came and picked it up."

"Interesting," George said, sipping his beer.

"It's amazing how many seals there are in the lake," I said, "especially on the logs at the marina. And last summer, there was one consistently swimming in front of our dock. David named it Bojangles."

"They swim from the ocean up the river and into the lake," Dieter explained, "But some are residents year-round."

"Speaking of the river," Helga chimed in, "our sons, Klaus and Pete, went all the way down the river one time, from the cabin to Fort Langley."

Dieter continued the story. "They each took a small aluminum boat with their wives, a bunch of camping gear, and their dogs. At the point where the Harrison River meets the Fraser, it creates big whirlpools. They were really scared when they got pulled into the spiral, it was so powerful."

George's eyebrows were raised, "That would be scary."

Dieter nodded. "Absolutely."

"What happened then?" I asked.

"They quickly put on their life jackets. Their outboard motors were barely strong enough to get them out."

I let out a sigh of relief.

"And right after they cleared the whirlpool," Dieter chuckled, "Klaus ran out of gas."

George responded, "Whoa, that could have been really bad."

"How long did the whole trip take?" I asked.

"Probably could have done it in about twelve hours, but they camped overnight somewhere near Chilliwack. So, they left here after breakfast and got there in the afternoon the next day."

We passed the snack bowl around, aware that the chocolate-covered pretzels were disappearing quickly. The rich, velvety chocolate with the salty crunch of the pretzel was a delightful fusion. I savoured one as I thought about my two favourite places, Harrison Lake and Fort Langley, being connected by water.

George and I sank into the hot tub, leaning back to gaze up at the star-studded sky. The contrast between the hot water and the crisp evening air added to the quiet beauty of the night.

Steam rose in delicate swirls around me. "Chris called me earlier, letting me know that Louisa passed away," I said.

"Oh... sorry to hear that," he said in a neutral tone.

"She had another stroke and didn't make it this time."

"How old was she?"

"Ninety-two." I pictured Louisa's warm, smiling face. I had always admired her resilience and the way she radiated kindness and optimism.

George nodded thoughtfully. "Time sure goes fast."

"That's why it's so important to live every day to the fullest and celebrate as much as possible," I said. "Speaking of celebrations, our anniversary in Tofino last weekend was so much fun."

"It sure was," George replied. "It's crazy that we haven't been there since our honeymoon."

"I know!" I said, shaking my head. "We kept saying we'd go, and somehow twenty-eight years flew by."

"That coastal scenery is stunning. I enjoyed walking barefoot in the sand, hand in hand with you."

"The water was cold, though. I love the ocean, but in the summer, this is the only place I want to be. The water here is so refreshingly clean."

George nodded in agreement. "We're lucky to have easy access to both. BC is the perfect place to live. We've got everything: beaches, mountains, lakes, rivers..."

As I listened to George gush about our home province, I couldn't help but smile wryly at him. "Do you realize you're like a different person when we're here? Especially when you have a few weeks off."

"Really? I don't feel any different."

I chuckled in a low tone, turning to face him. "All I know is, I like this version of you a lot better. You're much more... available."

I let him contemplate that while I closed my eyes, feeling utterly content in the abundance of natural beauty surrounding us.

Chapter Forty-Two

With the holidays falling just right on the calendar, George ended up with ten days off at Christmas. We decided it would be fun to spend New Year's at the cabin. The kids were excited to join us for part of the time. Mark even planned to bring his girlfriend, Tausha, so we could get to know her better.

David was home from university and offered to head up with us a day early to warm up the cabin, haul supplies, and get the water running.

We arrived at the marina in the late afternoon, braving the steady rain as we carried our provisions from the truck to the boat. George turned the key only to discover the battery was dead. It was a fifteen-minute drive to the nearest store that sold batteries, and it was almost closing time. George called ahead, begging the store owner on the phone to stay open until he and David got there.

I stayed with the boat, silently questioning our decision to venture to the lake in such weather. Still, we had come this far, and I knew that once we were safely inside, the effort would all be worth it. By the time they returned and replaced the battery, the weather had gone from bad to worse, and I was dreading the upcoming boat ride.

It was pitch dark, the wind was howling, and the rain had turned into sleet. George and I couldn't see anything at all. We tried shining a flashlight on the water, but the beam only obscured George's vision. David unzipped the front of the boat roof and poked his head through, yelling instructions back at his dad.

Enduring the stinging sleet on his face, David was able to guide us along the shoreline until we reached the bay. As we slowed down, I shone the flashlight toward the dock so George could moor the boat. The trip took forty minutes—twice as long as usual.

By the time we brought up the supplies, we were all soaked, and David's face was frozen. Huddled around the wood stove with blankets wrapped around us, it felt like an eternity before the chill finally gave way to warmth. We recalled the treacherous night, grinning now that it was behind us.

The storm showed no signs of letting up, and at some point during the night, I awakened to George throwing his clothes on in the dark.

"What's wrong?" I rubbed sleep from my eye.

"Something's up with the boat, I can hear it pounding. I probably have to re-tie it."

I awoke to a cold hand on my back, not even realizing that I had drifted off again. "It got a bit loose, but it's okay now," he mumbled, trying to warm himself against my body.

In the morning, the water was calm, a stark contrast to the turbulent waves of the previous night. At the dock, we were shocked at the size of the gouge our boat had made in the wood. As he untied the ropes, George pointed out how he should have properly secured it to avoid this kind of damage. Thankfully, the boat was unharmed, and he was still able to go down to the marina to pick up the rest of the family.

Winter at the cabin offered a different experience compared to summer. Instead of water sports, the kids—now all in their twenties—spent their days cruising through the trails on the ATVs. With darkness falling early, the cabin became a cozy haven of togetherness as we gathered for meals and games.

The infectious laughter of everyone around the table was pure joy to my ears. The game of *Nuscht* was a family favourite. It's a game of dice that can be played by any number of people.

It warmed my heart to see how naturally Tausha blended into our family dynamic. Her cascade of dark red hair reflected her vibrant energy, and her laughter harmonized perfectly with ours. It was evident that everyone was enjoying themselves. Tausha won every game of *Nuscht* that night.

We spent most of New Year's Eve around the table. A steaming pot of rich, golden cheese fondue took centre stage, surrounded by an array of dipping delights. As the clock struck midnight, we could hear the clatter of pots and pans echo across the bay, so we all went out onto the deck. At the far end, bursts of fireworks illuminated the night sky. We cheered as George popped the cork on the champagne. First we toasted to the year that had passed. Then we toasted to the year that was about to begin.

George and I dropped off the kids at the marina the next day, waving goodbye before boating back to the cabin for a few more days of peace and quiet. That night, as we soaked in the hot tub, we reflected on the past year.

"It's so different having adult kids," I said. "So much easier. Suddenly, they're all grown up, living their own lives. What I love the most is how well they all get along with each other."

George nodded. "I agree."

After a few minutes, he posed the question we had come to ask each other every New Year: "What was the highlight of the year for you?"

"It was an excellent year," I said. "But for me, Costa Rica was the biggest highlight. It feels like a long time ago, yet I can still hear the howler monkeys and the birds as if it were yesterday. Swimming in the warm ocean, surrounded by lush tropical foliage—I loved it. And I especially loved the whole concept of *Pura Vida*."

"What does it mean again? Pure life?"

"Well, literally it does, but for the people living there it's more of a philosophy. It means living life to its fullest and embracing joy, simplicity, and gratitude. It's more than that even. They have a deep connection to nature, living in harmony with all of life. It's about having a positive mindset and celebrating life's simple pleasures."

George chuckled. "You got all that from being there for three weeks?"

"Totally. I think we could learn from a culture like that. The older I get, the more I want to simplify my life."

George refrained from commenting, so I asked, "What were some of the highlights of the year for you?"

He thought for a minute. "It's hard to believe it's been almost a year since that trip. I'd say the highlight for me was Costa Rica too, especially the southern part of the Nosara Peninsula. That little rustic cabin you booked—how much was it again?"

"Twenty dollars a night."

"What a great deal! Watching the families of monkeys climb through the trees while we ate our breakfast, that was cool."

"And I liked sleeping under a mosquito net." For me it had been an important shield against the nighttime buzz of insects, like a protective veil. But the gauzy fabric also created a cocoon, bringing a sense of intimacy and adventure to the night.

George sat up on the step of the hot tub to cool off. "I liked hiking to those waterfalls, swimming in the cool water..."

"And that's where we saw those huge blue morpho butterflies. Those were my favourite." I could still picture the beautiful blue wings floating through the air.

"Montezuma was fun too, with that whole hippie vibe."

"You know what memory really stands out for me? Remember when we stopped for lunch at that little family-run outdoor restaurant? The place was packed, and the only two seats left were at the table with that mysterious Bohemian-looking guy sitting at one end, making wooden jewelry. Do you remember him– the guy with the long, dark hair?"

"Yup." George said as he sank back into the tub.

"When he asked us why we were visiting Costa Rica, you started talking about your hectic work schedule. You mentioned that we had five grown sons, then smirked a little and said I planned the trip around a yoga retreat."

"Yeah, so?"

"It was that man's response that really stayed with me. I clearly remember the way he fixed his deep, dark eyes on me, as if he could see straight into the depths of my soul. Then, in his French accent, he said, 'Ahhh, you are becoming a woman again.'"

George laughed. "I don't remember that!"

"Well, I'll never forget it. It almost made me cry. I was so amazed that a total stranger could sense what was happening within me and that you didn't—still don't—get it."

"Don't get what?" He seemed genuinely confused. After a minute, he ventured, "Is it like... a menopause thing?"

"No, it's not a menopause thing." I sighed, tired of the way my emotions were so easily dismissed, as if it was just a passing phase. "I think it's a natural progression for anyone as life changes and evolves. Being a full-time mother was my career—I poured so much of myself into motherhood. Our family will always be my top priority, but now that the boys are older, I need to rediscover myself and find a renewed sense of purpose. My world is changing, and I feel like I'm finally finding my own voice."

I took a deep breath and looked away, gathering my thoughts. In the distance, an owl called out, and somehow, the sound gave me strength to go on calmly. "I want to live in a way that's true to my values. To me, success isn't about how much money we have or the things we own—it's about being grounded in love and finding joy in everyday life."

There was a dense calm to the night, as if even the leaves dared not rustle while I shared what I felt. I glanced at George, waiting—hoping—for a response. But he said nothing, so I kept going. "I really believe there's freedom in simplicity."

I thought back to how often we used to talk about this when we were first married, when our focus was so clear. "Sometimes I feel like our lives have become too cluttered—not just with stuff, but anything that adds unnecessary complications or stress."

After a few minutes of silence, and with a subtle undertone of discomfort, George said, "It's late, I guess we should go to bed." He got out of the hot tub and headed to the outdoor shower to rinse off.

I knew this pattern all too well—his constant avoidance of anything deep or personal. I simply wanted to have a meaningful conversation. While I craved emotional depth in our marriage, physical intimacy seemed to be sufficient for him. I could practically feel the warmth draining from my heart, leaving behind an icy barrier.

The next morning, George and I slowly packed up. As I locked the cabin door, I felt the first cool drops of rain landing on my head. By the time we loaded the boat, the wind was kicking up whitecaps and the rain was pouring down in sheets. George drove with caution as we crested each swell. The storm had come up so fast.

At the marina, docking became a daunting task. The strong gusts pushed so hard, we almost collided into one of the other boats. On the third try, I jumped out onto the pier, rope in hand. The wooden boards were slick under my sneakers. The wind was relentless, draining my energy as I fought to pull the boat in.

My fingers, numb and frozen, clutched the soaked rope with all their might while the rain lashed at my face. With a determined pull, I was finally able to wrap it around the cleat a few times, enough so that George could hop out to help pull it closer. It took both of us a good half hour to get the boat secured.

After that struggle against the elements, we stopped at a coffee shop in town for warm drinks. I wrapped both hands around a steaming chai latte, holding it up to let the fragrant heat melt the chill from my face. George sat across the table, coffee in hand, steady and silent in his usual way. As I watched him, the stormy weather faded, and warmth slowly seeped back into my heart.

Chapter Forty-Three

Each winter brought its own challenges. George was still consistently consumed by his workload, leaving little room for anything or anyone else. I found meaning and purpose in my volunteer work, and the busy days passed quickly, yet I always longed for the calm, unhurried days by the lake.

Finally, spring blossomed, transforming the chaos of winter into another season of renewal and growth. With family Easter gatherings happening that long weekend, George and I contemplated whether it was worth going up to the cabin for the one night we had free.

When we pulled up to our dock and saw Dieter and Helga's delighted faces, I was immediately glad we had decided to come.

They were sitting in their usual spots at Dieter's homemade wooden table on the deck. A large wooden bowl overflowed with a mix of colourful eggs—both chocolate and hard-boiled. Nestled among them was a golden foil-wrapped chocolate bunny, creating an inviting Easter display. As we chatted about our latest family updates, Helga gave me a little nod to help myself.

I reached for a chocolate egg just as Dieter grabbed a hard-boiled one. He casually cracked it against his head and began peeling it. The unexpected act, combined with his deadpan expression, was so amusing that I couldn't stifle the chuckle that bubbled up within me in response.

As we caught up some more, Helga eventually glanced at her watch, then exclaimed, "Look at the time! Bruce and Joan invited us over for dinner. We've got to get going."

She put the eggs back inside, and they quickly got into their aluminum boat and puttered across the bay, leaving a wake of gentle ripples. George and I waved as we made our way back up to our cabin.

I was about to start preparing dinner when the phone rang. It was Joan, inviting us to join them. Touched by her thoughtfulness, I gladly accepted and went outside to let George know that our plans had changed.

We got into our aluminum boat, but for some reason, the motor wouldn't start. I called Joan back to apologize and express our disappointment. Just as I hung up, George spotted Dieter, already boating across to pick us up. We ran down to meet him at the dock.

Joan had gone all out. Not only did she have a turkey dinner with all the trimmings, but every corner of her cabin was adorned with festive decorations and cute bunnies. The table was beautifully set with candles, fresh tulips, pastel-coloured eggs, and cheerful springtime napkins. We ate, drank, and laughed late into the evening.

While helping clean up the dinner dishes, I thanked Joan profusely. "This was a really wonderful Easter."

Joan took the dish towel from me and smiled. "It's good to celebrate with neighbours, and you're part of our lake family now. Glad you could come."

On the boat ride back, George put his arm around me, and together we looked up at the bright, almost-full moon above.

"It's a good thing the moon is out so you can see where you're going," I called out to Dieter.

Over the steady hum of the boat's motor, he responded, "Wouldn't matter if it was pitch black. I could find my way home with my eyes closed."

I didn't doubt it.

I stepped out onto our deck with a pottery bowl full of freshly sliced strawberries. Our guests, Peter and his wife from England, were already seated at the brunch table, basking in the bright warmth of a typical July morning. Everyone eagerly helped themselves to the fruit and back bacon while I served the French Toast Raphael—a family-favourite, best enjoyed with a generous drizzle of pure maple syrup.

Laughter and conversation filled the air as we enjoyed our meal in the fresh outdoor breeze. I shared the story about the time Louisa, Peter's mom, and Joey visited the cabin before the renovations. Their smiles widened as I recounted the harrowing boat ride back.

The sun cast a golden glow over the lake, and we lingered at the table, savouring the last bites to the gentle chorus of birdsong.

A short while later, our guests reluctantly began to gather their belongings before heading down to the dock. They expressed heartfelt gratitude for the hospitality and the memorable stay. We exchanged hugs and well-wishes.

I untied the lines, pushed them off, and shouted my goodbyes as George manoeuvred the boat away. The water lapped against the hull, and I stood on the dock, waving, until the throttle increased, lifting the bow, and soon they were gliding into the distance toward the marina.

George would be back shortly after dropping them off. Usually, I would have used this time to clean up the dishes and tidy the cabin. Without thinking, I found myself walking left on the path—toward Dieter and Helga's cabin. As I topped the wooden steps to their deck, they smiled and pulled up a chair for me. It was barely one in the afternoon, but I couldn't help myself.

"Is it too early for sangria?"

Dieter rose without losing his grin and ducked into the cabin, the screen door slamming closed behind him. Exhausted from five days of entertaining guests, I adjusted the striped cushion and settled into their comfy deck chair. I angled the chair to maximize my view of the lake. Helga turned her body to gaze down the lake with me.

"Did your guests have a good time?"

"Yes, they loved it. We took them kayaking, ATVing, and boating to all our favourite places, including Rainbow Falls. They were so impressed. Neither of them had ever seen a waterfall in their lives!"

"Really?"

"I know, I couldn't believe it. Only in pictures, they said. They were blown away by all the natural beauty. When we kayaked around the bay, we saw bald eagles, geese, otters, ducks, and blue herons, all within half an hour."

Helga laughed. "Sometimes we forget how lucky we are."

"It's the best place on earth," I said, and I meant it.

Dieter came out with two large glasses of sangria.

"Does Dieter always make you drinks?" I asked Helga, then mouthed a thank you to Dieter.

She smiled. "I haven't poured my own drink in about fifteen years."

"Wow."

"He brings me flowers quite often too."

Just as I was thinking that George could learn a thing or two from Dieter, Helga said, "But it wasn't always like this."

"Oh?"

"There was a time when we got way too busy with work. It got so bad that I said to Dieter, 'I can't go on like this. Either we're taking a vacation or getting a divorce!'"

She saw the surprised look on my face and added, "And I wasn't joking. I was dead serious!"

Dieter chuckled and continued, "And I said, 'It's cheaper to travel than to get a divorce,' so I booked a trip to Costa Rica the very next day."

"And we've been travelling ever since," Helga concluded, giving Dieter a sweet smile as he went back into the cabin to get himself a beer.

I admired the older couple for finding a way to figure things out. I turned my attention to the drink in my hand. Like wind chimes in a gentle breeze, the ice cubes danced in the velvety red liquid.

Dieter returned, settling into his usual seat at the table. He raised his German lager, and said, "*Prost.*"

Helga clinked her glass to mine, shifting the conversation. "We haven't seen Mark up for a while."

"Maybe your cabin has been too full." Dieter laughed at his own joke, but he wasn't wrong. We had hosted dozens of people over the past month.

I smiled back. "Actually, Mark has a girlfriend."

Helga turned to search my face. "Really? What's her name?"

"Tausha." I gave Helga a reassuring glance. I knew they had a soft spot for my youngest. "She seems like a genuine, caring person. The two of them met on the Outtatown program, same as Tim and Sarah, and spent three months in South Africa together."

"Well," Helga nodded, "I'm happy for Mark."

"She came to the cabin with us at New Year's. They seem good together."

Just then, in typical Dieter fashion, he pulled out his high-powered binoculars and spied down the lake. "I see your hubby coming back. He should be here in eight minutes."

I spotted a black dot on the water just past the tip of the peninsula. To the naked eye, it could have been anything. The lake looked blue against the summer sky, but a hint of darker weather threatened on the far horizon, unusual for this time of year.

As George drew closer, the hum of the throttle easing down was my cue to head to the dock. I reached it just in time to catch the boat, and together we secured it before strolling back up to Dieter and Helga's deck. Dieter offered George a Holsten, one of his favourite German beers, which George gladly accepted.

A southerly wind began to whip up whitecaps while we finished our drinks. Dieter picked up his binoculars and fixed his gaze on the lake, then exclaimed, "Holy cow. I've never seen anything like this before."

The wind had suddenly intensified, causing the water to begin spraying up at least five feet in the air. We all sat there mesmerized as we watched the storm approach. By the time we got the deck chairs under cover, it had started to pour. George and I ran up the stone steps, laughing like children as the rain drenched us. We stripped off our wet clothes and wrapped ourselves in robes.

As I prepared a Mediterranean style linguine with shrimp and feta, George opened a bottle of wine. It was almost midnight by the time the storm subsided, its onslaught no longer audible on the cabin roof. I turned off the lights, ready for bed, but George was still looking out, silhouetted in the moonlight that spilled through the windows.

He spoke through the darkness. "It's not raining anymore. Let's go for a quick dip."

"Really?" I giggled, then headed to the laundry room to grab a few towels.

We walked in silence down to the water's edge. Droplets fell from the trees, splatting on stones below. In the distance, we heard the distinctive call of a barred owl. Its hoot filled the night air more frequently than that of any other type of owl, and it had become a comforting companion in the stillness of so many evenings at the lake. We placed our towels on a big rock and waded into the blackened depths.

The cool water was invigorating as we slowly swam around the dock. I listened to the haunting sounds of the owl, looked up at the stars and whispered, "This is total bliss."

"Might as well enjoy it now, because when we get home, we'll be in renovation mode again," George reminded me.

We had just moved into the one-bedroom suite above the garage of our Fort Langley home because the rest of the house was about to be gutted. George's plans included removing some interior walls and bumping out some exterior walls to create more space on the main floor. The idea was to make it the perfect gathering place, which made sense since we often hosted family events.

A part of me felt excited about the transformation, but another part couldn't ignore a lingering worry. We were expanding the house at a time when my heart was already leaning toward downsizing.

Although I wasn't comfortable with increasing our debt, the one positive outcome was that we were able to refinance with our bank, giving us enough funds to finally pay off what we still owed Dieter and Helga for the cabin. We didn't take no for an answer this time.

"It's nice to work with Erik Lacey and his crew again," George continued. "They did such a great job here."

Perched on the hill overlooking the bay, our cabin looked serene in the cloak of the crescent moon. "Just like this project," George said, "it will be a lot of hard work, but it will be worth it."

"Maybe," I murmured, gazing at the moon, "but nothing can beat this setting."

The following morning, I was watering my herb pots on the deck when a peculiar buzzing sound caught my attention. I peered over the edge to see where it was coming from and saw a little motorboat cruising around in the cove we shared with Dieter and Helga.

I spotted Dieter holding a remote control, his whole face lit up in a jolly expression. The small boat was zipping around in a circle, then in a figure eight, bouncing over the ripples it had made.

I marvelled at Dieter's ability to derive such pleasure from play—it made me laugh out loud. I couldn't imagine my father playing with a remote-control boat. The older adults in my world were more serious and didn't take part in "frivolous activities." But the pure joy on Dieter's face was priceless. I silently vowed that as I grew older, I too would allow myself the freedom to play.

In August, we celebrated Dieter's birthday on their deck. Helga made a beautiful Black Forest cake, and most of the neighbours stopped by. Some brought gifts or cards. Others stayed for a quick drink and a piece of cake. I wasn't surprised to see how many people came to show their appreciation of Dieter. He was very well loved in the bay.

I was still sipping my sangria after everyone had left. As usual, Helga pushed the bowl of pretzels my way before asking, "So what's new in that big family of yours?"

"We have some very exciting news. Tim and Sarah are expecting a baby, due next spring."

"Congratulations!" Helga and Dieter smiled broadly and raised their glasses in a toast.

"I'm going to be an *Opa*," George added proudly.

"That changes everything. You know why?" Dieter said, looking at George very seriously. "Now you're going to be sleeping with an *Oma*."

We all laughed.

I pivoted the conversation back to the birthday boy. "So, what was the highlight for you today?"

Dieter turned to Helga and said, "My wife gave me a kiss this morning. That was the best present."

Helga swatted his arm. "You get that every day."

Seeing their playful mood, I couldn't help but ask, "What's the secret to your happy marriage?"

Dieter smiled. "I always say, marry your best friend."

"And respect each other," Helga quickly added.

"Good advice," I affirmed.

In the quiet of the night, George and I slipped into the warmth of the hot tub. As usual, I initiated conversation.

"You know how Dieter said, 'Marry your best friend?'"

George was silent, so I hesitated, not knowing if I should continue my train of thought, but I persisted.

"Don't take this the wrong way... but I don't know if I would call you my best friend. I mean, I love you, but I think our relationship is a bit more... old-fashioned. Like we're stuck in traditional roles."

The silence stretched out for about a minute. Then he asked, sounding puzzled, "What do you mean?"

"I mean that we're a good team, and I'm totally committed to this marriage, but I don't feel like I can talk to you like I would talk to a best friend."

He gazed up at the sky. "Why not?"

"It's not that I can't share my thoughts and feelings with you, I do that all the time. It's that you don't share back, so it doesn't end up being a conversation. It's one-sided. It feels like you're so distant... especially when we're at home. Like you're physically there, but not fully present."

"If you're referring to my work," he said defensively, "you know how busy I am. That's what it takes to run a company and that's why we can afford a place like this."

"I know, I know. I appreciate everything you do. I'm not complaining. It's not necessarily a negative thing. I just wish we could talk about it and acknowledge that we're very different that way."

Silence.

My voice was tinged with concern as I tried to clarify. "We've been married almost thirty years. This feels like a pivotal time in our relationship. I don't want to keep waiting and hoping for a deeper level of connection if it's not going to happen."

"So... should we start our date nights again?"

I knew his love was genuine, so I found it hard to explain. "Even when we go out on a date, it feels like I'm talking to a business partner. You're very good at small talk and sharing thoughts about projects you're working on."

"Give me an example."

"Even the other night, during our magical midnight dip in the lake, we spent most of the time talking about the house renovation. I don't mean this as criticism—I just wish you'd share more about what's in your heart."

His agitated response came swiftly now. "I am who I am, but that doesn't seem good enough for you."

"That's not true." I felt bad seeing him get defensive. This wasn't the conversation I had hoped for.

He looked me in the eye and said, "I think your expectations are too high."

"Maybe they are..." My voice trailed off as I paused to think, feeling tired. My frustration about this had come up so often over the decades, I knew something needed to change. But I also knew I had to choose my words carefully to avoid escalating the situation.

Suddenly, two words emerged in my thoughts, almost as if they had been whispered to me. *Lass ihm.* Just let him be who he is.

I reminded myself that it was unrealistic to expect one person to meet all your needs in a relationship. I was grateful to have female friends I could talk to, friends who echoed my desire to be understood. Despite my yearning to have more of that in my marriage, I could feel myself choosing instead to appreciate all the aspects of his character that made him endearing.

I boldly stated, "From now on, I'm not going to have any more expectations."

"What do you mean?" He looked at me in bewilderment.

"I mean, I'm releasing myself from having expectations," I gazed into his eyes with genuine tenderness. "I want you to know that I accept you just the way you are, and I continue to choose you as my life partner. At the same time, I realize that loving you doesn't mean I have to lose myself."

Silence. Then, "I don't get it."

"I know! That's the problem!" I snickered, splashing some water at him. "You don't get it."

He splashed me back, and soon we were laughing.

George pulled me into a hug.

Still smiling, I tried to make my point so he would understand. "I want us to walk through life side by side, supporting each other as we grow—not just as a couple, but as individuals too."

In that moment of clarity, I realized I had held George to a different standard than anyone else in my life. I could accept others as they were, without expecting them to change—but with George, that acceptance didn't come as easily.

To truly see him with fresh eyes, I needed to shift my perspective. Instead of seeing him through the lens of what I thought a husband *should* be, I needed to see him simply as my closest neighbour—someone who just happened to live one pillow over.

Even when it felt like an invisible, unintentional fence stood between us, I knew I had to respect those boundaries—just as good neighbours do. What mattered most wasn't erasing the differences between us but cherishing the love and respect that bound us together despite them.

A sense of freedom washed over me. Then it hit me. Maybe this was another dimension of what it meant to *just be*.

Chapter Forty-Four

Dieter popped the cork and poured champagne into four long-stemmed glasses.

"To the next generation," he declared, holding up his glass.

"Here's to being an Oma and Opa," Helga said, completing the toast. Then she grilled me for details about Levi, our first grandchild.

"Spring is a nice season to bring a baby into the world," she said.

"Holding him for the first time brought tears to my eyes." I beamed. "It feels like I was just holding Tim as a baby, and now I'm holding his son! It's amazing!"

We chatted some more, finished our champagne, then George said, "Well, I'm going to head back up. I need to do an oil change on my generator."

For a second, I hesitated and thought about going too, but when Dieter replaced my empty champagne glass with sangria, I gladly stayed. It seemed as if I spent as much time on their deck as I did on ours. I toppled the orange slice in and took a sip. There was nothing like it.

Dieter settled into his chair slowly, and I could tell that Helga was watching him. A heavy silence hung between the couple. Suddenly, the atmosphere had shifted, taking on a more sombre tone. Their eyes, usually vibrant with laughter, now held a quiet sadness.

"Is something wrong?" I looked back and forth between the two of them.

Helga addressed my questioning look. "We had a lousy week this week."

Dieter's eyes grew glossy as the silence stretched out between us. Finally, he uttered the words that I wasn't ready to hear. "I just found out I have prostate cancer."

My throat caught. I couldn't speak. I could feel tears sliding down my cheeks, and the air pressed heavily around me. Helga started talking about next steps and treatments, but her words were distant, as though I were hearing them through a thick fog.

Eventually, I finished my drink, set the glass down and rose to my feet. Stepping toward Dieter, I wrapped him in a warm, firm hug, holding on just a little longer than usual.

I walked up to our cabin to find George. As soon as he saw the expression on my face, he pulled me into a comforting embrace. "What happened?"

I shared the news, my words blubbering through tears. "Dieter's one of those larger-than-life people. I guess I don't want to believe he's got cancer."

"It doesn't mean he's going to die. I've heard that prostate cancer is quite common in older men, and they've come a long way in treating it."

"I hope so." I couldn't help but think about Liz, and hoped Dieter would be spared the relentless cycles of chemo and radiation.

That evening, the sky was dark and crystal clear—ideal for our pre-bedtime soak in the hot tub. I was still reeling from the news of the day as I slipped into the water, but lying back under the stars and watching the satellites glide smoothly across the sky helped me to relax. I let out a deep breath.

"Every day is such a gift, yet we often take our health for granted—until something, or someone, reminds us just how precious life really is."

George moved closer and simply said, "So true."

In the quiet that followed, filled with mutual understanding, words became unnecessary.

Under a radiant sun, the day unfolded like a springtime masterpiece. Our two-week old grandson, Levi, came to the lake for the very first time. I reclined in the shade of a tree, swaying gently in our hammock, with Levi's little face snuggled against my shoulder. I loved the delicate aroma of a newborn baby and the feeling of holding him close as he slept.

I thought back on the events of the past week. Our family was growing quickly. Mark had surprised Tausha with a romantic marriage proposal by the river in Fort Langley. He did it on his twenty-first birthday so she wouldn't suspect anything. When they arrived back to our house that night, they walked into a surprise gathering of both her family and ours, all there to celebrate the engagement. Over desserts and drinks, Mark and Tausha shared their intention to wait until the following spring to have their wedding.

Levi squirmed slightly, and I changed his position, cradling him in my arms while humming a gentle lullaby. He was so cute, wrapped snugly in a soft, pastel-coloured blanket. I gazed down at his tiny face with a mixture of awe and tenderness, my heart swelling with an indescribable love. What a privilege it was to be a grandmother.

Slowly, my thoughts drifted again, this time to the upcoming responsibilities of the workday we had planned for next weekend.

There was plenty we needed to clean up, and the woodshed needed to be replenished. I was contemplating the menu for the event—envisioning the grocery list—when I interrupted my train of thought, opting instead to savour the present moment just a bit longer.

Holding Levi in my arms felt like the beginning of a new chapter, one filled with the joy of watching a new life unfold. I stared at him with a blend of pride, nostalgia, and the purest form of happiness. At the same time, thoughts of Dieter's diagnosis lingered in my mind like a gentle reminder of life's fragile balance.

Chapter Forty-Five

The very next morning, while I prepared breakfast, I was startled by the sight of a black bear outside my kitchen window. It had a yellow tag on its ear, just like the neighbours had described at the campfire last week. Rising on his hind legs to the height of at least six feet, the bear extended its heavy paws and swiped at the empty bird feeder, making it sway. Then he lowered himself, sniffed at the hammock, and eventually meandered away in search of better treasures.

At sangria time, I told Dieter about the bear.

"It was right there! I know they're usually harmless, but to think I was in the hammock with Levi less than twenty-four hours earlier!"

Dieter nodded. "Unfortunately, that bear is becoming a nuisance. It got into Mike's cabin," he pointed across the bay, "while they were out visiting. When they got back, the bear was sitting on their kitchen counter, eating peanut butter."

I laughed, picturing it. "That's a bit scary. What did they do?"

"They had to carefully chase him out."

Helga added, "The bear tried to get into John and Donna's cabin too. Scratched a hole in their screen door with its big paw."

Helga and I continued our conversation while Dieter and George started talking about plans for the new road. When Dieter pulled out a map, I got up to learn more about the latest developments.

"The logger's road ends here." He pointed. "We would need to hire some road builders to continue the road another eight hundred metres, along the back of everyone's cabins, and then we would all have road access." Dieter had already walked the route several times with an experienced surveyor who knew the region well.

"Makes total sense," George confirmed.

We needed to apply for a road licence with the Ministry of Forests, so George had helped to form an association with the twelve cabin owners on our side of the bay. Everyone was excited about making this road a reality, and everything was slowly falling into place.

The following evening, George invited a few of the neighbours to come over and watch the hockey game. Helga came up to be part of the fun, but I chose to go down and join Dieter at his campfire.

In the profound stillness of the evening, the bay lay motionless, reflecting the night sky like a polished mirror. I inched my chair a little closer, drawn to the warmth and glow of the crackling fire.

Dieter poured me a glass of his homemade wine, the rich aroma mingling with the scent of burning wood. As he sat back, he updated me about the bear.

"I contacted BC Wildlife, and they came right away to set up traps down the old logging road. It didn't take long before they caught it. They've already taken it up north, deep into the wilderness."

"That's a relief."

After that, we sat in silence, both of us relishing the peace and quiet. Every so often, a resounding cheer echoed from the cabin up the hill, and Dieter would say, "Canucks must have scored."

As the evening wore on, every moment felt suspended in the hushed stillness of twilight. Our conversation flowed easily, weaving between lighthearted stories and quiet reflections.

Without a sound, a magnificent owl swept down from the darkness, landing effortlessly on Dieter's flagpole right before our eyes. It radiated an air of majesty, its piercing gaze and ear-like tufts of feathers on its head giving it a regal presence.

Dieter whispered, "It's a great horned owl."

I had only seen pictures and was utterly captivated. "It's bigger than I imagined," I whispered.

Time froze as we watched the owl stare at us with intense yellow eyes. Then, just as silently as it had come, the owl flew off into the night. I gasped at its broad wingspan as it soared overhead.

"Wow!"

Dieter agreed quietly. "I would rather be watching this instead of TV any day."

"Me too," I whispered back.

Dieter added some more wood to the dwindling flames. I loved the peaceful stillness, where even the softest crackle of firewood felt like a whisper echoing across time. Gently nudging the logs in the fire, he took care to avoid sparking coals toward my sandalled feet. When he was done, he turned his attention to me, sincerity thick in his voice.

"I know I've said it before, but I am so glad you bought the cabin. I knew the first day we met that you were the right people. No ifs, ands, or buts."

"It's the best decision we ever made," I said, and I meant it. "Being here has changed our lives, and we couldn't have done it without you."

I blinked back my tears just as the hockey fans descended on our fire. Judging by the mood, I doubted that the Canucks had won.

Confirming my assumption, Donna broke into a rant about what the players had done wrong, disgusted that they had lost in overtime. Even Helga was frustrated, going on about the fact that they had been at the top of their division up to that point, and now they wouldn't even be in the playoffs.

Dieter and I exchanged a meaningful glance, a silent understanding between us. Every experience had its time and place, but tonight I felt deeply grateful to share the unforgettable, awe-inspiring sight of an owl with Dieter.

Chapter Forty-Six

I enjoyed hand washing the dishes at the lake. With a view of the water from my kitchen window and the sight of birds visiting our feeder hanging from a nearby branch, it didn't feel like a chore at all. Living off-grid and not having conveniences like dishwashers wasn't a drawback to me. Instead, it offered tranquil moments to let my mind wander freely.

I reflected on the news I'd received from my doctor the day before. I had finally gotten a biopsy done on an itchy red spot on my thigh that had been bothering me for some time. It was a form of cancer, the doctor said, basal cell carcinoma. He told me it wasn't life-threatening, but it was still cancer, and I would probably get more spots like these in the future. I had made an appointment to have it removed in November.

George was relieved that it wasn't worse news. Still, we agreed that the word *cancer* has a way of instantly shifting one's perspective on life. For me, it reinforced the importance of seizing every opportunity, embracing anything that could enrich my life, encourage growth, or inspire positive change.

I finished drying the last few cups and placed them in the cupboard. After wiping the countertop clean, I pulled the garbage bag out from under the sink. We were getting ready to leave, but there was no need to winterize yet, since the boys would be taking turns coming up on the weekends while we were away.

George and I had planned a trip to Turkey for September, our first major adventure without the boys. We were ready to start exploring some of the destinations we'd long dreamed about.

I put on my shoes and went down to spend some time with Dieter and Helga.

"Are you winterizing your cabin soon?" I asked.

"Not quite yet. We'll be staying for a bit longer to make food for the road builders," Helga said. "They'll be staying at John and Donna's, but we promised to help feed them."

Dieter got up slowly. "They'll get more done if they don't have to drive back and forth on the logging road every day." He went inside.

"That makes sense," I replied to Helga.

"We'll be here at least until after Thanksgiving," she added. "Then we'll close it up, and it can be your turn to feed them when you get back from your trip."

"George will be back after three weeks, but I'm meeting my cousin Rita in Rome. She's always wanted to explore Italy, so we decided to travel together for a whole month. When I come home, she'll spend another month in Crete, alone."

Dieter reemerged handing me a sangria and casually asked, "Why Crete?"

"Thanks, Dieter." I took a sip before answering. "It's warm and affordable at that time of year. And it's her forty-ninth birthday. She's planning to make her whole fiftieth year extra special."

"I see. And George is okay with you spending a month away in Italy?" Helga smiled knowingly.

"Well, I wouldn't say he's happy about it, but he's had eight months to get used to the idea. After three weeks in Turkey, I'm sure he'll be so swamped at work, he won't even notice. The boys are all men now, so he has nobody to look after but himself. The freezer will be full of food, and I think it will be good for him."

"I'm sure he'll be fine," she nodded.

"My mom thinks I'm crazy. She said my dad would never have allowed such a thing. The thought of me 'gallivanting' around Italy while poor George has to go back to work is totally absurd to her. She told me that George was being too good to me by *letting* me go."

"And how did you respond?" Dieter asked with a curious smile.

"I simply told her that times have changed."

Helga laughed. "Yes, times *have* changed."

"On another topic," I hesitated for a moment, then took on a more serious tone. "I had a doctor's appointment this week and it looks like I'm joining the cancer club."

"What?" Dieter looked at me with concern.

"I have a type of skin cancer—but not the life-threatening kind—it's basal cell carcinoma."

Helga didn't usually hug people, so when she came over and wrapped her arms around me, it caught me off guard and brought tears to my eyes. Like my parents, she was usually reserved in showing physical affection, no matter how deep the emotional bond. Her kindness and concern deeply touched me.

"Everything will be okay," she said. "Enjoy your trip and don't worry about anything."

"Have a good time," Dieter said. His hug was so comforting, like the embrace of a big, cuddly teddy bear. "And don't do anything I wouldn't do."

Chapter Forty-Seven

Back from our trip and with the Christmas season around the corner, George and I hosted the road builders at our cabin on several occasions. They were working on clearing a road, their machinery cutting through dense forest and rugged hillsides. Each tree felled and hill levelled marked another step closer to connecting us to the existing logging road that zigzagged its way up the side of the mountain and then meandered along until it eventually connected to the town of Harrison Hot Springs.

Early in the new year they began constructing driveways to each cabin.

"Hey, I'm hosting the road builders up at the lake this week. Are you busy?" I asked my cousin Rita over the phone. "Do you want to come help me cook for them? They're funny guys."

I heard her immediate enthusiasm through the phone. "Of course! I'd love to. We haven't had much time to talk since I came back from Crete!"

After securing the boat, we hauled up a cooler and a few bags of groceries. I could hear the excavator rumbling nearby as it dug into the earth, accentuated by the occasional loud clang when the bucket hit a large rock. They were working on a driveway a few properties down from ours.

Putting the groceries away, I turned to Rita and said, "I'm not sure if it's my turn to have them over tonight or if the other neighbours are feeding them dinner. I'll go check."

I made my way over a rocky hill just as the workers turned off the machinery. "I'm making pistachio-crusted salmon for dinner tonight. Are you planning on coming to my place this evening?"

Without hesitation, Norm grinned and replied, "You had me at pistachio!"

Our evening dinner conversation that night was hilarious. I hadn't laughed so much in a long time, and Rita fit right in with her quick wit.

The next morning, the men helped themselves to toast and coffee before they headed out. Other than bringing them sandwiches and coffee at lunch, Rita and I had the whole day to ourselves.

I opened the creaky door of the wood stove, releasing a burst of heat and the rich scent of burning cedar. Carefully, I placed a few more logs onto the embers, watching as the flames eagerly consumed the new fuel.

We sat facing each other in the sunroom, where the huge windows overlooked the lake. I poured steaming mugs of tea as Rita stretched her legs out on the ottoman and launched into memories of our trip.

"I'm glad I saw all the sights in Rome, and of course Michelangelo's *David* in Florence, since it was my first time in Italy, but I liked the smaller towns like Orvieto and Assisi. It felt like we were stepping back in time."

"I agree. Although I have to say, the best gelato we had was at that little shop across from the Spanish Steps in Rome."

"Oh yeah, that's when *bacio* became our favourite flavour!" Rita closed her eyes for a moment as if savouring a scoop of the delicious chocolate-hazelnut combination in her memory. "We ate gelato every afternoon. I'm surprised I ended up losing weight on that trip!"

"Walking up and down all those winding stairs and narrow roads in Positano was a full workout in itself," I reminded her as I laughed. "That's what I loved most-—just wandering around, happening upon things."

Rita's voice softened as she looked out the window of the cabin. "It was so peaceful in Positano, looking out over the endless sea. It felt like a holiday within the holiday. I know I thanked you many times during our trip, but thanks again for planning the whole thing, Anne. You taught me how to travel well—spending four or five days in each place to really experience its charm. By the time we left each town, even the staff at the local coffee shop greeted me like an old friend."

"It did work out well," I smiled, glad that Rita had enjoyed herself so much.

"My favourite memories will always be the conversations we shared. We could have been anywhere, but I have no doubt the beauty and history of Italy infused our talks about life and our hopes for the future." She took another sip of tea, then continued. "Remember that picture I took of you, leaning over that stone wall, peering out at the ocean? Let me find it." Rita quickly pulled up the photo on her phone and passed it over to me.

I studied the image. In it, my gaze was fixed on the shimmering expanse of water, my expression a blend of longing and contemplation, as if drawn by an irresistible pull to the ocean's mysterious depths.

"I can't remember what I was thinking, but I'll never forget that feeling."

"That picture," she said, "reminds me of that story you shared with me from the book you were reading at the time."

I knew immediately what she was referring to. "The one about the selkie."

"Yeah! How does it go again?" She settled back into her chair, draping her hand-dyed Italian scarf elegantly around her shoulders, ready for the story.

"It's a Celtic myth about a seal that sheds her skin and becomes a woman. One night, she's dancing in the moonlight and a farmer sees her and instantly falls in love with her. He steals her sealskin so she can't return to the ocean, but he promises her that if she marries him, he'll give the sealskin back."

"After seven years, right?" I liked the way Rita lit up over the details.

"Right. Then they have a son, and she gets pulled into domestic life, getting weaker and more lifeless as the years go by. Her deep longing for the water gets stronger and stronger. When seven years have passed, the farmer claims he doesn't know where the sealskin is. Life goes on—years pass until her son finds it hidden in a box in the basement. Because he's worried about his mother's health, he brings it to her."

"That part intrigues me, that her son was more in touch with her well-being than her husband!"

I nodded and continued. "And then—I love this part, the way it was worded in the book—she puts on the sealskin, and while part of her truly wants to stay with her son, something calls her, something older than she, older than time. She dives into the water, and then she's free. She is home."

"That story gives me chills. In this picture, you're looking at the water with that same look, like you long to be free."

I peered at the photo once more, understanding what Rita meant. "I can relate to that feeling of longing for something more than domestic life, for sure. I mean, I'm so grateful for everything I have—a devoted husband, amazing children, and now the privilege of being a grandmother. I wouldn't trade it for anything. And yet... there's this yearning inside. It feels like I'm finally reconnecting with a part of myself that I've kept suppressed for a long time."

I picked up the teapot and refilled our cups. "That trip felt like a real turning point—it gave me a sense of confidence."

"Makes complete sense to me," Rita replied in a knowing voice. "You were able to do something independently for the first time in how many years?"

"Exactly. It was totally different from going on a vacation with George, going on a yoga retreat, or visiting Louisa. Those were all great experiences, but..."

"But you were able to see, think, and feel exactly what you wanted without having to worry about juggling anyone else's opinions or needs." Rita's gaze met mine, and a soft shimmer filled her eyes. "It was an unforgettable gift to travel with you. I don't think we had a single disagreement that whole time. That's gotta be pretty rare."

"I know. It felt effortless." I wiped a tear from my cheek. "I'm so glad we had a whole month. Being away from the usual routines, exploring new places, and having so many meaningful conversations gave me a whole new perspective."

Rita inhaled a long breath and nodded, her eyes blinking back tears. "My month alone in Crete after you flew home was such an important time for me to figure out this next season of my life as well."

After more than twenty years of marriage and a few shorter relationships following her divorce, Rita was recently single again, rediscovering her own authentic self. She exuded a vibrant joy and a contagious energy.

"It felt like a total reset." She lingered for a moment, allowing her next thought to form. "We know what long-term marriage is like, a blend of joy and challenges. Over time, it gets harder to stay in tune with yourself when your attention is constantly centred on someone else."

I paused to reflect. "It reminds me of the verse we grew up with: 'Love your neighbour as yourself.' The emphasis always seemed to be on loving your neighbour—sometimes at the expense of taking care of ourselves—because that would be selfish."

Rita nodded in agreement. "Exactly. We were basically taught to give everything to others and forgot that loving ourselves is part of it too."

"I think it's about balance," I replied. "We need to show kindness and compassion to others, but it has to come from a place of wholeness and healthy boundaries. Otherwise, we just burn ourselves out."

"That's what I focused on in Crete." Rita's face radiated contentment as she spoke, "I worked through a lot of things, and gradually learned to be kinder to myself—especially in how I speak to myself and respond to my own thoughts."

I smiled. "When we nurture ourselves, we naturally have more to give to others, which makes us better neighbours in every sense."

In early March, as the rainy days grew further apart, Norm and Dave came back to carve out our driveway. They skillfully moved rock and soil, connecting the road to our home. Every time I wandered out to the back of the cabin, the men waved from atop their machinery.

As I approached, Norm shut off his excavator and hopped down to greet me.

"Hey Anne, how's the fam?"

"Great. Levi started walking this week!"

He smiled and the lines by his eyes creased deep. "He'll be runnin' in no time."

Dave joined us just as I pitched my idea. "If you come across any good straight logs, let us know. We're thinking of building a swing set over there." I pointed to a spot on the hill not far from the woodshed.

Dave nodded. "I'm sure we can find something."

"We can even help you build it!" Norm added.

Both men seemed excited about the project.

Less than two weeks later, three beautiful cedar logs were lying on one end of our new driveway.

"Wow! Those are massive!" I had imagined a much smaller swing set. "Where did you get them?"

Dave said, "We dragged them over from Vern's property across the bay."

I could tell they were pleased at my reaction.

"They were just lying there," Dave continued, "Vern said he didn't have any plans for them, so they probably would've just rotted or been burned."

"That's incredible." I ran my hand along the edge of one of them. "They're perfect."

The men went right to work stripping the bark off the cedar logs. Using the excavator, they dug deep holes and, with ropes and chains, skilfully manoeuvred the heavy logs into place. With precision, they cut the ends of the crosspiece with a chainsaw. Watching the excavator effortlessly place it on the top was nothing short of artistry.

The next day, they secured the top with huge bolts, attached hooks and chains, and used the extra wood to craft two seats. Once the seats were tied to the chains, the swing set was complete—and it exceeded all my expectations.

I was getting ready to take a picture to send to George when Norm and Dave scrambled onto the seats and, leaning back, started energetically pumping their legs. I laughed at these grown men swinging back and forth, their boyish faces gleeful. In a moment of playfulness, they reached out to grasp each other's hands while swinging, and I snapped a few pictures.

Throughout the spring, we hired Norm and Dave to finish a handful of other projects for us as well—a new septic tank, a massive firepit in our new yard area, and a rock retaining wall between our place and Dieter's. After countless backyard chats and shared meals, we had developed a comfortable friendship. When Norm asked if I wanted to try operating his excavator, I jumped at the opportunity.

I felt a mix of nerves and excitement as I climbed into the operator's seat of the massive machine. When the engine roared to life, I couldn't suppress my grin. Norm gave me some quick instructions, and then, with determination, I grasped the controls, feeling the power of the excavator beneath my fingertips. It took a few minutes to get the hang of it, but digging, lifting, and moving earth gave me an exhilarating thrill. I felt like a child playing with a new toy, awed by the sheer strength of the machine at my command.

One evening, George and I took a walk down the freshly laid gravel road. Its intrusion into the once-pristine forest felt a bit unsettling at first. Memories of navigating the narrow deer path that once meandered through dense foliage were now replaced by a view of a wide road that exposed the sky above.

While the transformation brought a pang of sadness, the convenience of having a proper road to our cabin—and the ease it afforded our children in visiting independently—outweighed the melancholy. No longer did we have to worry about weather conditions hindering our journey or taking our boat through a crazy storm to get home. It was a gentle reminder that every ending paves the way for a new beginning.

Chapter Forty-Eight

Dieter and Helga finally returned from their travels, and it felt good to reconnect. Gathered once more around the flickering flames of their campfire, we exchanged stories of our adventures.

Dieter enthusiastically recounted his recent sailing experience in Croatia. He described the thrill of navigating the Adriatic Sea, discovering rugged cliffs, and finding hidden coves that took his breath away.

Helga, who had chosen to stay with her sister in Germany, mentioned how Dieter seemed to be doing very well, living much the same as he had before his battle with cancer began.

George shared about our favourite highlights in Turkey, describing how we floated over the amazing rock formations of Cappadocia in a hot air balloon, and how much we admired the Blue Mosque in Istanbul.

I described the surreal thermal waters of Pamukkale, where aqua-blue pools cascaded down a white mountainside. I also shared how we visited the ancient ruins of Ephesus and saw a backgammon board carved into a marble sidewalk—dating back over two thousand years. It inspired us to learn the game ourselves.

When Helga asked about my month in Italy, I could tell George felt uncomfortable even before I could respond. His body tensed slightly, and he avoided eye contact. Trying to keep things light, I simply said it was great without offering any details.

After I returned from that trip, George admitted that it had been a difficult time for him. However, instead of talking about it, he buried himself in work. I could sense that an unspoken resentment was still simmering beneath the surface.

Later that evening, hoping to bring some closure to the topic, I waited until we were in the warmth of the hot tub, gazing at the night sky. It was where he seemed the most at ease, so I gently prompted him.

"I noticed you looked uncomfortable earlier when Helga mentioned Italy."

"I don't really want to talk about it."

"I think it's important for me to understand how you felt during that time."

His usual composure faltered before he finally voiced his frustration. "I felt lost," he said, "and lonely."

"But we talked almost every day through email or FaceTime."

"I know, but being in the house without you there didn't feel right."

"You know I love you, and extending that trip was never meant to hurt you." I looked him straight in the eyes and waited, making sure he was ready to hear me. "You know what became clear to me during that trip?"

"What?"

"Now that the boys are all grown up... I don't want to be in that role of a traditional Mennonite wife tending to your every need. I want us to be equal partners—I don't want to be like a mother to you."

There was a heavy stillness before he finally responded. "I know... I've been depending on you a lot, and I think I get it now—I've been taking you for granted."

I smiled, "To me, it feels like part of you woke up while I was away. You even surprised me with a love poem. But I can't help feeling like there's still something bothering you."

He hesitated again. "It was just so much harder than I thought it would be. I didn't function well while you were gone." His voice was barely above a whisper. "But I feel like I appreciate you now more than ever. And I don't want to take you for granted anymore."

George rarely expressed any emotions, so I was grateful he was finally starting to open up. Sincerity infused his words. "I know that I've only been able to get this far with the business because you managed everything and everyone at home all these years."

I reached for his hand, our fingers intertwining in a silent gesture of affection. In that moment, embraced by the stillness of the night, George's vulnerability made me feel closer to him.

Sensing the weight of his feelings, I tried to lighten the mood. "I don't want to take you for granted either. By pursuing your passion for work, you're giving me the opportunity to pursue one of my greatest passions—travelling."

He smiled. "Hopefully, we'll be doing a lot more of that together in the future."

"I would like that. And I promise I won't go away for a month again." I gave him a mischievous look and teased, "A week or two maybe, but not a whole month."

As he wrapped his arms around me, I knew that something had shifted in our relationship. There was a new-found appreciation kindling between us—a renewed sense of gratitude for our shared bond of love.

At the end of July, on one especially calm evening, I took my shepherd's harp down to the dock. George followed, carrying one of the chairs from the firepit. As I began to softly pluck the strings, a subtle vibration ran through my fingertips, drawing me into a quiet, timeless space where only the music existed.

The melodic notes echoed over the water as the sky turned from yellow to a warm orange, then transformed into a soft pink before deepening into a rich red. Neighbours gathered to listen. I heard clapping at the end of each song.

When it got too dark to see the strings, I carried my harp back up the ramp. Helga's brother, Franz, came over, his smile radiating sincerity as he greeted me warmly.

"I just wanted to say thank you," he said. "You touched our hearts and our souls with your music."

"I'm glad you enjoyed it," I said, as we went our separate ways.

Like a gentle breeze on a warm day, a quiet satisfaction washed over me as I walked up the stone path.

As the summer wore on, most of our projects had been completed and no more guests were expected to arrive. Dieter and Helga popped open a bottle of Prosecco to celebrate the end of summer. We lifted our slender, long-stemmed glasses and toasted.

"To the end of another season," Helga announced.

We sat on their concrete patio by the water's edge, sipping our drinks and watching the calm lake shimmer under the gentle haze of late summer light.

I could tell Dieter was feeling content when he used his classic line "Yeah, it's a tough life, but somebody's got to do it."

"It was nice to see your parents up on the weekend," Helga commented.

I chuckled, "It took me a while to convince them to come. They were always eager when there was a lot of work to do, but they didn't want to come just to relax."

George added, "Anne's mom never relaxes. She brought a cooler full of food for the weekend so that Anne wouldn't have to do any cooking."

Dieter smiled. "That must have been a real treat for you."

"It was wonderful. But she goes overboard in not wanting to be a burden. She brought her own sheets and towels so I wouldn't have to do any laundry because of them."

Dieter and Helga started laughing, but I wasn't finished yet. "Then, while I was out kayaking with my dad, she washed all the windows and floors."

Helga shook her head. "She's probably been a hard worker her whole life."

"That's for sure."

"And how did your dad like kayaking?" Dieter asked.

"I was surprised that he agreed to try it. He's eighty-four and has never done anything like that in his life. He admitted that he really enjoyed it."

Helga smiled. "I like your parents."

"The night before they left, I played my harp for them on our deck. One of my mom's favourite songs is 'Edelweiss.'" I looked over at Helga, knowing she liked it too.

"I thought I heard you playing that night," Dieter said.

We finished our Prosecco as the sun was setting.

As George and I walked back up to our cabin, I shared the real highlight of my weekend.

"I didn't want to bring it up earlier because I thought I might start crying, but when my dad and I were down at the dock, and you were getting the boat ready to take my parents back to the marina..."

"Yeah?" George prompted, positioning our deck chairs to face the lake.

"My dad turned to me and said, '*Du tust hier eine gute Mission.*' It was the way he said it, with affirmation, like he was proud of me."

"What did he mean, 'you're doing a good mission here'?"

"I think he understands the dedication and hard work it takes to host people," I said, "and sees the deeper purpose of not only creating lasting memories for our family but sharing this remote space with others."

My parents had always been generous with their time and their money, but praise had been rare during my upbringing. I assumed it was because they aimed to keep us from becoming conceited or boastful.

"I never imagined that even in my fifties, the opinion of my parents would still be so important to me." I could feel the emotions welling up inside and brushed away a tear. "For my dad to tell me that I'm doing meaningful work meant a lot to me. It felt like a genuine blessing."

I wondered then if George and I were praising our own children enough, or if we were simply passing down the emphasis on humility. I made a mental note to start voicing the positive qualities I saw in our boys rather than just noticing them silently.

George took my hand in his. We sat together, silently observing a group of turkey vultures gracefully gliding through the sky.

"All is well," I said aloud, feeling my body relax. I was embracing the best qualities passed down from my parents, allowing them to harmonize with the intentional changes I was making for myself. As I took a deep, cleansing breath, I felt the powerful connection of these generational threads—the legacy they carried and the clarity they brought to my life.

Chapter Forty-Nine

Rita and I shared a connection that went beyond mere cousinhood and friendship. Our grandmothers had been twins, binding us together with a familial bond that ran deep. It was as if our souls were attuned to the same frequency, making travelling together effortless and enjoyable. Our trip to Italy had solidified our decision to make annual excursions a tradition, a pact to explore new destinations and immerse ourselves in the joy of discovery even if just for a few precious days each year.

I usually looked for the most affordable deal I could find for a spontaneous getaway, mostly through my timeshare resources. There were always last-minute opportunities during the off-season, and finding a good deal somehow made it easier to justify going. For us, the destination didn't really matter. It was more about the adventure and the time we spent together. After all, beauty could be found anywhere.

In November, we found ourselves in Arizona on an exceptionally hot day. Even though neither of us cared much for shopping, we decided to go to the mall in Scottsdale to escape into the cool air conditioning.

"I could use a new dress," I said to Rita as we stepped into Nordstrom. "Maybe something I could wear to one of George's business events or the company Christmas party—something not too fancy but still sophisticated."

We slowly browsed through the racks. Suddenly, I noticed a knee-length dress in vibrant shades of blue and white, accented by a bold red banner that ran from top to bottom, resembling a giant Spanish fan. I wasn't sure why it had caught my eye—certainly not for its potential to be worn to a business dinner. The material felt like a wetsuit, yet the dress had a simple, elegant cut. I wouldn't normally wear something that colourful, but for some reason, I couldn't put it back on the rack.

Rita glanced over and saw me looking at it. "You should try it on," she said, intuitively sensing I needed her nudge.

Perhaps it was because I was in a different place, or maybe because we had a lot of time, but I decided to humour her. When I stepped out of the change room, I gave a little spin. The dress hugged my body, accentuating every curve and contour.

"Oh, Anne," Rita gasped, "it's your sealskin."

Surprising myself, I bought the dress, with an idea already brewing in my mind.

My friend and I had signed up for another Costa Rica yoga retreat in January. Since George was deeply immersed in a critical phase of a work project, he couldn't join me this time. So, Abby and I decided to extend our stay by a week to celebrate my fifty-fifth birthday.

I shared my idea for the dress with Abby over a cup of tea. "I feel like it's important to acknowledge the shift that's unfolding in my life, and the ocean seems like the perfect place to do it. I'm calling it Freedom fifty-five."

She chuckled, "Like that '80s insurance ad about early retirement?"

"It's definitely not about financial freedom," I smiled, "George and I are still far from that. This is about inner freedom, a new chapter in my life."

"I think it's a great idea. I'll bring my camera so I can capture the moment!"

On my birthday, I slipped into my sealskin dress and strolled toward a secluded corner of Playa Samara in Costa Rica. The wide, crescent-shaped beach stretched invitingly before me, each step on the hot sand drawing me closer to its beckoning shoreline.

As I reached the water's edge, the cool, damp sand offered soothing comfort to my feet. The rhythmic sound of the waves steadied my breath, aligning it with the ocean's pulse.

The water lapped at my ankles, then crept up to my calves as I waded in deeper. I paused when it reached my knees, welcoming the sea's invigorating touch against my skin. A soft laugh escaped me, carried away by the gentle breeze.

With my senses awakened, my thoughts quieted, letting my body take the lead. The gentle yet persistent tug of the water invited me further in, its refreshing embrace a perfect contrast to the blazing sun overhead.

I stood waist-deep, immersed in the endless expanse of the sea, lifting slightly with each larger wave that rolled in. The water cradled my body, buoying me up, as my dress hugged me tightly like a second skin. Soon only my head remained above the surface. Closing my eyes, I took a deep breath and submerged myself beneath the waves.

In my underwater sanctuary, all distractions faded away. I was weightless. A serene silence replaced all sound around me. In that moment, I was totally free, suspended in a tranquil world where time seemed to stand still.

When I surfaced for air, I turned my face toward the sun's warmth and floated effortlessly. Tears began to stream from my eyes, blending with the salty ocean water already on my skin. I drifted there, enveloped in contentment and calm peace.

Eventually, I felt a subtle shift, a quiet certainty that my symbolic act was now complete. Tears were still streaming down my face as I made my way back toward the shore, each step feeling like I was moving in slow motion through the crashing waves.

With joyful abandon, I scooped up handfuls of water and flung them into the air. In the cool, frothy surf, I continued splashing, the water dancing around me in wild, jubilant celebration.

I stepped onto the shoreline feeling fully grounded. A quote by Marcus Aurelius found its way into my thoughts. "Everything is interwoven, and the web is holy."

Abby was still snapping pictures as she walked toward me, then she glanced at my face and asked, "Are you crying?"

"Yes, but only because I'm so incredibly happy!"

She patiently waited for me to find the words.

"It felt like I was just a drop in the ocean, blending in and floating around."

"That's awesome," she smiled.

"Yeah, it was as if I disappeared for a moment." I stood there, still in a state of awe.

We began moving across the velvety sand. "In a way, it felt like a baptism," I said.

Abby looked at me with a curious gaze, "How so?"

"The past felt like it was washed away, and now I'm ready for a new beginning."

We kept walking in the warm sand, leaving an imprint with every step, my dress clinging to my body, "Somehow, by allowing myself to fade away, all that was left was a reverence for life."

Abby was still intrigued. "Sounds like you tapped into something really profound."

I reached for the towel I'd left on the shore, gently rubbing it through my damp hair. I grabbed my flip-flops, and we began walking toward our modest accommodation.

"It's hard to describe, but I think we make life a lot more complicated than it needs to be." I patted away the beads of water lingering on my face as I grasped for words, "It's like... instead of just reacting to life, I had a sense that... we *are* life."

Abby added, "Maybe it's like what our yoga instructor was saying about viewing life from the perspective of the sky, imagining yourself looking down at the weather, observing it as it passes by without getting caught in the emotional chaos of angry storms or clouds of sadness."

"Yeah, similar, but I think it's more about fully experiencing life—letting it flow without clinging to it or allowing circumstances to define you."

In that heightened sense of awareness, I knew this was the ultimate form of what it meant to *just be*—this state of existing without striving.

The entire experience had been far more transformative than I ever could have imagined, awakening a freedom and exhilaration I hadn't felt before. While I knew I couldn't live in this magical, dreamlike state forever, I could certainly carry with me the harmony and clarity it brought.

That moment became a touchstone, a reminder that even in the chaos of everyday life, within me there was always a place where my mind could find stillness and my heart could fill with peace.

Chapter Fifty

O n a calm Monday morning in August, I prepared a delicious picnic lunch, gathered some towels and other essentials, and met George at the boat. To celebrate our thirty-second anniversary, we had finally decided to take the boat to the far end of the sixty-kilometre lake, all the way to Port Douglas, something Dieter had been urging us to do for years.

We had only been as far as Long Island in the past, so it was fun to zip by it and keep heading north. We marvelled at the hues of the water, transitioning from a deep, dark green to a mesmerizing shade of aquamarine.

We couldn't resist stopping to snap pictures of the vibrant, lime-green lichen that clung to the rocky cliffs, adding a burst of colour to the serene landscape. George slowed the boat again, taking more pictures as the rugged terrain of Mount Breckenridge came into view.

A little farther along, we spotted the mouth of the river exactly as Dieter had described it, tucked into the shoreline like a hidden gateway. We slowly made our way up the narrow waterway until we reached Little Harrison Lake.

George eased the boat toward a dock where a lone fisherman was casting his line. The town looked much smaller than we'd imagined, so I asked the man, "Is this Port Douglas?"

"Yup, this is Port Douglas," he answered proudly, "the capital of British Columbia for two whole days. Says so in the history books."

In shabby attire and a baseball cap, the man exuded an aura of carefree living, as if the worries of the world were as distant from him as this small town was from the rest of society.

"Have you caught any fish?" George asked.

"Not today."

I looked around at the sparse buildings and was curious. "What's the population here?"

"Oh... 'bout nine or ten."

I smiled. "Well, have a good day," I said, and we pushed off to leave.

The man shouted, "Keep an eye out for the elk!"

We didn't see any elk, but we did stop at a beautiful beach on the way back. I spread out the picnic blanket and unpacked our lunch while George made sure the boat was secure.

"It's nice to have some quiet time after the busy weekend," I said.

George's eyes held a calm warmth as he joined me on the picnic blanket. "It was fun water-skiing and wakeboarding with the kids again." He took a chunk of the crusty baguette and a slice of prosciutto.

"I'm glad they could all make it." I said, handing George the marinated olives, then sliced myself a piece of Brie.

George took a sip of wine. "You sure spent a lot of time with Levi."

"I loved it. Seeing the world through the eyes of a two-year-old is so interesting. Cuddling baby Owen was fun too." Tim and Sarah's second son had arrived near the end of July. I loved every aspect of babies—their delicate scent, their irresistibly cuddly nature, and the tender moments spent rocking and singing them to sleep.

I picked up a fresh strawberry, pausing for a moment before taking a bite, "When I hold a baby, it feels like time stands still, like I can sense the eternal and ephemeral at the same time."

George gazed at me and smiled. "That sounds deep."

We continued snacking, dipping crisp carrots sticks, cucumber slices, and cherry tomatoes into creamy hummus, our conversation flowing as easily as the quiet rhythm of the afternoon.

After a while, we waded into the crystal-clear water, its cool embrace refreshing against the heat of the day. Then, we stretched out on our blanket, spread across the pebbled shore. The warmth of the sun was soothing, melting away any tension and easing us into absolute relaxation.

"This is so amazing." I sat up and looked out across the endless water. "There's not a single person as far as the eye can see. No signs of civilization at all!" It felt as if we had the entire world to ourselves. Our own secluded paradise.

"You're amazing too," George said, his eyes shining with love. "With all the books you've been reading, you seem excited about learning."

"I am," I admitted. "I never used to have the time, but suddenly I have this insatiable thirst for knowledge."

Recently I'd immersed myself in a variety of subjects, from philosophy and science to religion. I delved into the works of great thinkers and scholars, captivated by new insights into the mysteries of existence and the complexities of the universe. Ever since my Freedom fifty-five experience in Costa Rica, I felt stronger, freer, and more alive than ever.

"And you're learning Spanish too," he added, his voice full of admiration.

"Finally," I laughed. "I've always wanted to learn Spanish, and it feels great to have the time to pursue it. But it's not just about learning something new—it's about rediscovering what matters to me and shaping my life through my own choices."

"I like the new you." George's eyes were full of reverence. "I can honestly say it feels like I'm falling in love with you all over again, more and more every day."

I looked at my husband, the man I'd been sharing my life with for thirty-two years, and a wave of affection washed over me. His face, familiar and dear, carried the marks of our journey—laugh lines and gentle creases that spoke of both trials and joys.

He added with heartfelt sincerity, "I know I've neglected you in the past, and I regret that. But now I want to start treating you like a queen."

I pressed a kiss to his lips, a simple gesture that held the weight of decades. Our bond had deepened, growing richer with every chapter we had written together. As our marriage continued to evolve, I realized that the layers we were discovering about each other only strengthened our connection. At the same time, I understood that my own journey was vital—not only for my personal growth, but for the health of our marriage as well.

"I love you," I said, and leaned in again for another lingering kiss that spoke more than words ever could. We spent the rest of the afternoon on the blanket, our eyes eventually drawn to the slow, graceful dance of clouds wandering across the endless blue sky.

The following day, when I went down for sangria time, Helga asked, "So what did George get you for your anniversary?"

I smiled. "Nothing."

"What!?" Helga gasped.

"But we did have a very romantic day," I added.

"Still, Dieter has always given me gifts for our anniversaries. And he buys me roses all the time for no special reason. I need to have a talk with George. That's just not right!"

Her serious tone made me grin.

Just then, George came down, beer in hand, ready for happy hour. Helga didn't hesitate to give him a lecture. As she spoke, her eyes often drifted to Dieter, who sat across from me chuckling softly whenever she showered him with praise. It was clear how deeply she loved him.

George laughed it off, but I noticed a flicker of unease in his eyes. I knew Helga cared about both of us and that she just wanted me to experience the warmth and attention that had brought her so much joy in her own marriage.

When it got dark, George and I stretched out on our dock, gazing up at the heavens as flashes of light danced across the sky, resembling a flurry of fireflies in motion.

"What did you think of the lecture you got from Helga this afternoon?" I teased.

"Sorry I didn't get you anything." George's voice was laced with remorse.

My response was sincere. "You know I didn't expect anything. Spending quality time together is worth far more to me than material gifts."

Just then, a spectacularly bright light with a long tail streaked across the darkness like a brushstroke of fire. We both gasped in delight. As we watched, another appeared some minutes later, then another, and another.

"This meteor shower is better than any fireworks display we've ever seen." I reached for George's hand, gently squeezing it so he could feel the depth of my words. "It's actually a great metaphor for our marriage."

"What do you mean?"

"Some couples have a fireworks marriage, expressing their love in bright, flashy ways, giving the perfect gifts at just the right moment. There's nothing wrong with that. But I think we have more of a meteor shower marriage." I giggled. "The dazzling moments might not happen as often, but it doesn't mean that our love isn't just as beautiful. In fact, I prefer not having expectations to exchange gifts on specific dates. For me, it feels more natural to enjoy the gift of being together, sharing the awe and beauty of moments like this."

As we watched another luminous streak of light cross the night sky, a single thought echoed in my heart: all is well.

Chapter Fifty-One

Our growing family, including Dieter and Helga, gathered on the deck, where the warmth of the sun mingled with the cool spring air. With our eyes on the birthday boy, we sat in a circle, singing together and drawing out his name for effect when we reached it.

"Happy birthday dear Leeee-vi, happy birthday to you."

Levi sat patiently in his tiny chair, looking adorable with his mop of wavy blonde hair. Sarah lit the three candles on his birthday cake and placed it in front of him on the small table. With a deep breath, he leaned forward, cheeks puffing out as he blew as hard as he could. Cheers and applause made him grin as he clapped his little hands.

He opened one gift after another—a new bouncy ball, a book, a bubble blower—his excitement growing with each surprise. Then he unwrapped the gift I had chosen for him and inhaled sharply. He wrapped his tiny fingers around the handle of his new blue toolbox, and when he lifted the lid, his eyes shimmered with pure delight. Inside, it was filled with real little tools.

For the rest of the day, he proudly walked around with his toolbox looking for things to fix. George showed him how to hammer nails into the old logs we used as end tables by the firepit.

I could tell by the way he moved around and wielded his tools that he felt like a real worker.

That evening, as we gathered around the crackling fire, Levi clutched his beloved toolbox, opening and closing the lid, inspecting his tools anew each time. When he had to go to the bathroom, Sarah had a hard time persuading him to leave his toolbox behind. After much cajoling and some reluctant grumbling, he finally relented, placing the toolbox on a nearby chair.

He took a few steps toward the stairs, then turned around, locking eyes with Helga. With a serious face, he warned, "Don't touch my toolbox."

We all burst into laughter.

An entire year passed, and the seasons came full circle once again. In no time, we were back at the cabin, sharing our wonderful news with Dieter and Helga. Two new grandchildren had joined the family, bringing even more joy to our lives. In October, Lyell and Tania had welcomed little Adeline, while in November, Mark and Tausha had celebrated the arrival of Finley. After a life surrounded by boys, the thought of having two little girls in the family filled me with a fresh wave of excitement.

George and I joined Dieter and Helga for happy hour on their deck once again. Helga spoiled us with a wonderful array of cheeses, crackers, red pepper jelly, olives, and spinach dip. She opened a bottle of Prosecco to celebrate our newest grandchildren. As we enjoyed the indulgent spread, she recounted some of the other memorable celebrations that had happened at the lake over the years.

"Elmer and Kay, who owned this cabin before us—their daughter got married right there on the grass." She pointed to a spot in front of their deck.

"And right after they were pronounced husband and wife, she put on a white bikini and went water-skiing," Dieter laughed, amused by the memory of it, which made us all laugh.

Helga nodded toward me, "You've sure had your share of family weddings over the last few years."

"I know." I dipped a carrot into the spinach dip. "I can't believe how quickly things have changed, with three of the boys married and four grandchildren already!"

"I had never been to that part of Maple Ridge before," Helga said, "... where Mark and Tausha's wedding was."

"Oh, Whonnock Lake. Tausha's parents live just down the street from there."

Helga put blue cheese and homemade jelly on a cracker. "Levi sure looked cute with his little white shirt and pink bowtie."

"He was adorable." I reached for a cube of Gouda, a grin spreading across my face at the memory of how proudly Levi strode down the aisle, clutching the ring-bearer pillow, then came to sit on my lap when he reached the end.

"The dinner you had in your backyard for Lyell and Tania was very nice too," Dieter added. "That salmon was delicious."

"Thank you. We had to wait over a year to host their reception. That's how long it took for Tania to get her papers so she could come to Canada."

"Remind me how Lyell met his wife?" Helga asked.

"Lyell had been dating on and off for a while, but he was getting frustrated. A Ukrainian plumber he worked with told him about a friend in Ukraine that he thought would be a good match for Lyell. They started writing to each other, and when he went there to meet her, they decided to get married right away."

"She's very striking," Helga said. I thought I detected a hint of concern in her voice. "She has an eye for fashion and is always so well put together. And you know Lyell. He's... very practical."

I chuckled to myself, noting how Tania had already made significant improvements to Lyell's wardrobe. "I know what you mean. At first, I wondered how their styles and cultures would mesh, but they both have sincere hearts and have found a way to build a loving relationship."

George spoke up. "Feels like such a long time ago that we were at the actual wedding in her hometown of Lviv." He glanced in my direction. "Was it only last spring?"

I nodded and turned to Dieter. "You should have seen the extravagant feast we had in Lviv. I've never seen anything like it! The food just kept coming like an endless banquet. I'm so glad we could be there."

"And the amount of vodka that was served," George laughed. "It was an unforgettable experience."

"The most important thing," Dieter said, smiling, "is that your boys found good partners. They all seem happy."

We lifted our glasses and toasted to the boys and their wives.

After a while, George headed back up to our place, and Dieter retreated into his cabin to lie down. Though he never spoke of his cancer, the changes were hard to miss. He had begun spending more afternoons napping that summer.

During those quiet hours, Helga had introduced me to Canasta. With her patient guidance and a touch of humour, the game became more than just a pastime—it became a comforting ritual.

The steady rhythm of dealing cards and laying down sets continued that afternoon. I finally said, "I can see that Dieter isn't feeling well," hoping she would be willing to give me an update about his health.

Helga sighed. "He's taking some pills. It's a form of chemo, and it doesn't agree with his stomach."

I shook my head. "He's been living as if nothing has changed."

"That's Dieter," Helga agreed. "I think he's in denial."

A noise by the lake caught our attention. Two eagles had swooped down from the trees, trying to take a mother duck's babies. The ducklings cheeped and paddled in circles, and the mother quacked urgently as she spread her wings wide and fought back. One of the eagles managed to grab a duckling and flew off, leaving the mother quacking loudly in their direction long after they had gone.

"That's so sad," I said as I turned back to Helga.

"Not really." She met my eyes. "Those eagles probably have babies to feed too. That's the cycle of life."

Chapter Fifty-Two

Sunlight filtered through the trees on the hill where the big wooden swing set stood. With each push, my grandsons' giggles filled the air. I loved watching their excitement mount as I pushed them higher.

Levi yelled, "Under-duck Oma, under-duck!"

I pushed him high and ran forward and under him, listening to his little voice go, "Wheeeeeee."

The scent of Helga's doughnuts frying reached us long before the little bell rang. I took Owen out of the baby swing, holding him with one arm, and Levi clasped my other hand with his tiny fingers, his grasp a delicate blend of trust and affection.

Levi's eyes lit up when he saw the platter full of doughnuts, golden-crisp with sprinkled confectioner's sugar. When he bit into one, the white powder coated his lips and puffed onto his nose. It struck me how, in the blink of an eye, the next generation was already experiencing some of the same joys my sons had when they'd been kids.

When the last doughnut had been devoured, I shuffled my grandsons off to their parents, sensing that their energy was a bit much for Dieter right now. I took some soiled napkins and plates into the kitchen where Dieter was preparing my sangria. He seemed extra slow and took long breaths as he walked.

I asked him directly. "It's getting worse now, isn't it?"

Helga answered for him. "We had an appointment with the oncologist. He told us that the cancer has spread into the liver. There is nothing more they can do."

I instantly teared up and looked at Dieter's glistening eyes. "So you just keep on going as if nothing is happening?"

His smile hinted at a deeper understanding of the bigger picture. "That's all you *can* do," he said. I leaned in for a hug, tears now flowing freely down my face.

The following weekend, Helga asked David and Mark to take her up the mountain on the quads. It had been a while since she'd been up to the lookout, and she wanted to see the lake from that vantage point again. Meanwhile, I seized the opportunity to enjoy happy hour alone with Dieter. We settled into our usual places at the table on the deck.

"You know," Dieter started, sipping his beer, "last June the doctor told me I had four months to live, yet a year later, I'm still here."

"I had no idea you received that prognosis last summer already."

His face appeared resolute, quiet acceptance etched into his features. "Other than feeling more tired than usual, I don't feel too bad."

I held up my sangria, feeling mixed emotions as we toasted to the bittersweet reality—his prognosis was bleak, but he was still here with us.

Dieter never stopped his projects, but he visibly slowed. He'd taken it upon himself to create a first aid box that the whole community could access. Crafting it from sturdy wood, he painted it white and emblazoned a bold red cross on the front. He strategically positioned it at the back of his cabin, visible to everyone in our bay who used the new road. Despite his health challenges, his dedication to helping others remained strong.

Water retention caused his feet and stomach to swell, but if he caught anyone looking, he just rubbed his big belly and declared, "I'm about eight months pregnant." It was funny and sad at the same time.

I started to feel guilty about sangria time, but Helga reassured me that her husband still found joy in making the drinks. I heard Dieter's shallow breathing every time he rose to get my glass, and although I insisted that I didn't need more than one, he always waved away my protests and refilled the "top half" for me anyway.

That summer, I spent a lot of time on their deck. We spent hours playing cards or Yahtzee, listening to the soft calls of owls in the night. The conversations stayed light. We never spoke of Dieter's obvious struggles. I observed Dieter and Helga exchanging tender, affectionate glances with each other more often than usual, their love shining brightly even as they faced the reality of his imminent departure from this world.

One afternoon, Helga turned to me and said, "I need a distraction. Let's have an end of summer party."

"Sure. I can make the invitations," I offered.

"I want it to be a crazy theme," she said. "People should dress up in whatever kind of ridiculous costume they want."

We hosted the party in our backyard, drawing a crowd of forty-six neighbours, about half of whom dressed up in something silly. Most of the people in the bay didn't even know about Dieter's condition, and that was the way he wanted it. He and Helga maintained privacy when it came to personal matters, a trait I speculated was at least partially cultural.

The afternoon was filled with refreshing drinks, an abundance of tasty dishes on the potluck table, and a lot of games.

Helga stood in her flowing, rainbow-coloured dress and called out with a grin, "Alright, I need ten women to join me over here."

I opted to sit back and watch, but the response from the rest of the crowd was swift and eager. Helga quickly paired up the ten participants, arranging them to face each other about five feet apart. With a mischievous smile, she handed each woman a large tablespoon. The crowd buzzed with anticipation as Helga carefully placed a raw egg on one partner's spoon per pair, sparking laughter and cheers from the onlookers. Once everyone was ready, Helga announced the challenge with a glint in her eye.

"You have to toss the egg to your partner, who has to catch it with her spoon. If it breaks, you're out. Then you each take a step back, and you keep tossing the egg to each other until the last pair with an unbroken egg wins."

Everyone cheered, and the game began. With the first toss, eggs sailed through the air, and while some caught theirs effortlessly, one slipped past the spoon, landing with a splat on the ground and eliciting groans and giggles. One by one, pairs were eliminated. Helga burst into laughter when an egg hit a woman's leg, cracking open on impact, leaving a yellow smear that oozed down her jeans.

The crowd joined in with playful teasing. I glanced at Dieter, his eyes soft with a quiet smile. It was clear he took comfort and joy in seeing his wife so full of life.

Finally, with a careful toss and a skillful catch, one pair won the game. They stood beaming, holding their unbroken egg as the group erupted in applause and cheers.

It was great to observe Helga having a good time. I admired her ability to know what she needed. It almost seemed as if, in that moment, that fleeting instant, all her worries and cares melted away, replaced by a profound sense of happiness. It was a testament to the power of laughter and the simple pleasure of having fun in the company of friends.

Chapter Fifty-Three

September was always a time of transition. There was a subtle shift in the atmosphere as a delicate mist hung over the vibrant lake in the early morning hours. Some of the leaves on the alder trees had begun to blush with a gentle touch of yellow.

I sauntered down the stone path like so many afternoons before, pausing briefly once I was in view to make sure I wasn't intruding. Dieter smiled and waved me up onto the deck. As he rose to get me a sangria, I started to protest, but Helga stopped me.

"It's okay," she said with tired eyes.

Dieter's complexion had yellowed, and his body didn't move like it used to. While he was in the cabin, I sat with Helga. We didn't talk. We simply shared a silent understanding that spoke volumes.

Dieter returned, handing me the sangria with a faint smile.

"Thank you, Dieter."

"I'm going to go lie down for a bit," he said apologetically.

I watched him shuffle into the darkness of the cabin. I looked at Helga with growing concern. Her deep sadness was evident.

She turned to me, tears teetering on the brink. "He's been sleeping a lot lately and is starting to lose weight fast. He doesn't have an appetite anymore." She said it stoically, factually, but her face added the emotion her voice lacked. "We're going home first thing in the morning. I don't know if we'll be back."

Over the next two weeks, the landscape continued to transform. The forest, once cloaked in the deep greens of summer, began to weave in rich hues of amber and gold. Every fall, even the lake water changed colour to a vivid blue-green.

George was reading the newspaper out on the deck, and I was in the middle of folding laundry when the phone rang.

After hanging up, I looked out at the bright sun reflecting off the lake, thinking that rain would have suited the day better. I stepped out onto the deck. George took one look at my tear-stained face, and he knew. I said it aloud anyway.

"Emily just called. Dieter passed away peacefully."

We embraced for a long time, tears flowing freely down our cheeks. The moment felt surreal, the finality of it all not fully sinking in, as if my mind didn't want to accept it. Dieter's soul had been such a big part of these cabins, this land, and the people here. I couldn't imagine this place without Dieter.

Eventually, George and I eased into the deck chairs. We sat in silence for a few moments. My eyes drifted to George's stack of newspapers on the side table, and I said, "Remember when Dieter used to kayak all the way to town just to get the newspaper?"

George smiled. "He did it quite often, especially when they were up here for longer stretches of time. And then he had us trained to bring him the weekend newspaper."

"I wanted to go visit him last week," I said, "but Helga told me over the phone that he had taken a turn for the worse." Deep down, I knew he'd want me to remember him as he once was—strong, good-humoured, and full of life. Tears welled up again in my eyes. I felt at peace knowing that he had been surrounded by his loving family.

At four o'clock, George went into the cabin, returning with a bottle of wine and two glasses.

"Let's go sit down on Dieter's bench," he said.

We walked slowly down the path. From the bench, the view down the lake was nothing short of breathtaking. George uncorked the bottle and poured us each a glass.

"To Dieter."

Clinking my glass to George's, I felt a deep gratitude for all the happy hours we had shared with Dieter. The bench beneath us, sturdy and enduring, was a testament to his life. The world felt quiet without him, yet in this moment, surrounded by the beauty he so loved, his silent presence lingered. The memories washed over me like gentle waves, each one carrying the warmth of Dieter's laughter, his strength, and the kindness in his eyes.

Later that evening, George built a bonfire in Dieter's honour. As if the massive fire insisted on joining in on our conversation and our grief, it crackled loudly, blowing smoke in our direction.

George coughed as he said, "I love white rabbits."

We chuckled and sat in silence for a few moments.

"I'm glad we were here when he passed." I looked around, adjusting my eyes to the darkness, and began to sniffle again. "This is where we first met Dieter, and this is where we saw him last."

George put his arm around me as I leaned into his shoulder. An owl called from the forest, bringing with it more tears and memories of Dieter.

When the logs had burned down, creating a bed of glowing embers, George added more wood. He had a designated fire stick, much like the one Dieter had used. Then he asked, "Do you want anything to drink? Maybe some sparkling water?"

"Sure."

From that day forward, George took it upon himself to pour my drinks for me. It warmed my heart to think that a bit of Dieter had rubbed off on him after all.

Looking at my husband, I said, "There's a comfort in knowing that no matter what life throws our way, we'll face it together, like they did."

George nodded and poked at the fire. "Dieter and Helga were a great team."

"When you've shared a lifetime with the same person, it's only natural to develop a deeper kind of understanding."

He smiled, but as was his manner, he remained silent, and I was okay with that. George had his own way of processing. In his quiet way, his steadfast presence offered a comforting sense of stability, and I'd come to respect that.

A few days later, we drove out to Abbotsford for Dieter's celebration of life. I recognized many familiar faces, including cabin owners, friends, and relatives who had travelled all the way from Germany. The room brimmed with guests, all united in their purpose to honour and remember Dieter.

I watched Dieter's life play out in the slideshow. Though he had told us many stories, seeing the images strung together added a new layer of depth: Dieter as a young man, Dieter in military clothes, Dieter in a ski suit. Black-and-white memories then took on colour, and a more recent Dieter flashed on the screen, bright and full of life: Dieter out on a sailboat, Dieter wearing his dive gear, Dieter at the lake... countless pictures of Dieter at the lake.

It all made me think about the transience of life and the fleeting moments that shaped our existence. Soon the next generation would be creating their own memories at the lake. We were all part of a continuous cycle, with each new wave of life leaving its unique mark on the ever-unfolding story. If only there were more neighbours like Dieter in this world.

Chapter Fifty-Four

I awoke to find George gently touching my arm.

"Sorry," he whispered, "but you have to see this."

Confused, but trusting him, I grabbed my robe and followed. He eagerly led me to the sunroom. The hardwood floor was cold under my feet, sending a shiver through my body. Looking out of the floor-to-ceiling windows, I was in awe. The landscape was draped in a blanket of freshly fallen snow.

It was a winter wonderland. Two feet of fluffy white snow was piled on the deck and clinging to the cedar bows. A smile spread across my face. Ever since my childhood days on the farm, I had always loved being snowed in. Snow meant the hard work had to stop. You couldn't go anywhere. You *had* to slow down. You had to *just be.*

In quiet contemplation, I watched the shimmering icicles hanging from the edge of the sunroom roof. "I guess our company won't be coming up for New Year's Eve," I said, pulling my robe tighter against the chill.

George came closer, wrapping his arms around me for warmth. "Well, isn't that a shame."

I heard the smile in his voice.

George made his coffee, and a pot of tea for me. We set up the backgammon board in the sunroom and played for over an hour, our eyes frequently drawn to the view beyond the glass—a perfect portrait of winter's quiet magic. We allowed the day to unfold with no schedule.

Sometime in the late afternoon, as daylight was waning, I peered over the top of my book and observed George. The soft light highlighted how much greyer his hair had become, a subtle reminder of the years that had passed.

"There's nobody I'd rather be snowed in with."

George lowered his newspaper as his eyes met mine. "Same."

"Let's make a conscious effort to create more moments like this. It doesn't happen very often where we're just together, enjoying whatever the day brings, without the need to fill it with plans."

"I agree," he winked.

As dinnertime approached, I prepared two steaks with lemon and garlic, ready for George to grill on the barbecue while the vegetables roasted in the oven. I drizzled olive oil into a small bowl, adding a splash of tangy vinegar, a touch of Dijon mustard, a hint of maple syrup, and a pinch of sea salt. With a quick whisk, it blended into a light dressing. I tossed our simple green salad and topped it with a sprinkle of freshly ground pepper.

With a satisfying pop, George released the cork from a champagne bottle and filled our glasses.

"Here's to Dieter," I said, raising my glass. "And to all our neighbours—past, present, and future."

"And here's to our growing family," George said. "Can you believe it? By this spring, we'll have six grandchildren."

"It's unbelievable." Our glasses clinked together.

He took a bite of his steak and let out a satisfied sound. "Mmmm, this is delicious."

I acknowledged his compliment with a nod before continuing. "As our family gets bigger, we're only going to get busier. But it's different—the good kind of busy."

"I wouldn't trade it for anything."

"I think we're finally finding our rhythm, everything feels a bit more manageable. Let's try to make this next year even better."

I held up my glass for another toast, "To a year of fun," I declared with conviction.

"Does that mean you've got another trip in mind?" he smirked.

"You know me well," I laughed. "Since I've been studying Spanish, I've been thinking Barcelona would be a good place to go."

"Perfect! I've always wanted to see the architecture there."

"I'll start working on the travel plans when we get home."

After tidying up the kitchen and finishing the last of the dishes, we put on a CD, letting the smooth voice of Michael Bublé set the mood as we danced our way into the New Year.

Awakening to another foot of snow, George started to get worried. He shovelled a few feet ahead of the truck and tried putting chains on the tires, but it was no use. The snow was too deep. It became clear that we weren't going to be able to leave the same way we had come.

"I've got enough food to last at least a couple of weeks," I said, secretly hoping we could stay.

"I can't. I have to get back to work."

"But it's so beautiful. Can't we enjoy it a bit longer?"

I could tell by the look on George's face and the frantic way he scrolled through his contacts that he was determined to find us a way home. "I'm calling the water taxi first," he said.

When he learned their boat was out of the water for repairs, he began calling everyone he could think of in the area. Finally, he reached Greg, who lived down the Harrison River. We had gotten to know him during our renovation. He was the one who had done such a great job creating the peeled cedar railing in the loft of the cabin.

After arranging details with him, George turned to me. "We're so lucky I called today. He's taking his boat out in the morning. The only time he can come pick us up is later tonight around midnight."

Secretly disappointed, I began packing, knowing we'd spend the rest of the day winterizing the cabin. I decided to carry some provisions down to the dock, but as I stepped onto the path, I couldn't help but laugh. The snow was up to my thighs, making every step a struggle. I tried lifting my legs high, only to sink back down with every stride, my boots filling up with snow. After a few clumsy attempts, I gave up and waited for George to clear a path before hauling everything down.

By the time we finished cleaning up, emptying the propane fridge, draining the water system, adding antifreeze to the pipes, and shutting off the power, it was late evening. We settled into the warmth of the sunroom and noticed a tiny light flickering in the distance.

Greg's twenty-six-foot cabin cruiser was an older model, so it would take a while to reach our dock from where he was. While we waited, I was lost in introspection, my thoughts wandering to the past, to the events that had led us here in the first place.

"Isn't it interesting," I said to George, "how often things shift in life to create new opportunities?"

"What do you mean?"

"I was just thinking, we never would have found this place if it hadn't been for that first trip to Europe with the boys. When your vacation time ran out, I tried to find something close by. And the fact that you bought a boat just the year before... it all came together so perfectly."

"That's true."

"And the way Dieter and Helga made it all possible for us... Every choice set off a chain of events, shaping our path in ways that weren't obvious at the time."

I kept reflecting, "Even our perspective on church evolved over time. When we were immersed in it, we couldn't imagine life any other way. But gradually our views shifted, and eventually, letting go became a natural step. It's not about being right or wrong—everyone's journey is unique, and everyone's path unfolds in its own time."

George nodded. "The church gave us a great foundation to build on. I have no regrets or negative feelings about those experiences."

"Neither do I. I value all the relationships we've built. You know what has surprised me the most?"

"What?"

"The power of love."

"How do you mean?"

I inhaled deeply, relaxed into the cushion, and let my eyes wander up. The thick timber beams supported the warm wood finishes of the vaulted ceiling, creating an ambience reminiscent of a sacred space. "It's that the love I've known and been taught all my life feels even more powerful when it's not limited by a religious belief system. It's incredibly freeing."

"I agree," he said reassuringly, "and I'm glad we're on the same page."

"If someone had told me that years ago, I never would have believed it was possible."

The lake stretched out in perfect stillness, its surface gleaming like polished glass beneath the night sky. In the distance, Greg's boat glided closer, its soft light casting a shimmering glow across the water. He was probably only ten minutes away now.

I reflected on my relationship with George. For so many years, I had hoped he would change. But I came to realize that a person's growth is a gradual process that ripens in its own time, with moments of insight that can't be rushed or forced. Over time I discovered that it was my own quest for change and personal growth that truly empowered me to accept George just as he was.

I stared at the lake, deep in thought. There was no question that this cabin had transformed our lives as a couple and as a family. All the time and energy we had invested was undeniably worth it. I felt a deep sense of gratitude for what George's talent and vision had helped create.

"This is definitely my happy place," I said, sliding my hand into George's warm grip, giving it a squeeze. "Thanks for everything you did to make it happen."

His gaze had been fixed on the slow approach of the rescue boat, but at that moment he turned to me and said, "I love you."

We embraced, sharing a tender kiss before he, ever-practical, pulled away and said, "Now we better lock up and make our way down to the dock."

From the warmth inside Greg's old boat, I looked out the window at the shoreline, sparkling with icy brilliance. It was a magical night. We slowly puttered back under the radiance of the full moon, its luminous glow bathing the lake in a lustrous sheen.

Our son David came to pick us up at the marina, and our truck remained snowed in at the cabin for another six weeks.

Chapter Fifty-Five

In March, the snow-capped peaks of Whistler beckoned, so George and the boys planned a weekend ski trip. Last year I had joined them, but this year I felt it was time for the boys and their dad to start making their own memories and create their own traditions. Besides, I had an idea about how I wanted to spend the weekend that pulled my heart in a different direction.

I invited Helga out to the lake—just the two of us—which would be a first in our friendship. She wasn't quite ready to stay in her cabin alone but agreed to come stay with me in ours. As we drove the logging road, scarred by winter's harshness, the weight of grief made the journey feel heavy.

When we reached the cabin, we began unloading the truck. Helga paused, looking at me earnestly. "I need a bit of time."

She didn't have to explain. "Of course," I said. "Take all the time you need."

As Helga walked toward her cabin, I could only imagine how difficult it must be. Dieter's presence lingered in every detail. His handiwork, the smell of the wood, even his jackets and hats would still be hanging by the door.

I busied myself with unpacking and lit a fire, the crackle of the flames a small comfort against the cold air inside. My thoughts kept drifting to Helga, to the lakeside experience she had shared with Dieter for the past forty-eight years, now profoundly altered by his absence.

An hour or so later, I heard the back door open, and Helga appeared in the kitchen, a bottle in hand. "I brought some of Dieter's last batch. I thought we could make mulled wine."

I accepted the bottle from her. "Sounds great, I love mulled wine."

The aromatic spices filled the air as I filled two steaming mugs. Helga shuffled the deck and dealt the cards for our Canasta game. After a series of well-played hands, with Helga winning the first few games, she became noticeably quiet. "I need another break."

She stepped outside and paused at the railing, her eyes drawn to the cabin she and Dieter shared. Noticing her trembling shoulders, I went out and stood beside her, gently wrapping one arm around her, tears streaming down our faces. After a while, I went back inside, giving her the space she needed to face her new reality.

When the sun began sinking lower in the sky, we prepared a cheese fondue for dinner. With chunks of fresh baguette, crisp vegetables, sweet apples, and tender prawns, we savoured every bite, dipping them into the rich blend of melted Gruyère, white wine, and fragrant herbs. We ate until every morsel was gone, our stomachs full from the indulgent feast.

"We should do this every year," Helga proposed, "as a way to start the cabin season."

"That's a great idea!" I held up my wine glass. "A toast to our new tradition."

When the dishes were done, we resumed our Canasta game. For dessert, Helga brought out an assortment of German chocolates.

"Mmmm," I murmured, letting one melt on my tongue, "This chocolate is so good."

"I always say," she snapped a bar in half, opening the wrapper like a present, "Eat good quality chocolate or don't eat chocolate at all."

The next day, after clearing away the remains of winter from our gardens, enjoying lively rounds of Canasta, and indulging in more chocolate, we set out for a walk. Part way down the road, Helga drew my attention to a giant fir tree.

"That tree has an eagle's nest on the top."

I looked way up and saw it. "I've never noticed that before."

"And look at the trunk. You see that black part there?"

"Yeah?"

"That's where it was struck by lightning many years ago."

I paused to admire the ancient tree, once deep in the forest but now standing beside the new gravel road. Despite all the storms and trials it had endured, the tree stood tall and proud, rooted deep within the earth like a living monument. I wondered how many more generations would walk beneath its branches, and how many more neighbours would share the privilege of its timeless presence on this land?

By Sunday morning, we were packed and ready to leave. As we drove down the bumpy logging road, Helga summed it up. "That did me a world of good."

A warm smile lit my face. "I'm so glad."

"I'm going to be okay." Helga let out a slow breath. "And I think I can keep coming to the cabin alone. I'll ask Klaus to help me with the things Dieter used to do. I'm not helpless, but there are some things that men are better at."

"That's true," I said, navigating through a series of deep potholes.

The lake held its timeless beauty in every season, but as we passed green clusters of early buds and new growth, I knew there was an undeniable allure to the awakening of spring. It brought with it a sense of renewed vitality—a reminder that hope could be found once more.

Upon arriving the next weekend with George, I glanced toward Dieter's place, half expecting him to be there, smiling and waving like he used to. Instead, I was surprised to see a white rabbit. I stared in disbelief as the rabbit nibbled at the grass right behind their cabin.

"George, look!"

He followed my pointing finger and grinned. "In all the years we've been here, I've never seen wild rabbits before."

"Let alone a white one," I added.

As if he was right beside me, I could hear Dieter's low baritone voice in my head saying, "I love white rabbits." I could almost smell the smoke from the campfires we had shared over the years.

I looked at George, "Remember the time Dieter said, 'I love white rabbits,' and the smoke didn't clear out of his face? And then he said, 'I absolutely *adore* white rabbits,' hoping maybe that would do it. The boys still laugh whenever they tell that story."

We both laughed out loud.

Throughout the weekend, the rabbit made frequent appearances, always in Dieter's yard, calmly munching grass, looking like he owned the place.

Klaus and Helga arrived in separate vehicles the following weekend. Klaus helped his mom prepare the cabin for the summer season. He made sure that the water pump was working and there were no leaks in the lines, hooked up the propane tanks so she could cook, started up the hot water tank, and replenished the basket of wood by the hearth. I heard the rumble of his truck leaving in the afternoon but waited until four o'clock to go down for a visit.

The first thing I noticed as I walked in the door was Helga's wooden bowl filled with its customary Easter chocolates ready to be shared. I told her about the white rabbit we'd seen the previous weekend and how it had been a comforting reminder of Dieter's infamous phrase.

She had seen two rabbits as well, but their white winter fur was already changing to a brownish colour. Helga missed Dieter deeply, and as we reminisced, our tears fell freely. Yet she carried on with quiet strength, embracing her routines with a determination that inspired me.

"I want to plan a small event here at the lake this summer," she said, "a ceremony to spread Dieter's ashes—but with family only." She looked at me with warmth and conviction. "You're family," she said. "Your whole family is."

On a perfect July afternoon, the sun hung high in the sky, casting dappled shadows beneath the canopy of trees. In that warm embrace, we stood together by the serene lake, along the patio by Dieter's bench, united in our grief yet strengthened by our shared love for him.

Carrying a beautiful wooden box, handmade by her brother-in-law, Helga walked slowly from her cabin to the lakeside. She made her way past Dieter's loved ones: his children, his granddaughters, a few close relatives, me and George, and our boys. We formed a semicircle around Helga, and with her voice clear and certain, she spoke a benediction.

"Dieter, my one love, my only love, this is your final resting place, this view that you always loved so much."

Helga placed the box of ashes in a concrete case that had been fashioned by Dieter's sons, nestled among the rocks behind Dieter's bench. The reality of that action, the memories infused in that location, and the spirit of the man we were all there to honour left everyone wiping tears from their faces.

I was feeling too emotional to speak, but a few others shared some sweet words about Dieter. Ruth, his daughter-in-law, placed a seashell beside the wooden box and spoke briefly. "This is to symbolize Dieter's love of the water and diving. I always felt safe diving when Dieter was nearby." Other members of the family nodded in agreement.

Helga had told me earlier that her sister, Petra, was planning to spread some of Dieter's ashes in the Adriatic Sea out by Croatia where he loved sailing. Helga had also saved some ashes for Dieter's sister, Inge, to take to Germany.

Dieter's sons, Klaus and Peter, carefully lifted a stone slab and placed it atop the concrete case, sealing it with quiet reverence and a solemn sense of finality. After exchanging heartfelt hugs, we gathered on the deck to share food, drinks, and stories—some of Dieter's greatest pleasures.

Klaus handed me a glass of sangria and tears instantly welled up in my eyes. Noticing my emotions, he gave me an inquiring look.

"My last memory of Dieter is of him handing me a sangria," my voice quivered. "I never saw him again after that."

Ruth threw one arm around me as she clinked her glass to mine. "And that's exactly how we should remember him."

She was right. From that moment on, sangria would never taste the same. Not only could no one make it like he did, but its sweetness would be laced with the absence of a friendship I would deeply miss.

When it was finally time to go, I ascended the rock steps to my cabin, taking each one in a deliberately unhurried way. I kept thinking about how important it was to tell stories, knowing that through them, we preserve the legacy of the departed and keep their memory alive.

After a flurry of bedtime activity and much pitter-pattering of little feet, the grandkids finally fell asleep. Gradually, the adults followed suit one by one, until a peaceful silence enveloped the wooden cabin. Thoughts of Dieter lingered in my mind—how he'd chosen us to be his neighbours, forever changing and shaping our lives.

As George got ready for bed, I volunteered to go turn off all the lights. The cool tiles felt refreshing beneath my feet as I made my way into the kitchen. This was the heart of the cabin, always the busiest place. As I flicked off the light, Liz came to mind. Even here, I was learning to *just be*. Could it really have been two decades since she passed?

I walked into the sunroom to turn off the reading lamp, which reminded me of Stan and the lamp over Silvia. He had been a window into another world. I realized then that it probably wouldn't be long before Stan and Louisa's story would be forgotten.

Lastly, I switched off the deck light, but a sudden impulse pulled me toward the darkness outside. I grabbed a small blanket and, draping it over my shoulders, stepped out onto the deck. There, bathed in the soft glow of a crescent moon, I tilted my head back and gazed up at the stars. With each passing moment, the panorama above me grew more magnificent.

Amidst the vastness of the cosmos, I thought about future generations, each twinkling light representing a potential journey waiting to unfold.

I pictured each of my grandchildren's faces and wondered what kind of lives they might build. I hoped their paths would be filled with love and kindness, rich in curiosity and open-mindedness, and that they'd see failure not as a stumbling block, but as a stepping stone. Most of all, I trusted they would have the freedom to *just be*.

In the quiet of the night, I longed for a world where we could all embrace the values of peace and love. A world where we'd see the worth of every person we meet and understand that every individual has a unique story. On this earth, we are all neighbours after all.

Feeling a weariness settle over me, I turned away from the captivating night sky and headed back inside, my eyelids growing heavier with each step. Just before I shut the door behind me, I heard the distant call of an owl.

Ah, the owl. It would always remind me of Dieter, its quiet presence a reflection of how wisdom so often arrived—softly and when least expected.

I nestled beside George, my mind still churning as I drifted off to sleep.

In the early morning hours, before I even opened my eyes, I felt the stirring of a powerful notion taking root within me. It resonated deeply, beckoning me with a compelling call that I couldn't ignore.

As George began to awaken, his body inching closer to mine, I turned to face him and calmly but confidently declared, "I'm going to write a book."

Acknowledgments:

Bringing this book to life has been an incredible journey, and I'm deeply grateful to those who helped make it possible.

To Emily Hoefner, thank you so much for being there from the very beginning. Your insights, encouragement and expertise not only made me a better writer but gave me the confidence to begin this project in the first place. You're amazing.

To Rita Kampen, your sharp eye for detail and thoughtful questions pushed me to dig deeper and make this story more personal. Your dedication, hard work and invaluable contributions made writing a rewarding experience. I couldn't have done it without you, dear Twypsy.

Finally, to my husband George, thank you for standing by me every step of the way. Your unwavering love and support gave me the determination to see this through. I look forward to the ongoing adventures we'll share as we grow old together.